THE GREAT CRUISING COOKBOOK

By the same author

THE MARINE ELECTRICAL AND
ELECTRONICS BIBLE

THE GREAT CRUISING COOKBOOK

An International Galley Guide

John C. Payne

S

SHERIDAN HOUSE

This edition first published 1996 by
Sheridan House, Inc.
145 Palisade Street
Dobbs Ferry, NY 10522

Library of Congress Cataloging-in-Publication Data

Payne, John C., 1954-
        The great cruising cookbook : an international galley guide /
    John C. Payne
            p. cm
        Includes index
        ISBN 0-924486-92-9 (hardcover : alk. paper)
        1. Cookery, Marine I. Title
    TX840.M7P37 1996
        641.5'753--dc20   96-6095
                                                             CIP

Illustrations by Greg Horder

Printed in the United States of America

ISBN 0-924486-92-9

This book is for Judith, who always tried out the results, both good and bad.

CONTENTS

Introduction

Chapter 1:
Cooking at Sea   3
Rough weather foods   4

Chapter 2:
Galley Equipment   7
The cooking stove   9
Refrigeration systems   10
Cooking equipment   13
Galley safety   15
Galley cleaning   16
Trash control and disposal   17
Cooking data   18

Chapter 3:
Provisioning   19
Planning   21
Length of shelf life   22
Food preservation   22
Storage   25
Provisioning checklists   28
Herbs, spices and condiments   31
Cooking oils   33
Fresh food substitutes   34
Worldwide provisioning guide   37

Chapter 4:
Breakfast Ideas and Eggs   43

Chapter 5:
Seafood   49

Catching fish   51
Buying fish   54
Fish storage   55
Basic fish cooking   56
Shellfish   67
Fish soups and stews   84
Canned fish   88

Chapter 6:
Meats   93

Chicken   95
Pork   101
Goat   103
Lamb and beef   104
Stir fry   107
Sausages   108
Rissoles   110
Casseroles   111
The Barbecue   112

Chapter 7:
Rice, Pasta and Legumes   115

Rice cooking methods   117
Pasta cooking methods   122
Pasta sauces   127
Legume varieties   129
Legume cooking methods   130

Chapter 8:
Vegetables   139

On board gardening   141
Produce names   142
Some vegetables   143
Leaf vegetables   145

Chinese vegetables 146

Mixed vegetables 148

Eggplants 151

Okra 153

Potatoes 154

Pumpkins 159

Tomatoes 160

Zucchini 163

Breadfruit 165

Taro 167

Chapter 9:
Fruits and Salads 169

Tropical fruit guide 171

Apples 173

Avocados 174

Bananas 175

Coconuts 179

Mangoes 181

Papayas 181

Pineapples 184

Salads 185

Salad dressings 188

Chapter 10:
Baking 189

Breads 191

Scones 196

Muffins 197

Basic pancakes, crêpes and waffles 198

Cookies, cakes and tarts 200

Puddings 206

Chapter 11:
Curries, Salsas, Dips, Marinades,
Jams, and Pickles   209

Chapter 12:
Drinks   223
    Tea   225
    Coffee   227
    Social icebreakers   228
    Alcoholic drinks   229
    Home Brewing   233

Acknowledgements and References   234
Index   235

Introduction

Preparing a cookbook is the ultimate self indulgence, and you have to be careful not to focus on your favorite foods too much. Cruising puts you back in touch with your taste buds. Remember what fresh food used to taste like before processing came along?

Cruising cooking is an exercise in ingenuity, experimentation and adaptation. What is more, it is about improvisation, using strange raw materials in strange places under difficult circumstances.

One of the great joys of cruising is the swapping and collecting of recipes from a vast range of cultures. There is always someone with a great little recipe or hint that makes life that much easier or more enjoyable. You collect valuable mementos with stories attached.

The early explorers and sailors discovered fruits, vegetables and spices, then sailed home with them where they were incorporated into their national cuisines. Finding and eating local foods while cruising is like a retracing of those early voyages, and part of the fun, excitement and sense of discovery we all share.

This book is a result of years of accumulating and adapting recipes. It contains therefore a variety of recipes and food ideas that keeps you away from a life of cans, or bland food covered with sauces. Be bold, if in doubt then definitely try it. You will be surprised.

Bon Appétit, Bon Voyage

Chapter 1

Cooking at Sea

Rough Weather Foods

Most sailors travel on their stomachs. On an ocean going vessel, when the cook goes bad, so do most other things.

Cooking at sea on a yacht presents many problems, and these are encountered whether at anchor or under way·on passage. Most sailors travel on their stomachs. On an ocean going vessel, when the cook goes bad, so do most other things.

The first major problem is the lack of space. Galleys are generally small and cramped. If you are lucky enough to be taking delivery of a big new vessel, you will have that dream galley, but if you are like the rest of us, you'll have to make do with what you find. A small galley must be well organized, with everything in its place, and everything required to cook a meal easily located at hand.

The second problem is that of movement. Movement impacts on galley safety. Movement results largely from the prevailing sea conditions, but it also depends very much on the sea kindliness of particular vessels. A light weight racer cruiser may be very tender and bounce around, while a heavy displacement vessel will be more stable.

The third problem is that of limited resources. Generally, passage making and rolling anchorages represent only 25% of cruising time, so in most cases the biggest problems will come from resources and the cruising budget. Without a local supermarket or favorite deli close by, cruising food requires a significant amount of long-term planning, and a change in eating habits. As stocking up in foreign places generally means that the original provisioning list has to be modified, it becomes an exercise in adaptation and improvisation. If you want to stick to your home based diets and favorite foods, you will have to pay a lot more, if you can find the foods at all.

Nutrition requirements vary when cruising, and it is easy to fall into a snacking or grazing habit. Energy expenditure is often underrated; in heavy weather, as the energy levels fade, the results of poor nutrition will soon show up. When you sail, you will need lots of energy foods and a well balanced diet.

ROUGH WEATHER FOODS

While many are happy to subsist on canned food, which in all fairness these days is quite good and palatable, some veteran cruisers and others prefer "home cooked" sustenance in rough weather.

Rough weather eating brings on special nutritional requirements. The body is subject to significantly lowered temperatures, with subsequently greater demands on energy reserves. A generally increased rate of activity means greater fatigue and therefore greater energy input is required to replace it. Simply hanging on is demanding, as we all know. So many cruisers end up in trouble as they simply run out of steam during protracted bad periods.

The simplest things to make as the weather rises are thermos bottles (vacuum flasks) of soup and sandwiches. Eating dried fruits and nuts (pecans have the highest energy rating) is also good. In extended weather periods, however, you will run out of these backup meals. The quest then becomes one of spending a minimal time in the galley while preparing the most soul restoring hot foods or good energy foods.

Carbohydrate Loading

The athletes' way of "energizing" the body is equally important to cruisers. When bad or severe weather is in the offing, it is important to prime the body with energy foods and those foods capable of sustaining the body through a physically demanding rough period. Some of the regimes used by athletes are pretty drastic and are not really that necessary to a cruiser. Ideally, increase carbohydrate intake to around 60 to 70% of total calorie intake in the period leading up to the weather if advance knowledge is available. If the bad weather is coming on quickly then load up as soon as possible. This is important as galley preparation is that much easier. Fluid intake during bad weather is also important; if possible add a small amount of fruit cordial to water, as it contains some liquid carbohydrates, or drink fruit juices. The long life ones are ideal. Drink small amounts regularly.

Carbohydrate Sources

- **Porridge oats**. Porridge oats are an excellent source of slow release sustaining energy food, if you get the one-minute variety you can be in and out of the galley in about three minutes. See the breakfast recipe chapter for porridge preparation.

- **Pasta**. If you use the vacuum flask method you can have a sustaining meal with minimum time in the galley. Ideally a pasta soup is a great reviver.

- **Rice**. Again use the vacuum flask method to prepare and vary the taste by adding soup mixes.

- **Bread**. Ideally make bread and butter slices. Many people can get a little queasy and the munching of things like wholemeal crackers will fill you up as well as settle your stomach.

- **Bananas**. The great hand eaten energy food, indispensable as a quick meal, and good as a rough weather snack.

Recipes for Rough Weather

Vacuum Flask Rice
(Alex and Rob on *Monteza*)

This requires a little initial experimentation, but it is well worth the effort.

Put boiling water in a wide mouthed vacuum flask. Optionally you can add a one-cup soup mix to give flavor; tomato or cream of mushroom taste great. Add a serving of rice. Allow to "cook" for a couple of hours, and out comes ready made boiled rice.

Vacuum Flask Pasta

Follow the instructions for rice using any spiral or shell type pasta. You may have to experiment a little to get times and quantities correct but it is worthwhile. Again add a one-cup tomato soup or similar to enhance the flavor.

Pasta Frittata   *Serves 4*

This can be made beforehand or when it gets bumpy. It is very quick to make and can be hand eaten hot or cold. It has good carbohydrate levels, and settles well in the stomach. You can substitute rice for the pasta.

1 cup milk
6 lightly beaten eggs
2 tablespoons oil
1 boiled and diced potato
1 diced tomato
½ pound (250g) dry shell pasta

Whisk the milk into the eggs. Heat oil in a skillet and add the potato and tomato. Add the pasta and pour over the egg mixture. Pasta can be cooked in a vacuum flask as can the potato. Cook until mixture sets, and if you have a broiler put the pan under the broiler to set and brown the top.

Energy Drink

A great pick-me-up drink, and your body will be forever grateful for it.

1 fresh egg
1 teaspoon honey
1 cup fruit juice (orange, tomato)

Beat the raw egg and honey into a cup of juice. Pour and drink. In rough weather use a Tupperware™ Shake-and-Pour to prepare.

10 Minutes Pressure Cooker Hot Pot

Serves 4 to 6

This is an easy, quick, and soul restoring dish.

3 pints (1½ lt) water
½ teaspoon salt
1 beef stock bouillon cube
1 can tomatoes
2 diced potatoes
¼ pound (125g) rice
¼ pound (125g) shell pasta
2 tablespoons dehydrated peas
½ cup diced canned ham (optional)
Parmesan cheese
Chunks of bread

Bring the water to a boil, then add the salt. Add the crumbled bouillon cube, tomatoes, diced potatoes, rice, shell pasta and peas. Add diced ham. Bring up to pressure on a moderate heat setting. Cook for 4 minutes (6 minutes if a non auto cooker) at 15 pounds pressure. Reduce pressure slowly. If non auto cooker, reduce pressure quickly. Sprinkle with Parmesan cheese and eat with chunks of bread.

Chapter 2

Galley Equipment

The Cooking Stove

Refrigeration Systems

Cooking Equipment

Galley Safety

Galley Cleaning

Trash Control and Disposal

Cooking Data

The successful galley consists of
sensible equipment, generally a
few tried and true implements
that save work and store easily.

The successful galley consists of sensible equipment, generally a few tried and tested implements that both save on work and store easily.

THE COOKING STOVE

Type of Fuel

The stove is the heart of the galley. While most vessels are increasingly turning to LPG (Propane) or CND (Compressed Natural Gas), nevertheless many users of other types of fuels are happy with them. The real problem of cruising in foreign areas is that the particular fuel you are using may be difficult to obtain.

- **Gas Propane** This the preferred gas since you find refills easily worldwide, although compatible fittings might be hard to locate. Calor Gas and Camping Gaz are found in Europe, but difficult to refill in other areas. Take as many differing adaptors as you can. There are many good makes around and budget will often dictate the choice.

- **Kerosene** (Paraffin) This is known under a variety of names, so ensure that you are getting the right thing. It used to be easy to obtain fuel worldwide but that has changed, making gas the preferred option.

- **Methylated Spirit** (Alcohol) Alcohol is harder to get in most cruising areas. As a result the stove types using alcohol are less common although there are still plenty around. They are often a little difficult to handle and require a little skill to use.

- **Diesel** There is now a diesel stove available. It is made by Wallis-Marin in Finland. It is a ceramic hob only; it has no open flame, and is soot free. Rated at 1800 watts and adjustable, it also backs up as a heater.

Stove Gimballing

The more weight you put on a stove the more unstable it becomes. Regrettably the vast majority of stoves are not ballasted. On most you open the door and the oven tilts considerably. This is unfortunate as you cannot remove a baking tray or whatever onto the door top to rest with risking serious injury. This stability problem also has implications when cooking at sea with a heavy

pot or two on the top. One solution is to secure 40-50 pounds of lead to the bottom. Alternatively place a couple of divers weights into the base of the oven.

The Microwave

Microwaves are rapidly appearing on cruising yachts. Coupled with inverters they allow quick cooking and easy conservation of other cooking fuels. Before investing in an inverter to power a microwave remember that with most square wave, trapezoidal or quasi sine wave output units, the microwave will operate at considerably reduced efficiency, generally in the order of a 20 to 40% drop. Get a sine wave inverter if at all possible; everything else will operate more efficiently as well.

REFRIGERATION SYSTEMS

The refrigerator is essential to an acceptable lifestyle, even if only for a cold beer in the tropics. The following is excerpted from my previous book *The Marine Electrical and Electronics Bible*, also available through Sheridan House.

Iceboxes and cool boxes are rapidly being replaced by both refrigerators and freezers. Cruising in comfort entails a well-found galley, and an occasional steak on the barbecue. On cruising yachts the decision is usually for one of two different eutectic refrigeration systems, and the big question is generally electric or engine driven. This is the most common and efficient method of vessel refrigeration. Unlike domestic systems the evaporator is replaced by a eutectic plate or tank. The period of time that the space will remain within required temperature ranges before refrigeration is required is called the holdover period. When specifying a system, the holdover time and the temperature required are critical to the size of the plates or tanks and of the type of eutectic solution required.

Electric Refrigeration The principal reason given for choosing electric systems is the intent to operate them off wind- and solar-energy sources. In practice this is not entirely successful, and some engine charging is often necessary, at least every second day. The facts are as follows:

- **Battery Demand** Electric refrigeration systems are power hungry. No matter how many systems put forward attractive consumption figures (most are often optimistic), average usage is at least 50 amp-hours for a refrigerator, and around 100 amp-hours for freezers on a 50% duty cycle. I have a new Isotherm system fitted which I have found to be very efficient.

- **Battery Charging** A far greater run time is required to restore battery capacity involved than for an equivalent engine driven system. You will definitely require a higher output alternator, and a fast charging device is essential. The average vessel recharging time with electric systems is typically around one hour morning and night. Remember that you have to replace 120% of the power used.

- **Efficiency** The majority of electric systems use hermetically sealed, Danfoss-type compressors. Glacier Bay uses reciprocating units. The reciprocating compressor system is far more efficient, more reliable and robust. It is almost universally found on engine driven systems. An engine driven compressor applies a greater load onto the engine, which along with an alternator and a fast charge device, allows reasonably economical engine use instead of damaging, light load conditions. There is however a more intangible efficiency gain with an electric system because it keeps temperatures stable, so the actual run times to pull down temperatures are relatively small. The Isotherm system has an innovative feature: When the control module detects the engine running through an increase in voltage from the charging system, the compressor motor runs at twice the speed pulling down the temperature quickly.

- **Economics** The engine driven system is generally more expensive to install, requires more engineering, pipework, etc. Engine maintenance is lower than simple battery charging duties, because the run times have greater loads and are for considerably shorter periods. Electric systems are initially cheaper to buy and install, but they do require much greater battery capacity, and thousands can be spent on solar and wind systems, high output alternators, etc. Also, longer engine run times are often required when wind and sun do not deliver, generally costing in maintenance and fuel.

Engine Driven Eutectic Systems The engine driven compressor is probably the most efficient, and is able to pull down temperatures quickly. Selection factors are as follows:

- **Economics** Engine driven compressors make more economical use of the engine by imposing a substantial load, which reduces maintenance costs. If you have to run the engine for battery charging, it makes good sense to fully utilize the energy source. The extra load also gets the water hot if you have a calorifier.

- **Dual Circuit Systems** An engine driven system also enables both refrigerator and freezer to run off the same refrigeration plant. There is a growing trend to incorporate engine driven compressors with small electric systems. The main refrigerator space can be pulled down initially and every second day using the engine compressor. The electric unit, sustained by alternative energy sources, can then maintain the temperature for a significantly increased period.

- **Disadvantages** The capital cost of installation is relatively high, as are the installation time and work involved. If an installation is not properly done, gas leakage problems are common.

Energy Saving Measures A few energy saving, efficiency increasing measures can be implemented:

- **Void Spaces** Fill any empty spaces in the refrigerator compartment with either blocks of foam, or inflated empty wine-cask bladders. This will decrease the refrigerator space and reduce energy requirements.

- **Food Covers** If all frozen goods are placed at the bottom of the compartment, place a mat over the food so that cold air is retained within the food below the mat.

- **Battery Voltages** Ensure that battery voltage levels are maintained. Low battery levels will cause inefficient compressor operation. Do not let the battery level sink to the normal minimum level of 10.5 volts. It takes far more energy and engine run time to charge a nearly flat battery than one half charged.

- **Ventilation** See that the compressor unit is well ventilated. Installing a small solar fan will ensure positive ventilation. Water cooled condensers are essential for refrigerator system efficiency in tropical waters.

- **Insulation** The thicker the insulation the better the performance. I have installed 4 inches of urethane insulation and I am very happy with the results.

Reduced Holdover Times This is by far the most common problem. Causes are as follows:

- **Warm Foodstuffs** A refrigerator or freezer system pulled down to the required temperature and then loaded with unfrozen food or warm drinks will not remain cold for as long as a system where the contents are pre-cooled.

- **Climate Change** More often than not the system works well in a temperate climate, but the first extended cruise in to tropical waters results in a dramatic reduction in apparent efficiency. A liveaboard opens the refrigerator sparingly, while the people new to the liveaboard lifestyle are probably opening it far more than is necessary and far more than they did on a normal weekend cruise. Keep access to a minimum.

- **Mechanical Causes** Engine drive belts are not retensioned. Belt slippage under load causes decreased refrigeration. Make sure the refrigerator access lid seals well.

COOKING EQUIPMENT

The real art of cooking depends on the equipment used on the stove burners. The following offer the most energy efficient ways of preparing great meals quickly.

The Pressure Cooker

The pressure cooker is a savior for cruisers, especially the many who do not have a broiler (grill) or an oven. Whether it is the cheaper aluminum unit with automatic timer and vent, or a heavy old-fashioned cast one like mine with a brass weight on the vent, it is both a time and fuel saver. The nutritional advantages are also well known in pressure cooking. The Cuisinart® stainless steel cooker from the Cruising Equipment Company of Seattle is top of the line for cruising. Do not leave port without a pressure cooker, it is an indispensable part of the cruising galley.

The Wok

The wok is one of the most versatile and quickest ways to cook on board. The stir fry method of cooking is quick and easy, and what is more it is very economical on fuel. On a moving yacht, it really does become wok-and-roll cooking (Ha!). Ideally you will need to find a wok with a wooden handle and a small enough diameter to get over the burner and fiddle rails.

Seasoning your wok Your new wok requires seasoning. This will stop food from sticking. Any self respecting Chinese cook has a wonderfully blackened wok.

- First, wash in hot and soapy water to remove any traces of machine oil.

- Dry the wok well and place over a low flame.

- Ideally rub the wok with a paper towel soaked with peanut oil (never use olive oil). Heat the oil; repeat a couple of times.

Cooking with a wok Successful stir frying requires high heat, a small amount of oil, and constant tossing and stirring. See stir frying recipe chapter.

- Get the wok really hot before cooking.

- Meats and vegetables should be thinly sliced so they cook quickly to get that mixture of crispy vegetables and juicy meat.

- Introduce ingredients into the wok according to the time required to cook them.

Knives

Every galley needs a good knife set. The set should include a good paring knife. Wide bladed and well balanced, the paring knife is the essential cook's knife for all those regular tasks that range from slicing and chopping of vegetables to poultry. A good flexible filleting knife for the fresh catch is also a must. A broad-bladed cleaver will also be very useful. Essential is a sharpening steel. The quality of any knife cutting edge is dictated by the cutting angle of the blade. Most knives have an angle of 40 to 45 degrees, but the more flexible boning and filleting knives have an angle of about 55 degrees. When using the sharpening steel, move the knife blade on the steel at an angle between 20 to 22 degrees. Do not apply too much pressure. Six to eight strokes on each side are all that is necessary.

Pots and Pans

Space is at a premium in any galley, and finding pots and pans with accessible handles, that fit burners, is often quite a problem.

Stainless Steel Cookware Many people opt for a set of corrosion-resistant stainless steel cookware. I have a 5-quart stockpot with a narrow base that fits neatly on the stove top. Cuisinart® Stainless Nesting Cookware have a stainless steel cookware set that is ideal for a cruising yacht. This is a nine-piece set nesting into each other; it comprises a 3-quart, 2-quart, and a 1-quart saucepan that double as mixing bowls and baking dishes. They come with quick release handles. The set also has a great 5-quart stockpot and a 9-inch skillet as a lid. It measures a compact 13 inches across the handles, and is only 7 inches high. Contact the Cruising Equipment Company in Seattle.

Non-Stick Cookware A number of people prefer non-stick cookware. Usually non-stick cookware is relatively inexpensive. The big advantage is ease of cleaning, and cleaning with salt water is a great water saver. I have one good non-stick saucepan. Make sure you do not scratch your pots and they will last a long time.

Cast Iron Cookware While a full set of the French Le Creuset cookware is generally out of the question, a good cast iron skillet is a great companion; typically a skillet of about 7-inch to 10-inch is ideal. Season well with corn oil. Many also prefer a cast iron Dutch oven. Another great item for those without a broiler is a ridged griddle pan. This allows easy dry frying of meats and fish, and is great for indoor barbecues.

Hand Appliances

There are some really useful things around and most have their origins in camping equipment. I have a griddle which is great. Put in the bread and fillings: for rough weather meals it is unbeatable and fast. These days toaster ovens are quite popular.

Electric Appliances

For those on larger yachts, with a genset or an inverter system, these appliances will speed up galley preparation times:

- **Blenders and food processors** They are worth their weight in gold. You can opt for DC equivalents. While not cheap, they are a viable way to dispense with AC. These are primarily U.S. made.

- **Toasters** Again these are useful if AC is available.

- **Kettles** The most efficient way of boiling water is the stovetop kettle. If you opt for an AC powered domestic unit, you must be careful. The quick boil units pull a large current, in many cases equating to domestic hot water systems. Get a unit with a smaller element, typically around 1.2kW.

GALLEY SAFETY

If ever there is a dangerous workplace, it is the galley on a cruising boat. Some major safety factors must be considered.

Gas Safety

With a large amount of yachts converting to or installing gas, safety is of paramount importance. Explosions are thankfully rare, and this may be due to the inordinate fear of gas. I have seen first hand what gas can do, while working on an offshore oil drilling rig that suffered a massive explosion from leaking gas, with sad loss of life and massive destruction. It only takes a small quantity of gas in the bilge of a yacht to literally blow it apart.

- First and foremost, install a reliable gas detector, with solenoid shut-off valve. It should be left on all the time, not when you are about to cook.

- Treat any alarm as a problem, not as a false alarm. Ventilate the boat to be on the safe side before cooking and satisfy yourself that no gas is around.

- Gas sensors have a tendency to degrade: make sure you have a spare to replace it with, preferably every couple of years. If the sensor head has been wet with seawater, replace it as well.

- Always turn off the gas at the bottle as well as the local valve.

Galley Fires

Fire is the major enemy afloat. As on land, a great many fires start in the kitchen. Be prepared with the proper safety equipment and more importantly know how and when to use it. Always have a fire extinguisher mounted on the adjacent bulkhead. Have a fire blanket mounted on the adjacent bulkhead.

Hot Liquids

Always wear an oilskin apron or jacket at sea. Spilling hot liquids is a real danger and a common cause of burns and scald. Ensure that the stove has properly installed fiddle rails and pot clamps to hold everything in place, in addition to gimballing. Many galleys still do not have them.

Balance

Continuous gyrating movement is the major source of difficulties. Install a "buttstrap" so that you can lean back into it and have both hands free to cook. The stove should have a strong fixed bar mounted in front to grab onto.

GALLEY CLEANING

Environmental cleaning methods are a great way to look after the ocean itself and save a little money into the bargain. The following well-known products and tried methods are recommended:

- **Borax** Borax is used as a water softener, disinfectant and insecticide. It is slightly toxic and can enter the body through skin breaks, so use sparingly. To control cockroaches, mix with honey or jam and place in infested areas.

- **Bicarbonate of soda or baking soda** This is a versatile and very efficient cleaner.

- **Cloudy Ammonia** Never use in enclosed spaces or the vapors can cause respiratory problems and eye irritation. Wear a surgical mask during use.

- **White Vinegar** White vinegar is a natural and mild disinfectant and can be used for most cleaning.

Stoves and Ovens

Mix 1 cup water and ½ cup of ammonia and put into an ovenproof dish or bowl. Place in a warm oven for 10 to 15 minutes, then wipe off grime with scourer and bicarbonate of soda. Wipe over with cloudy ammonia. When the worst of the grime is off, clean with bicarbonate of soda and a scourer.

Stainless Steel Sinks

Rub with bicarbonate of soda on a damp cloth, followed by warm soapy water.

Refrigerators and Freezers

Wipe insides with bicarbonate of soda on a damp cloth. For a shiny finish give a wipe with white vinegar. Put an open container of bicarbonate of soda inside the refrigerator to eliminate smells

and odors for up to 3 months. Wiping the inside of the refrigerator with vanilla essence will also deodorize it. Or you can leave a cotton wool ball soaked in vanilla to absorb odors.

Work Surfaces

Rub with bicarbonate of soda on a damp cloth. Ceramic tiles are best cleaned with white vinegar on a cloth.

Pots and Pans

There a few ways to clean them, so try the following:

- Burnt saucepans are best cleaned by covering the bottom with a layer of cooking salt and white vinegar and letting stand overnight. Heat until boiling, simmer for 10 minutes, then wash normally when cool, or

- Sprinkle the burnt area with bicarbonate of soda and let it stand, or

- Simmer the pot with a strong solution of cream of tartar and water for 30 minutes.

General Washing Up

Use a cake of pure soap ideally in a wire shaker or a small can pierced with holes. Shake in the water to raise a lather. For heavy grease washing loads, add some bicarbonate of soda to neutralize the grease. If you prefer off the shelf washing up liquids, get concentrated ones that take up minimal space and make up a batch as required.

TRASH CONTROL AND DISPOSAL

The management of trash is an important consideration on any yacht, and the following are some simple suggestions.

Plastics

Plastic is the most environmentally destructive of all packaging materials. When provisioning, remove all the excess plastic wrapping ashore. Plastics still on board should be placed in a bag for disposal ashore. As they will compress well, little space is used. PET and other plastic drink bottles should be cut into strips or small squares with scissors and similarly stored for later disposal.

Papers and Cardboard

When provisioning, remove all cardboard packaging possible ashore. Store provisions in airtight containers or in resealable plastic bags. As papers and cardboard are a popular source of cockroach eggs and stowaway bugs this is a useful exercise. While cruising the best way of disposal is the use of the barbecue as an incinerator.

Cans

The disposal of cans poses the greatest dilemma. Aluminum cans should be crushed for disposal at a shoreside recycling point. Tin cans should also be washed out and they can be often stowed inside larger cans to reduce stowage space. Many people punch holes in the can and throw it overboard: yes, it'll sink, but it is still pollution.

Food Waste

It is biodegradable, and can be thrown over the side. If you can, save it for a couple of days and use as bait over the stern when fishing.

COOKING DATA

Weights and Measures (U.S., U.K., Metric)

US Standard	=	Metric	US Standard	=	Metric
⅓ ounce	=	10 grams	½ ounce	=	15 grams
1¾ ounces	=	50 grams	1 ounce	=	30 grams
3½ ounces	=	100 grams	¼ pound (4 ounces)	=	120 grams
8¾ ounces	=	250 grams	½ pound (8 ounces)	=	230 grams
			1 pound (16 ounces)	=	460 grams

Fluid Measures

US Standard	=	Metric
1 teaspoon	=	5 milliliters
1 tablespoon	=	20 milliliters
1 ounce	=	30 milliliters
1 pint	=	475 milliliters

Cup and Spoon Conversions

US Standard	=	Metric	US Standard	=	Metric
1¼ cups	=	1 cup	¼ cup	=	2 tablespoons
1 cup	=	¾ cup	3 teaspoons	=	1 tablespoon
¾ cup	=	⅔ cup	1 cup(8 fl oz)	=	250 milliliters
⅔ cup	=	½ cup	½ cup(4 fl oz)	=	125 milliliters
½ cup	=	⅓ cup	⅓ cup	=	80 milliliters
⅓ cup	=	¼ cup	¼ cup(2 fl oz)	=	60 milliliters

Gas Temperature Equivalents

Very Slow	250°F	120°C		Moderately Hot	375°F	190°C
Slow	300°F	150°C		Hot	400°F	205°C
Moderately Slow	325°F	160°C		Very Hot	450°F	230°C
Moderate	350°F	180°C				

These measurements have been rounded up in the recipes for ease of use.

Chapter 3

Provisioning

Planning

Length of Shelf Life

Food Preservation

Storage

Provisioning Checklists

Herbs, Spices and Condiments

Cooking Oils

Fresh Food Substitutes

Worldwide Provisioning Guide

Provisioning is a major undertaking. Stocking up is of critical importance, whether for a weekend cruise, a two week vacation or a circumnavigation.

PLANNING

Provisioning, or to use the old fashioned term, victualling, is a major undertaking. Ask anyone who has gone through the exercise before a cruise. Storing up is of critical importance, whether it is for a weekend cruise, a two weeks vacation, or the circumnavigation. Remember last time you did your provisioning, that seemingly endless procession of boxes? It was frightening, wasn't it? There are two basic provisioning philosophies:

Option 1. Menu Based Planning

This method is by its nature fairly rigid. Menu based planning only makes sense for a short cruise. It is comparatively easy then to work out a series of menus for the entire trip, and base the provisioning around the required ingredients. These menu based plans often involve the use of readily available deli and fresh food items.

Option 2. General Food Base Planning

On an extended cruise in foreign countries, the menu goes out the porthole when you find you cannot get the items you need unless you pay an exorbitant price. The reality is that once you run out of the prime menu ingredients, it is often near impossible to obtain them elsewhere. I feel that for the longer voyages storing up on a broad range of staples and basic items will give you the scope to prepare a greater range of meals and adapt them to local ingredients. It will be much cheaper to buy bulk amounts of staples such as rice, pasta, selected canned foods, etc.

Whichever method you choose, be meticulous in your planning, allow for some wastage, for extra days, extra people, and make sure you stock up on foods you will eat. So, fill up your tender, and start ferrying it out.

LENGTH OF SHELF LIFE

Under various governmental legislation and requirements, the dates until when the foodstuffs may be consumed are written clearly on the containers; often food is useable within a reasonable period afterwards. Manufactured foods with preservatives must be watched because the food-stuffs break down as preservatives age. Typical shelf lives are as follows:

- Canned Foods   18 months

- Flour   12 months

- Rice   12 months

FOOD PRESERVATION

More than a few resourceful cruisers preserve food wherever possible. The most common methods used are as follows:

- **Drying** Choose a warm sunny day, slice meat or fish into thin strips and hang well spaced on a drying line.

- **Smoking** A small smoker, or dual purpose barbecue, can be used. Food will last up to a month.

- **Bottling** The pressure cooker is a valuable friend in this task. The method requires proper bottling jars and seals. By heating the jars, you create a vacuum seal that preserves the cooked food. Mostly fruit and tomatoes are suitable for bottling. Bad seals may be a problem. Also, glass bottles run the risk of breaking.

- **Pickling** Fish and vegetables are suitable for pickling. You will need pickling vinegar. The flavor is enhanced by the addition of herbs and spices.

- **Salting** Used for fish, meat. You will require cooking salt. Store in sealed liquid brine or between layers of salt. Keep the food in thin strips to allow salt to penetrate properly.

Dry Food Preservation

Dry foods should be stored in air tight containers if at all possible. Humidity is the greatest problem; it penetrates quickly paper packaging, a pound of sugar soon goes solid. Add some rice grains to the flour to absorb moisture.

Canned Food Preservation

Varnish and mark cans to use by dates and store them in cool areas. Do not allow cans to rust or damage. Personally I use hair spray, and give them a few coats to form a layer. It is less messy and cheaper than varnish and it dries quickly. If you mark cans with a marker pen, make sure it is a waterproof one. The idea of stowing cans of food in bilges is common but as wrong as

letting water into the diesel tanks. Bilges are for water, not food. Food is your fuel, look after it.

The Long Life Vegetable Bag

The green bag is a cruiser's best friend. The green plastic is impregnated with a natural mineral ingredient called Maxifresh™. It can be reused several times, although effectiveness decreases gradually with each wash.

Suitable perishable produce include asparagus, green beans, broccoli, Brussels sprouts, cabbage, cucumber, lettuce, mushrooms, peas and tomatoes. Fruits include peaches, apricots, cherries and grapes. Less perishables include avocados, carrots, cauliflower, celery, parsley, parsnip, pumpkin, and snow peas. Fruits include apples, grapefruit, lemons, oranges and pears. There are a few basic rules when using green bags:

- Use separate bags for different produce.

- Where possible refrigerate as well.

- Store fresh and undamaged produce.

- If the bag is being reused, it should be dry.

- Only store dry produce in bags.

- After placing the produce in the bag, get the air out and seal with a twist tie.

- Do not overfill the bag with produce.

Fresh Vegetables and Fruit

If you want maximum life and quality out of your fresh produce, observe the following simple guidelines:

- Always select vegetables in varying stages of ripeness, so that you do not suddenly end up with a glut of produce that has to be eaten immediately or otherwise thrown away.

- Wash all fruit and vegetables well either before or after bringing them aboard, and if preserving see notes on preservation dips below.

- Store produce in dark and well ventilated areas.

- Install hanging nets and plastic vegetable trays.

- Inspect daily, and eat anything that is about to go off to avoid waste. Longest lasting are garlic, onions, potatoes, cabbage, carrots, cauliflower and pumpkins.

- Remove leaves from root vegetables before storage.

- If you are going to foreign countries, do not purchase more than you need for the voyage as it will probably be confiscated on arrival under local quarantine rules. It is worth checking on appropriate quarantine rules before you head off.

Companion Storage

Some vegetables and fruit do not store well next to each other. The ethylene gas generated during ripening can seriously shorten the life of other produce.

Do not store the following adjacent to each other—observe how various vegetables and fruits react to each other:

- Onions and potatoes

- Apples and carrots

- Bananas and apples

Fruit and Vegetable Preservation Dips These methods have been around for many years and many cruising folk are more than happy with the results.

- **Potassium Permanganate** Prepare a dilute solution of potassium permanganate and water. Dip the vegetables in the mixture and allow to dry before storing.

- **Bleach** Prepare a dilute solution of bleach and water in the ratio of 1 tablespoon bleach per gallon of water. Place each item into the solution and soak for around 10 to 15 minutes. Pat dry and leave in the sun to dry for 30 minutes. Stow in appropriate location. The theory is that the bleach solution kills off surface bacteria and this is assisted in the drying stage by the sunlight.

STORAGE

Typical Average Vegetable Storage Life

The following table is a guide to the typical shelf life of vegetables. It may vary depending on ripeness when purchased, actual storage practices, and ambient temperatures.

Vegetable	Unrefrigerated	Refrigerated	Green Bag
Artichoke	14 days	21 days	Not required
Asparagus	4	7	14 days
Beans	3	7	14
Beets	7	14	21
Broccoli	2	7	14
Brussels sprouts	5	7	14
Cabbage	28	42	35
Carrots	10	14	21
Cauliflower	10	14	21
Celery	5	8	14
Chocho (Chayote)	7	14	21
Cucumber	10	14	21
Eggplant	10	14	21
Garlic	28	42	56
Leaf greens	4	7	14
Leeks	7	10	Not required
Lettuce	7	10	14
Mushrooms	4	7 (brown bag)	Not required
Okra	7	10	Not required
Onions (yellow)	3-12 weeks	Not required	Not required
Parsnip	21	Not required	Not required
Peas	4	7	14
Potatoes	2-12 weeks	Not required	Not required
Pumpkin	4-14 weeks	Not required	Not required
Scallions	7	10	14
Squash	7	10	Not required
Sweet corn	5	7	14
Sweet pepper	7	10	21
Sweet potato	2-14 weeks	Not required	Not required
Taro	2-10 weeks	Not required	Not required
Tomatoes	14	21	28
Zucchini	5	10	14

Sweet pepper (also green, red or yellow bell pepper) is also known as capsicum.
Zucchini is known in some countries as courgettes.

Typical Average Fruit Storage Life

The following table gives the typical storage life for various fruits. Obviously this depends on the stage of ripeness of the fruit when purchased. Some fruits are easily stored at room temperature.

- Fruits such as apricots, nectarines, peaches, pears, persimmons and plums usually require ripening at room temperature.

- Fruits such as avocados, kiwis, mangoes, papayas and rockmelon are ripened at room temperature and then stored in the refrigerator.

Vegetable	Unrefrigerated	Refrigerated	Green Bag
Apples	14 days	21 days	28 days
Apricots	4	7	10
Avocados	4	7	10
Bananas	4	7	10
Cherries	4	7	10
Citrus	14	Not required	Not required
Custard apples	3	5	7
Grapes	7	10	14
Grapefruits	21	Not required	Not required
Mangoes	4	7	10
Nectarines	4	7	10
Papaya (paw paw)	4	7	10
Passion fruit	10	14	21
Peaches	4	10	14
Pineapples	7	Not required	Not required
Plums	4	7	10
Rockmelon	5	10	14
Strawberries	4	7	10
Tamarillos	7	10	14
Watermelons	14	Not required	Not required

Egg Storage

Eggs are versatile and a great pantry addition. See the recipe section on eggs for some great ideas.

- If refrigerator space permits, store the eggs as deterioration is much slower. Put the small end down in the carton.

- Eggs will last up to two months if covered with Vaseline and turned weekly. Alternatively use glycerine which works well. Storage should be in as cool a place as possible.

- Buy fresh eggs at farm or market, especially those that are unwashed and have never been refrigerated as they last significantly longer.

- Do not wash eggs you purchase as the shell acts as a barrier to harmful bacteria. Only wash in warm water prior to use.

- Freshness Test. Place eggs in cold salty water. The really fresh eggs sink immediately; the older the eggs are the higher they float. Any egg that surfaces is bad and should be thrown away. As eggshells are porous, the internal liquids evaporate, and the egg becomes progressively lighter.

- Storage Hint. Instead of buying expensive plastic egg storers, simply paint and seal the paper ones, it is just like papier-mâché.

- For really long term egg storage, albeit with a little bit of work, try the following: Boil a large pot of water. Add 2 pounds (1kg) of limes in a covered enamel pot and pour over the water. Let stand for 2 days and strain off limes. Add 1 ounce (30g) of cream of tartar and 4 ounces of salt. Dip the fresh eggs every day into the solution. The eggs should be used only for baking.

Cheeses

- Waxed cheeses last up to two months.

- Muslin covered cheeses last up to a year, a favorite for long cruises.

Meats

Cured hams and smoked meats and salamis last well if hung in a cool, well ventilated area.

PROVISIONING CHECKLISTS

The following list covers most of the items used in this book. You can add your own provisions in the blank spaces.

Item	Qty	Exp. date	Item	Qty	Exp. date
Baking			**Rice**		
Plain (All purpose) Flour			Long grain		
Self-raising flour			Basmati		
Corn flour			Jasmine		
Dry yeast					
Compressed yeast			**Pasta**		
_____			Fettuccine		
_____			Lasagne sheets		
Baking soda			Pasta shells		
Salt			Spaghetti		
Instant gravy			_____		
White sugar			_____		
Brown sugar					
Powdered sugar			**Legumes**		
_____			Chickpeas		
_____			Lima beans		
			Navy beans		
Beverages			Red kidney beans		
Skim milk powder			Red lentils		
Condensed milk			_____		
UHT milk			_____		
Cocoa					
Coffee - instant					
Coffee - ground			Taco shells		
Coffee - beans			Instant noodles		
Tea - leaf			Packet soups		
Tea - bags			Soup in a cup		
Cordials			Porridge oats		
_____					
_____			Raisins (sultanas)		
_____					

Canned and Bottled Stores

The following list gives all of the items used in this book. You can add your own provisions in the blank spaces.

Item	Qty	Exp. date	Item	Qty	Exp. date
Baked beans			Olives		
Corn kernels			Peanut butter		
Creamed corn			Pickles		
Mushrooms					
Red kidney beans			Honey		
Tomatoes			Jams		
			Pineapple pieces		
Corned beef					
Ham					
Salmon					
Sardines					
Tuna					
Condensed Soups:					
Cream of mushroom					
Tomato soup					
Vegetable soup					
Pasta sauces					

Miscellaneous Stores

The following list covers all of the items used in this book. You can add your own provisions in the blank spaces.

Item	Qty	Exp. date	Item	Qty	Exp. date
Olive oil			Beef stock cubes		
Peanut oil			Brown sauce		
Sesame oil			Chicken stock cubes		
Vegetable cooking oil			Lemon juice		
			Minced coriander		
			Minced garlic		
Light soy sauce			Minced ginger		
Soy sauce			Sweet chili sauce		
Thai fish sauce			Tabasco sauce		
			Tomato ketchup		
Coconut cream					
Vanilla essence					

HERBS, SPICES AND CONDIMENTS

One of the catalysts for seagoing exploration was the quest for a reliable and cheap supply of spices. The great Dutch East India Company was created for this reason. In 1519, Ferdinand Magellan headed out with five ships to circumnavigate the globe, and only one vessel with 18 out of an original 230 men made it back to home port. Spices were so precious that the cinnamon, nutmeg and mace carried home made the voyage financially viable.

Pepper

Pepper is a condiment. Whether you grind the peppercorns with your own grinder or it is already ground, it has a beautiful aroma. It is the most popular of spices in the world. It was once a rare and expensive spice and, like salt, was used as a currency. If you cruise the Pacific and visit Ponapei in the Caroline Islands, stock up on the superb gourmet pepper grown there.

Nutmeg

The spice that started it all. The Dutch controlled the spice islands (Moluccas) and even tried to eradicate the trees from other islands to increase their monopoly, without success.

The Essential Herb/Spice List

As any visit to a modern supermarket will show, the spice racks are enormous. Spices are not cheap, so limit yourself to those you will use within a reasonable period. Remember that the spices lose their flavor as they age. The following list includes all those found in this book, and what I personally regard as the essentials in any galley. Include your own in the list.

Herb/Spice - Traditional	Qty	Herb/Spice - Asian	Qty
Basil		Cardamom pods	
Bay leaves		Cinnamon sticks	
Cayenne pepper		Coriander	
Chili powder		Curry powder - Madras	
Cloves		Curry powder - Thai	
Cumin		Curry leaves	
Fennel		Five-spice powder *	
Nutmeg		Garam masala	
Oregano		Ground ginger	
Paprika		Saffron	
Parsley flakes		Turmeric	
Peppercorns			
Rosemary			
Sesame seeds			
Thyme			
_____			
_____			

Five-spice powder is a combination of cinnamon, star anise, fennel, cloves, and peppercorn.

Herbs

Herbs have a very wide range of uses. If you can get fresh herbs, great, but like most cruisers, you will probably need to substitute dried herbs in recipes.

Basil A big player in Italian cuisine, it goes well with egg and tomato dishes, mushroom, rice, tomatoes, pasta, octopus and fish. It has a strong flavor, so use sparingly. Fresh basil is great in salads and dressings—see the pesto recipe. For a tasty lunch with fresh bread, put some chopped basil leaves on sliced tomatoes with a drizzle of virgin olive oil over it all.

Bay leaves One of three herbs used in a bouquet garni, best with meat, stews and soups.

Coriander (Chinese parsley, cilantro) One of my favorite herbs, it is an essential part of Middle Eastern, South American and Asian cuisine. Dried coriander is used in curry powder. Add fresh coriander into seafood dishes, scrambled eggs and green salads.

Mint A traditional partner for lamb.

Oregano A major part of Italian and Greek food. Great with pizza sauces and pasta dishes.

Parsley Great on pasta, in casseroles, and with omelettes.

Rosemary It is used with lamb. Also tasty with eggs and cheese.

Sage A strong flavor that livens up stuffings and bread, potatoes, chicken and turkey, also great with pork, duck and stews. Be careful not to put too much in.

Thyme A strongly flavored herb, used with meats, fish soups, stews and pasta sauces.

COOKING OILS

The oil used will make or break a meal. Change the oil and you change both the flavor and the texture of most dishes. It is a good idea to include a variety and get the most from your dishes.

Olive Oil

The heart of Mediterranean cooking is olive oil. Besides being very healthy for you it adds great flavor to cooking. If you cook Italian or Greek food, then always use olive oil. There are a few basic and different types. Sources vary, but most olive oils are Spanish or Italian; my own preference is for Bertolli, an Italian brand.

- Extra Light This is highly refined and the ideal alternative to vegetable oils.

- Pure Olive Oil A blend of extra light and pressed oil.

- Extra Virgin This is from the first pressing and retains much of the olive fruit flavor.

Vegetable Oil

Safflower, peanut, canola and a variety of other such oils are general purpose cooking oils that do not rely on the oil taste to form part of the dish. Buy in bulk if you can as it is significantly cheaper that way.

Palm Oil (Dende)

Palm oil primarily comes from South America, principally Brazil. It has a red color and is rather "unique" in taste. Wherever it is used it adds a strong flavor to any dish.

FRESH FOOD SUBSTITUTES

A number of substitute items can be successfully used afloat.

Butter Substitute

Fresh butter belongs to the luxury list together with fresh milk, but you have to forego it when cruising.

- Tinned Butter Lasts up to one year in a cool place, but it not always easy to find.

- Margarine Many people are already converts to margarine. It will last up to a month or so in the refrigerator.

- Ghee Used in Indian cookery. You can get tins of liquefied ghee that lasts well.

Eggs

I have never thought much of egg substitutes. However powdered egg mixtures are good for baking. Use the egg preservation methods for the fresh ones.

Tomatoes

Canned tomatoes and tomato products are an essential part of cooking. Brands of canned tomatoes, tomato pastes, and tomato sauces vary greatly as consistency and added seasonings are different. Tomato sauce has added salt, spices, etc., whereas tomato paste is concentrated.

Tomato Purée To make purée from paste add one part water to the paste. If using canned tomatoes in recipes, add a teaspoon of brown sugar to the recipe to cut the acidity and sharp taste.

Instant Foods

There is a bewildering choice of instant foods and it all comes down to personal choices and tastes. Most cruisers carry some easily prepared foods. Speed and energy savings are worth the effort when you feel too tired to do anything else.

Packet Soups

Dried packaged soups are versatile, in particular the one-cup instant soups. Try these quick ideas:

- Layer sliced potato in a small casserole dish, sprinkle over a one-cup French onion soup pack, pour over a cup of hot milk, and bake in the oven.

- Mix melted butter and one-cup tomato soup and toss over some hot pasta.

- Add one-cup tomato soup to a marinade.

Instant Noodles

I personally prefer those from Maggi, although there are a range of Chinese varieties that are excellent. It is easy to turn a small package into a quick 5-minute meal for two by adding some vegetables to the boiling water, or perhaps some meat or seafood leftovers, before the noodles are added. Carry a large selection.

Dairy Products

Reducing dependence on dairy products is not easy for some, but there are many alternatives. A pint of fresh milk is hard to beat, but one can easily survive on the alternatives.

Condensed Milk

A great standby. Some people love it and others hate it and find it too sweet. Approximately 60% of the water has been removed from whole milk, then cane or corn sugar is added. You can buy it in skim and "light" types as well. Try these simple ideas and recipes.

Some Recipes with Condensed Milk

Quick Mayonnaise

1 pound can (500g) condensed milk
1 cup vinegar
1 teaspoon dried mustard powder
Black pepper and salt

Combine all the ingredients well. Cover and chill for 2 to 3 hours.

Papaya Mold

Serves 6

1 pound can (500g) condensed milk
½ cup orange juice
3 cups ripe papaya

Put all the ingredients in a blender for 3 minutes until smooth. Pour into molds and allow to set for 1½ hours. Pour into serving dishes before chilling and serving.

Coconut Mousse

Serves 6

1 tablespoon gelatine
2 tablespoons boiling water
1 pound can (500g)
   condensed milk
1½ cups shredded coconut
3 egg whites

Dissolve the gelatine in boiling water, then put in a blender with the condensed milk and the coconut, and mix until smooth. Beat the egg whites until stiff and fold into mixture in a bowl. Pour into serving dishes and chill for 3 hours until set.

Coconut Fingers

Serves 4 to 6

1 loaf sliced bread
1 pound can (500g)
   condensed milk
Fresh milk (if available)
¾ cup shredded coconut

Cut off the crusts of the bread and cut slices into three pieces each. Combine the condensed milk with some fresh milk, if available, then dip each finger into the mixture. Roll the fingers in the coconut and place onto a baking tray. Bake in a moderate oven until brown.

Powdered Milk

Both skim and full milk powders are quite acceptable if mixed properly and chilled. Expiration date is typically a year from purchase. Generally packaged in plastic bags of about 10 pints (5 liters), powdered milk is less prone to damage and deterioration. For best results always follow the instructions, in particular add powder to the water, not the other way around or you will end up with lumps.

Long Life Milk

Long life milk lasts well but takes up a lot of space and on long cruises you eventually run out and it is hard to replace. Typically shelf life is around 6 months.

Soy Milk

Packaged as long life milks. It is also difficult to replace.

Vacuum Flask Yogurt

Sterilize the flask in boiling water. Boil 2 pints of milk in a double saucepan. Simmer at boiling point for 30 minutes. Cool the milk by placing the saucepan in a sink full of cold water, swirling continually to ensure hot milk contacts the pan sides. Cool the milk to exactly 113°F. Pour into the flask a small pot of plain yogurt (goat yogurt if you can get it)—the flask will maintain the temperature for a sufficient time to allow optimum culture growth. Leave the flask for 6 to 12 hours depending on the required acidity. When yogurt is ready, pour into a jug and refrigerate. Close the flask leaving some yogurt inside to act as an inoculant for the next batch, or save some of the yogurt. Remember that the life of the yogurt as a culture for successive batches will gradually decrease.

WORLDWIDE PROVISIONING GUIDE

What can you expect to find when you get to that perfect paradise or dream destination? When you do, can you afford it without blowing out the budget? Remember that every dollar saved is a little more cruising time before you have to return home to earn more cruising dollars.

The Caribbean

Bananas, leaf vegetables (dasheen), okra, and a large range of tropical fruits and vegetables are always available.

Bahamas

Best for in season fruit and vegetables. Seafood tops the list for quality and variety. Rum of course is good value. Imported goods are prohibitively expensive, so stock up well.

Best Fruit and Vegetable Source: Local markets.

Best Grocery Source: Stock up at any of the major supermarkets in Nassau.

Water Quality: Good.

Antigua

Best Fruit and Vegetable Source: Malones Food Store, English Harbour. There is also a large outdoor market in St John's.

Best Grocery Source: Carib Marine, English Harbour. Call large orders on VHF 68; orders can be delivered to the boat.

LPG/Gas Refills: The Chandlery, Falmouth Harbour and Bowl Consumer Gas Service in St John's.

Water Quality: Good.

St Lucia

Best Fruit and Vegetable Source: There is a large outdoor market in Castries.

Best Grocery Source: Julie'n Supermarket in Gablewood Shopping Mall.

LPG/Gas Refills: Sunsail, Rodney Bay Marina.

Water Quality: Okay.

Grenada

Grenada is also called Isle of Spice, and for good reason. Nutmeg, cinnamon, cloves, etc., are to be found. Fresh fruits are superb, in particular bananas, pineapples and papayas. Local vegetables include the spinach-like callaloo and calabash. Seafood is plentiful. Take a trip across the island to Grenville and visit the Nutmeg Co-op: the local nutmeg syrup is delightful, try it on waffles instead of maple syrup.

Best Fruit and Vegetable Source: There is a large outdoor market in St George's.

Water Quality: Okay.

Pacific Islands

Many food items are imported so it is better to stock up beforehand on canned goods and toiletries. Locally produced fruit and vegetables are the best in many countries.

Polynesia (Central and Western Pacific)

The Society Islands
Tahiti

Much of the food is imported from France or New Zealand and can be terribly expensive. Nevertheless fresh local produce is plentiful and reasonably priced. If you plan on dining ashore, fixed price menus offer the best value. Local produce include seafoods of all types, breadfruit, cassava, mangoes, pamplemousse (grapefruit), papaya, pineapples, sweet potato, taro, tomatoes, onions and yams. Meat includes pork and chicken. Try local freshwater shrimp (called crevettes) when available.

Best Fruit and Vegetable Source: Municipal Market in Papeete (especially Sundays).

American Samoa

Pago Pago is a reasonable place to store up in mid Pacific.

Best Fruit and Vegetable Source: Fagotogo Market.

Water Quality: Good.

Western Samoa

The local market in Apia has a good array of local produce; get to the fish market early (around 0500) for best choice and freshness. Buy a bottle of the uniquely Western Samoan Talofa Ginger Liqueur.

Best Fruit and Vegetable Source: Local market for fish and vegetables.

Water Quality: Questionable.

Tonga

In Nuku'alofa on the main island of Tongatapu fresh fruits and vegetables are plentiful and reasonably priced. Fresh fish and seafood are available at the wharf, direct from the fishing boats, on the southern side of Faua Harbour. Up in the Vav'au Island group, supplies are less plentiful and more expensive if imported, but are available due to local charter operations.

Best Fruit and Vegetable Source: Daily market in Nuku'alofa.

Best Grocery Sources: Burns Philp, Morris Hedstrom, frozen meat available from the Tonga Cold Store.

Melanesia (South Pacific)

Vanuatu

A very large range of locally grown produce that includes breadfruit, cassava (manioc), paw-paws, lemons, limes, mangoes, oranges, bananas, pineapples, guavas, soursop, watermelons, avocados (badafrut), taro, Chinese cabbage, sweet corn, tomatoes, pumpkins, yams. The locally produced beef is excellent and well priced, so steak is a viable menu option. More recently a much wider range of locally grown "European" vegetables are becoming available.

Port Vila

Best Fruit and Vegetable Source: Vila market on Wednesday, Friday and Saturday, 0600-1200. Cheaper produce is available off street market on Rue Carnot on market days.

Best Provisioning Sources: Au Bon Marché and Burns Philp supermarkets, or Better Price.

Water Quality: Okay in Vila only.

Luganville

Best Fruit and Vegetable Source: Market Tuesday, Thursday and Saturday from 0730. Fish market is next door, with excellent fish, crabs and lobsters.

Best Grocery Source: Au Bon Marché and Burns Philp supermarket.

Water Quality: Questionable.

Solomon Islands
Honiara

Best Fruit and Vegetable Source: Central Market.

Best Grocery Source: Joy Supermarket.

Water Quality: Questionable.

Fiji

Fiji has a lot of locally grown produce. It includes eggplants, taro, sweet potatoes, onions, cabbage, avocados, bananas, cassava, papaya, pineapple, oranges, guava, as well as a variety of leaf vegetables similar to spinach. Seafoods are of course excellent, tuna is an export. Poultry, pork and beef are the most economical meats. Local dairy products are reasonably priced. Like most places in the Pacific, imported goods, in particular canned foods, are relatively expensive. Having a large Indian population, Fiji is excellent for Indian food and spices. Full provisioning (and all other services) can be made or arranged through Yacht Help in Suva; they monitor VHF Channel 71.

Best Fruit and Vegetable Source: Markets in Nadi, Lautoka and Suva. In Suva try Joes Farm Produce on Ragg Avenue. At Musket Cove Resort on Malolo Lai Lai Island you can obtain some fresh produce through Musket Cove Trader.

Best Grocery Sources: In Suva, all do dockside deliveries. Apteds in Bau Street, Flagstaff, Morris Hedstrom. In Lautoka, Morris Hedstrom.

New Caledonia

Most food is imported from France or nearby Australia, nevertheless fresh local produce is plentiful.

Noumea

Best Fruit and Vegetable Source: Market Monday to Saturday (0500-1000).

Best Grocery Source: Prisunic Barrau.

Water Quality: Fair Only.

Micronesia (Western North Pacific)

Micronesia consists of over 200 islands in the North Pacific. Basic local produce varies between the different island groups. Coconut and mangrove crabs are plentiful, reef fish are also plentiful, but ciguatera poisoning is a risk; tuna is the best buy, it is plentiful and not a risk fish. I was fortunate to first visit some of these beautiful places back in the 70's when employed on a small Nauruan passenger/cargo vessel. My second visit on a cruising yacht was even better.

Marshall Islands
Majuro

Breadfruit, coconuts and pumpkins, with limited amounts of other greens.

Water Quality: Tap water unsafe to drink. Lagoon water polluted, do not fish.

Federated States of Micronesia

This is the richest area in the world for tuna fishing so indulge where possible.

Kosrae

Bananas, breadfruit, coconut, citrus, mangrove crabs, taro.

Best Fruit and Vegetable Source: Public Market on road to Lelu.

Best Grocery Source: Websters at Tafunsak.

Water Quality: Fairly safe (has high rainfall).

Pohnpei

Gourmet pepper is wonderful, stock up. Produce includes bananas, breadfruit, limes, watermelon, yams and seafood (tuna).

Best Fruit and Vegetable Source: Public Market.

Best Grocery Source: Gibsons.

Water Quality: Tap water unsafe to drink.

Truk

Breadfruit, cucumbers, limes, mangoes, taro and shell fish. Sail to nearby Fefan Island for best fresh produce.

Best Grocery Source: Truk Trading Store.

Water Quality: Tap water unsafe to drink.

Yap

Bananas, breadfruit, oranges, papaya, tapioca, taro and yams.

Best Fruit and Vegetable Source: Waab-Mak'uuf market.

Best Grocery Source: Yap Co-operative Association.

Water Quality: Tap water unsafe to drink.

Republic of Palau
Koror

Mainly seafood (fruit bat and crocodile are local delicacies).

Best Fruit and Vegetable Source: Yano and Sons Produce market.

Best Grocery Source: WCTC Shopping Centre.

Water Quality: Tap water unsafe to drink.

Guam

Guam is the home of the Chamorro culture, or rather the remains of it. Local cuisine is a blend of Spanish, Filipino and Pacific Island foods. Sample Chamorro foods at public market stalls. Roast pig is a feast specialty, a variety of fruits and seafoods also are available. The large population and military presence ensures that a large amount of food is imported directly from the United States.

Best Fruit and Vegetable Source: Public market close to marina.

Best Grocery Source: Agana Shopping Center close to marina, or the Safeway at Micronesia Mall (take a taxi).

Water Quality: Safe to drink and treated.

Northern Marianas
Saipan

Seafood, particularly shellfish.

Best Fruit and Vegetable Source: Farmers Market.

Best Grocery Source: Hafa Dai store is the closest.

Water Quality: Tap water unsafe to drink.

Australia and New Zealand

Australia and New Zealand are probably the best places on earth to store up. Quality is very high, range is large, and what is more it is affordable. For exotic local tastes, try some kangaroo meat, or perhaps crocodile or emu steaks. Quality red meats are very economical.

Best Fruit and Vegetable Source: Any produce store or large supermarket, as well as Franklins Big Fresh Stores.

Best Grocery Source: Best value supermarkets are Bi-Lo, Franklins and Jewel while Woolworths and Coles New World supermarkets offer a greater range, particularly with gourmet or rarer items. For fresh seafoods, most small port towns have a fisherman's co-op. In Sydney do not miss out on the fish markets every day at Pyrmont, a seafood heaven.

Water Quality: Tap water safe everywhere.

The Mediterranean

The Med is the home of cuisine. Around its shores are the great culinary styles of France, Spain, Italy, Greece, and the Middle Eastern countries for good measure. Every town and every port have markets as sources of local produce and provisions. For instance in Italy you can stock up chiefly on tomato products, and likewise every other place has its bargains. I have therefore covered some of the less famous destinations.

Tunisia

If you are having a break or wintering in Tunisia, you can survive at a reasonable cost. Best places are Monastir and El Kantaoui. Fresh fruit and vegetables are of good quality, and very cheap in season. Bread is also cheap as are some other items such as UHT milk, dried fruits and nuts.

El Kantaoui The Magasin Général is the best place for reasonably priced stores, other places border on extortion. Sousse and Hamman Sousse are only 10 kilometers away and offer better value for fresh fruit and vegetables, meat and seafood.

Monastir Reasonable shops with Magasin Général and Monoprix being the larger ones. A daily market in the town, which is a leisurely 15 minutes stroll from the marina.

The Balearics

Tourism in these Spanish islands has ensured a ready supply of local and imported produce and stores, although local dishes are harder to find when dining ashore. Try and taste, and purchase some of the excellent local sausages from markets or butchers, in particular "llonganisa" and "botifarro." Pork is the main feature in local cuisine.

Palma

Fresh meat, fruit, vegetables and seafoods are available in the main market Mercado Pedro Grau. These include cheese, tomatoes and potatoes, citrus and almost everything else at reasonable prices. If you like fresh rabbit or poultry, this is the place. You have to get down there early for best choice—0500 is the startup time, by 0730 it is probably too late for the best quality. For fresh seafood visit incoming trawlers for good value. Haggling over prices is normal everywhere.

Gibraltar

As the exit or entrance to the Mediterranean, it is an important provisioning point.

Best Fruit and Vegetable Source: Go across the border to La Linea municipal market, held every Wednesday.

Best Supermarket: Stock up at Safeways, it is far better value and up to 50% cheaper than in Spain or elsewhere. In particular canned foods, meat and packaged or processed stores are best buys.

Azores

If you are stopping off at Horta on a transatlantic voyage, storing up is good, with plenty of fresh produce. The municipal market has a wide range of fruit and vegetables and excellent fish if you get there early. Good bread is also available and very good local cheese that keeps well.

Madeira

A lot is imported from Portugal so can be expensive. Obviously Madeira is reasonably priced, and I just cannot bring myself to open up my two bottles of 1942 vintage. Nelson had the "good fortune" to be transported back to England interred in a barrel of Madeira (although some accounts say rum!). If ashore try the local beef which melts in the mouth and some of the local extra deep sea fish, you'll see the ugly critters at the market. Even Jacques Cousteau hasn't figured out the life cycles of these tasty denizens.

Chapter 4

Breakfast Ideas and Eggs

Breakfast is an important meal. It provides the energy to sustain you through the day.

BREAKFAST IDEAS

Breakfast is an important meal, and provides the energy to sustain you through the day. It is well known that a good breakfast makes you more alert and feel more positive, especially on long and demanding passages. The cereal and milk breakfast is fine, and still a favorite among many cruisers, but many just skip breakfast. Try these breakfast ideas.

French Toast

Single Serving

1 egg
1 tablespoon skimmed milk
Pepper
2 slices bread
1 teaspoon oil

Beat the egg, milk and pepper lightly. Cut the bread slices into half and dip into the egg mixture. Brush a skillet with oil and heat. Put in the coated bread along with rest of egg mixture. Cook over medium heat until golden on both sides.

Pacific Toast

Serves 2

3 eggs
½ cup coconut cream
½ teaspoon white sugar
2 tablespoons lemon juice
Sliced bread
2 tablespoons butter or
   margarine

Beat the ingredients all together. Dip the bread slices into mixture and soak well. Melt butter in the skillet, then cook slowly on each side.

Porridge Oats

Single Serving

3 tablespoons rolled oats
1 cup skim milk
1 tablespoon sultanas raisins
Cinnamon powder to taste

Mix the oats, milk and sultanas in a pan. Bring to a boil slowly, and simmer gently for 10 minutes, stirring regularly. Add water to adjust consistency. Serve and sprinkle with cinnamon (I prefer soft brown sugar).

Quick Bubble and Squeak

Serves 2

1 teaspoon oil
1 small diced onion
1 cup leftover vegetables
½ cup cooked potato
1 egg white
Salt and black pepper to taste

Sauté onion until golden. Add the cooked vegetables and heat through. Lower the heat and stir the egg white and pepper. Cook the underside of vegetables until slightly crusted.

Breakfast Fritters

Serves 2

3 rashers bacon
1 cup self-raising flour
½ teaspoon salt
1 lightly beaten egg
1 cup milk

Finely chop the bacon, and fry until crisp. Sift flour and salt in a bowl, make a well in the center and add the egg. Mix until smooth, and gradually add the milk, beating well. Add the bacon. Heat margarine in a skillet and drop in tablespoons of the mixture into pan. Cook until golden brown and crisp, turn and cook the other side.

Fish Flapjacks

Serves 6

4 tablespoons self-raising flour
1 beaten egg
1 cup fresh or canned flaked fish
2 teaspoons lemon juice
¼ teaspoon grated lemon rind
1 tablespoon finely chopped parsley
2 teaspoons melted butter or margarine
2 tablespoons milk
Oil

Sift the flour into a bowl. Add the egg, fish, lemon juice, rind, parsley, butter and milk. Mix ingredients well. Drop a tablespoon at a time on a hot greased skillet, cook until golden brown on each side.

Norris Family Scottish Hotcakes
(Pauline on *Ruahatu*)

Serves 2

1 cup semolina or breakfast grain
1 cup oats
1 cup self-raising flour
½ cup powdered or fresh milk
2 eggs
Pinch of salt

Blend dry ingredients with the eggs and enough milk to form a pancake mixture consistency. Pour approximately ½ cup of mixture into a hot buttered or oiled skillet. Spread to form a thin pancake. Cook for about 2 minutes per side. Serve with honey or maple syrup.

EGGS

Eggs have many uses on the cruising menu; not only are they part of many recipes, but egg dishes also offer some great variations. One can tire of scrambled eggs or omelettes, but the following give a few useful and tasty extra ways to enjoy eggs.

Egg and Bacon Pie

Serves 4 to 6

½ cup melted butter
¾ cup self-raising flour
1½ cups milk
3 eggs
1 cup grated cheese
3 tablespoons fried crisp bacon
Seasonings, carrots, peas
  (optional)

Beat the butter, flour, and milk together with the eggs. Add the grated cheese and the bacon, and if you wish, seasonings, grated carrots, peas, etc. Put the mixture into a quiche dish and cook in the oven at 350°F (180°C) for 30 minutes.

Basic Frittata

Serves 4 to 6

2 tablespoons butter
2 tablespoons olive oil
1 diced onion
½ cup diced red pepper
½ cup diced green pepper
½ cup diced ham
1 tablespoon fresh herbs
  (oregano, basil)
8 eggs
Salt and pepper

Melt half the butter and olive oil together in a large skillet. Add the onion and cook until soft over low heat. Put in the red and green pepper and coat with oil and butter. Stir in the herbs and ham. Beat the eggs in a bowl and pour into the pan. Cook only until the bottom is firm. Coat the top with the rest of the butter and put under the broiler until the top sets and is golden. Alternatively you can combine all the ingredients and cook in a casserole dish in a moderate oven.

Rice and Vegetable Frittata

Serves 4

2 cups cooked brown rice
½ cup diced onion
1½ cups sliced zucchini
1 cup grated carrot
¼ cup fresh chopped parsley
Ground black pepper to taste
4 lightly beaten eggs
1 tablespoon margarine

Combine the rice, onion, zucchini, carrot, parsley, pepper and eggs and mix well. Heat the margarine in a skillet, and add the mixture. Cook over a low heat for 30 minutes until golden underneath. Finish under the broiler until top is browned.

Frittata Pottatta

Serves 4 to 6

This is great as main meal, or eaten cold as a snack.

2 tablespoons butter
2 tablespoons olive oil
1 diced onion
2 small cooked and diced
   potatoes
1 small sliced tomato
1 slice diced ham
1 tablespoon fresh herbs
   (oregano, basil)
8 eggs
Salt and pepper

Melt half the butter and olive oil together in a large skillet. Add the onion and cook until soft over low heat. Add the potatoes and coat with oil and butter. Stir in the herbs, ham, and the tomato. Beat the eggs in a bowl and pour into the pan. Add salt and pepper to taste. Cook only until the bottom is firm. Coat the top with butter and put under the broiler until the top sets and is golden. Alternatively combine all the ingredients and cook in a casserole dish in a moderate oven.

Fettuccine Frittata

Serves 4

1 cup milk
1 cup cream
6 lightly beaten eggs
2 tablespoons fresh chopped
   parsley
1 chopped red pepper
½ pound (250g) dry fettuccine

Whisk the milk and cream into the eggs. Stir in parsley and red pepper. Cook fettuccine in boiling water until tender, and drain. Stir fettuccine into egg and cream mixture. Pour into greased flan dish, and bake at 350°F (180°C) for 25 to 30 minutes.

Tropical Scrambled Eggs

Serves 2

4 eggs
½ cup milk
½ fresh squeezed orange
Fresh mango or paw paw

Crack eggs into a bowl, whisk in milk. Squeeze in orange juice. Drop mixture on hot skillet, use spatula and move around as it thickens. When half done, add slices of mango or pawpaw and continue cooking until done.

Chapter 5

Seafood

Catching Fish

Buying Fish

Fish Storage

Basic Fish Cooking

Shellfish

Fish Soups and Stews

Canned Fish

The best part of the cruising diet is seafood.

The best part of the cruising diet includes a lot of seafood, generally of a widely varying nature. Obviously you can catch your own, and in many cases you can purchase at local markets at reasonable or even cheap prices.

CATCHING FISH

A lot of people say that they do not catch many fish, but this is generally because they don't know how. Simply throwing a line off the stern is not going to keep you well fed. The most common fish caught off the stern are pelagic fish such as Spanish mackerel, school and spotted mackerel, bonito and tuna. These are migratory ocean going fish that surface feed on smaller bait fish. Top anglers will also tell you that fish bite better on the full moon, or the periods just before or after, so give it a try. This applies to ocean, reef and estuary fishing. Some clever digital watches will also help you to work out optimum fishing periods.

Here is a quick guide on how to recognize the various fish. For quick reference, invest in a fish identification chart and laminate it.

- Mackerels generally have triangular, sharp teeth and rigid, crescent shaped tails.
- Barracuda have long needle looking teeth prominent on the top jaw and a soft tail similar to bream.
- Tuna and bonito have a cigar-shaped body with dark blue or green backs and silver bellies. Bonito usually have horizontal stripes.

The ocean is often a barren place for fish, and you will want to fish where the fish will be feeding. These areas include the following, so it pays to keep a close eye on your chart depth contours, sometimes a minor course deviation can pay dividends.

- Reef systems These are natural locations for fish to concentrate.
- Sub sea mountains, plateaus, and pinnacles A rise in the seabed of only 50 feet can produce results on the surface 300 feet above particularly where currents rise off that feature and cause eddies on the surface.
- Current lines Fish are often seen foraging along these lines.
- Temperature occlusions This is generally on the continental shelf where deep and colder waters meet inshore warmer shelf waters. A series of tacks across the line is often very useful.
- Weed rafts The fish often travel with the raft using it as protection, or as a source of food. (If you are ever unfortunate enough to end up in a liferaft, try and secure yourself to a weed raft if you drift into one, as it has abundant lifesaving life.)

Visual signs of fish

- Flocks of seabirds wheeling and diving are a sign that fish is nearby. Generally they are feeding on surface schools.

- Signs of surface fish schools jumping as predators chase them. Often schools are chased by sharks, dolphins and other larger predatory fish.

Trolling

Trolled lures are the general method of fishing for pelagic fish. Here are a few basic recommendations:

- A braided line is a lot better as it kinks a lot less—I personally fish with at least a hundred pounds breaking strain line as well. Use stainless or black swivels to join the trace.
- A reel with a variable clutch is essential. Most fish are lost (the ones that get away!) as they break the line on the initial run. Set the tension so that it pays out under medium pressure. When a fish strikes, just wind in hard, do not tighten up the clutch.
- The best catches are always taken along reef edges and close to deep passages, around islands. Best boat speeds are about 3 to 6 knots, with around 150 feet (50 to 60 meters) of line paid out astern.
- Gaff the fish before landing since many are lost at this stage as hooks straighten out, lines break or traces are severed.
- When you land the catch, dispatch the victim with something heavy and blunt between the eyes. Bleed the fish straight away. This is done by cutting either under or behind the gills. Bleed and put straight on ice or in the refrigerator. If you don't, rapid softening and discoloration of the flesh will happen.
- There are many brands of lures. Some prefer spoons, others more lifelike lures that imitate fish movements and colors. For best lures use Rapala Magnums, Yo-Zuris, and Rebel Jaw-breakers. Contact the following mail order offshore tackle catalog suppliers. They supply worldwide and their advice is also invaluable:

Murray Bros., 8087 Monetary Dr., Suite El, Riviera Beach, FL 33404 (tel. 1-800-845-3474)
Offshore Angler Catalog, Dept. NE36, 1935 South Campbell, Springfield, MO 65896-0140

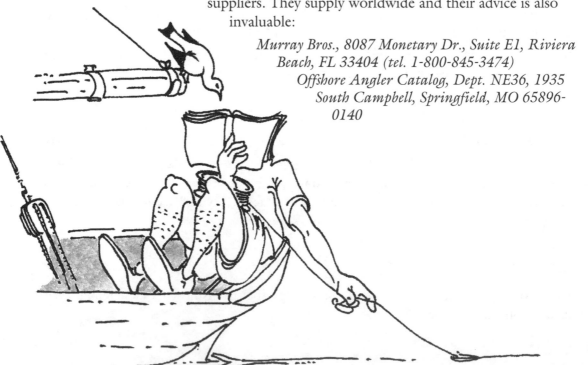

Ciguatera Poisoning

This normally non-fatal but debilitating poisoning occurs from eating some reef fish in tropical areas. Two to three percent of severe cases result in respiratory system paralysis and failure and are fatal. Fish become poisonous when they feed on organisms called dinoflagellates which grow on specific algae, notably blue-green. There are approximately 300 fish species suspected of causing poisoning. These include surgeon fish, coral trout, red snapper, mackerel, queen fish, red emperor, sweet lip, barracuda and grouper. Current research shows that fish above 5 pounds (2.5kg) are the most dangerous as the toxins concentrate and are stronger the larger the fish becomes. There is a significant risk of poisoning in areas where major reef disturbances have occurred, usually after cyclones and hurricanes, but pollution and any major natural disturbance also play their part.

Symptoms: The symptoms usually appear in anything from one to 12 hours. The first stage lasts around 40 hours and is characterized by tiredness and profuse perspiration. Usually this may be accompanied by vomiting, diarrhea and stomach cramps. Longer lasting effects include blurred vision and sore eyes, tight chest pains, lack of muscular co-ordination and blood in the urine. There are long term effects that may last years that include tingling or numbness of the lips, hands and feet, aching joints, severe headaches and aching teeth. Also there is a strange effect of temperature sensory reversal, which means hot feels cold and vice versa.

Detection and Cures: One method I have been told of (thanks Gail!) is that you should rub the fish liver on the lip and tongue, as this is where toxins accumulate. If the lip goes numb or tingling, the fish is suspect. It does work, so don't be squeamish. There has also been a treatment devised based on mannitol, which alleviates the symptoms.

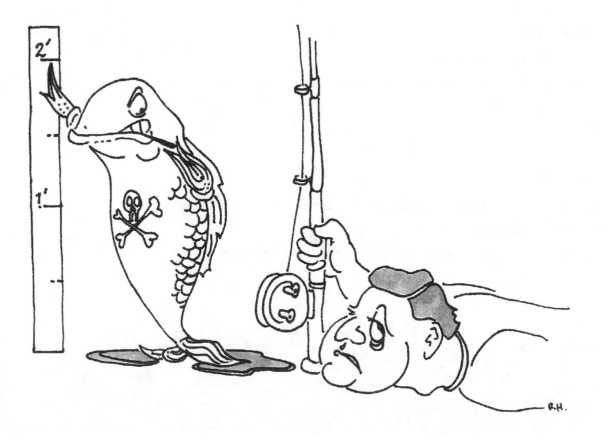

BUYING FISH

First and foremost, get there early, preferably as soon as the local markets open. In most cases the fish is not refrigerated or on ice. The later you come, the more suspect your purchase. Some local sellers will at least keep sluicing salt water over the fish (but where is the water from, you may ask?). Observe the following when purchasing fish:

Whole Fish

- The fish should have bright red gills.
- The flesh should be firm, and will spring back to the touch; scales should be tight.
- The eyes should be bright and unclouded, not sunken or milky.
- The skin should be bright and lustrous.
- The fish should have a pleasant sea smell.

Fish Fillets

- Flesh shiny and firm, not soft and dull.
- Flesh should not be "waterlogged."
- Pleasant sea smell.
- No discoloration.

Crustaceans

- No discoloration at the joints.
- Prawns should have no discoloration along edges of segments or legs.
- Pleasant sea smell.
- When buying live, pick out those that are most active.

Mollusks

- Mollusks such as mussels and scallops should be tightly closed.
- Pleasant sea smell.
- Squid, calamari, octopus and cuttlefish should have a mottled brown skin.

FISH STORAGE

Scale, remove gills and gut. Wash in cold water and dry well. Wrap in aluminium foil or place in covered container. Store in refrigerator. Eat within 2 to 3 days.

Freezing Fish

Freeze fish only when absolutely fresh. If you want to have fillets, do the filleting before freezing. Gut and gill whole fish first. Wrap each fish in plastic food wrap, label, date and freeze. As soon as fish is frozen, remove and dip in cold water and return to freezer. This puts a protective glaze over it that prevents drying out and an off flavor.

Freezer life at 0°F (- 18° C)

- Lean fish 3 to 6 months
- Oily fish 2 to 3 months

BASIC FISH COOKING

Baking Wrap fish in lightly greased foil. Bake at 350° F (180°) for 20 minutes per 2 pounds (1kg) weight.

Broiling (Grilling) Grill under medium heat on lightly greased or oiled aluminum foil. Turn fish once and baste with fruit and vegetable juices. Cook fillets 2 to 3 minutes and small whole fish 3 to 4 minutes per side. Always incise skin to allow heat penetration, and brush with marinade, butter or lemon juice while cooking to prevent drying out. In a restaurant kitchen that I worked in, we simply brushed the fish fillets with margarine, rubbed in a small amount of minced garlic, a light sprinkle of ground chili, and then squeezed fresh lemon juice over.

Microwaving The key to microwaving fish is not to overcook. Always arrange thickest parts to the outside. Pierce the eyes of whole fish. Cover tail ends to prevent overcooking. Cook on 70% power, with whole fish 2 to 3 minutes on high and finish with 70%. Allow 2 minutes standing time after microwaving to finish cooking.

Poaching Place fish in simmering and unsalted fish stock or water and cover. Turn once during cooking. Fillets 1 to 2 minutes, whole fish 3 to 4 minutes per side.

Steaming Place fish in a steamer, sprinkle with fresh herbs, and cover. Turn once during cooking only. Fillets 2 to 3 minutes per side, whole fish 4 to 5 minutes.

Fish Foil Recipes
(per serving of fish fillet)

Smear a coating of margarine or oil over the foil, and if using whole fish, cut the skin two or three times first to allow juices and flavors to penetrate. Put the foil packages under the broiler for about 5 minutes per side for fillets, or about 10 minutes for whole fish. The following variations are delightful, or experiment yourself. You can add:

- Slices of lemon, black pepper, chopped parsley.
- 1 tablespoon sherry or mirin and toasted sesame seeds.
- Slices of tomato, sprinkle of curry powder and sultana raisins.
- Chopped shallots, soy sauce, minced ginger, minced garlic.
- Slices of orange, minced garlic and ginger, a dash of soy, freshly squeezed juice.
- Minced ginger and garlic, a dash of soy and lemon juice and a smear of honey.

Thomo's Gameboat Fish Recipe

This method is from friend and top Cairns gameboat skipper Frank Thomson:

Slice up fish fillets into small segments about 1-inch wide and not too thick. Put the fillets in a bowl and marinate in lime or lemon juice for about an hour, preferably in the refrigerator. Coat the fillets in a mixture of plain flour with a dash of salt and black pepper. Melt some butter (margarine or oil) in a skillet. Bring to medium heat and gently sauté the fillets, turning once until flesh starts to give. Serve and eat immediately.

Marinated and Grilled Yellowfin Tuna

Serves 6

1 cup olive oil
4 tablespoons soy sauce
4 cloves crushed or minced garlic
4 tablespoons finely chopped ginger
1 teaspoon salt
½ teaspoon ground black pepper
6 tuna steaks

Whisk all the ingredients together in a bowl. Add the fish steaks, coating them on both sides. Cover with plastic wrap and leave in the refrigerator to marinate for at least 2 hours. Heat a griddle pan or heavy skillet or bring barbecue to smoking hot. Sear the steaks on each side for 1 minute then turn the steaks on their sides and sear all round for 1 minute. Do not overcook. Steaks should only be sealed and cooked on the outside, and should be served rare.

Tropical Snapper or Bream

Serves 4

1 cup pineapple juice
½ cup white wine
¼ cup Worcestershire sauce
2 tablespoons brown sugar
1 large whole snapper or bream
½ cup seasoned flour
2 tablespoons olive oil
2 tablespoons American mustard
1 tablespoon extra Worcestershire sauce
½ cup crushed pineapple
1 tablespoon chopped mint

Combine the juice, wine, Worcestershire sauce and the sugar. Mix well. Make 1 or 2 cuts into the thickest parts of the fish flesh. Add the fish to the mixture and marinate, preferably overnight. Drain the fish, and pat dry. Reserve the marinade. Coat the fish in flour and dust off excess. Heat the oil and sauté the fish 4 to 5 minutes on each side until crisp and golden. Drain and keep warm. Pour the marinade into a saucepan, add the mustard and extra Worcestershire sauce, and gently reduce by a third. Add the crushed pineapple and mint. Pour sauce over the fish.

Creamed Fish with Rice
(Pauline on *Ruahatu*)

Serves 4

1 pound (500g) fresh fish
2 teaspoons minced or crushed
   garlic
Oil
1 teaspoon soy sauce, or 1
   teaspoon curry powder
1½ cups coconut cream
Fresh herbs (optional)

Slice fish into bite sized pieces. Sauté garlic in oil and blend in soy sauce or curry powder. Add fish pieces and fry quickly, do not overcook. Lower heat and stir in cream and fresh herbs, stir until hot, do not allow to boil. Serve on boiled rice or with salad.

Banana and Ginger Fillets

Serves 4

1½ pounds (750g) fish fillets
½ cup water
¼ cup sultana raisins
¼ cup lemon juice
Fresh ground black pepper
1 peeled and chopped banana
2 teaspoons minced ginger
2 tablespoons sour cream

Remove all bones from fish fillets. Put water, sultanas, lemon juice and pepper into a skillet. Bring to a boil, reduce heat and add the fish fillets. Cook for 2 minutes. Remove the fillets, and add the banana and ginger to the pan. Cook for 2 minutes. Add the fish, cook until it starts to flake. Stir in the sour cream.

Ika Mata

Serves 4

Visit Rarotonga and try this fish in coconut cream in paradise itself.

1 pound (500g) fish fillets
Salt
1 cup lemon (or lime) juice
1 cup thick coconut cream
Diced spring onions
1 finely chopped tomato

Slice fillets into ½ inch pieces. Sprinkle with salt and set aside for 5 minutes. Pour the lemon juice over the fish. Refrigerate for 2 hours. When fish is white, strain off the juice and pour over coconut cream. Sprinkle with chopped tomato and onions. Chill and serve.

Indian Fried Fish

Serves 4

4 fillets or steaks white fish
2 teaspoons finely grated fresh
   ginger
1 teaspoon salt
1 teaspoon turmeric
½ teaspoon white pepper

Coating:

1 beaten egg
4 tablespoons plain flour
1 teaspoon salt
½ teaspoon turmeric
½ teaspoon garam masala
Oil

Wash and dry the fish with absorbent paper. Rub each side with the ginger. Sprinkle evenly with salt, turmeric and white pepper. Rub it well into the flesh, and let it stand for 10 minutes. Dip each piece of fish into beaten egg, then into flour mixed with salt, turmeric and garam masala. Heat oil in a heavy skillet, and sauté on medium heat until golden, turning once.

Kokoda

Serves 4

This dish is delightful on a balmy afternoon in a beautiful Fijian anchorage.

1 pound (500g) white fish
   (snapper, cod)
4 tablespoons lime juice
1½ cups coconut cream
1 large Spanish onion
1 teaspoon chopped fresh chili
1 medium diced red pepper
1 cup chopped shallots
1 large ripe finely chopped
   tomato
Salt and fresh ground pepper

Put the fish pieces in a stainless bowl. Coat fish with lime juice and marinate in the refrigerator for 4 hours. Add the coconut cream and the other ingredients. Stir gently to mix all ingredients evenly, and serve cold.

Steamed Fish in Banana Leaves

Serves 4

1 pound (500g) white fish
2 lightly beaten eggs
1 teaspoon chopped chili
2 chopped shallots
1 tablespoon chopped
  coriander
1 tablespoon corn flour
1 cup coconut cream
Salt and pepper to taste
8 pieces of banana leaf (8"x 8";
  20cm x 20 cm)

Mix all ingredients together, and put a couple of spoonfuls onto each banana leaf. Wrap in foil and steam for about 10 minutes.

Oka

Serves 2

This dish comes from Western Samoa.

½ pound (250g) fish fillets
  (yellowfin, tuna, bonito)
Lime juice
Coconut cream
1 chopped onion
1 chopped cucumber
Salt
1 chopped tomato

Cut the fish into small cubes. Add lime juice, coconut cream, onion, cucumber, salt and tomato. Mix together and allow to marinate for about an hour. Serve traditionally in a coconut shell.

Seafood Laksa

Serves 4 to 6

½ pound (250g) fish fillets
1 tablespoon corn flour
1 egg white
2 tablespoons finely chopped
   onion
1 tablespoon fresh coriander
3 cups fish or chicken stock
Sesame oil
1 teaspoon minced garlic
1 teaspoon minced ginger
1 teaspoon Thai sweet chili
   sauce
1 teaspoon lemon rind
1 teaspoon peanut butter
1 teaspoon turmeric
1 cup coconut milk
1 pack instant noodles
½ pound (250g) cooked
   prawns

Chop the fish into fine pieces. Put the corn flour and egg white into a bowl and mix well. Add onion, coriander and the fish. Mix well. Put the stock into a pan and heat. When very hot, drop spoon-size balls of the mixture. Cook these dumplings for 30 to 40 seconds and set aside. Heat sesame oil in wok or skillet. Sauté the garlic, ginger, chili sauce, lemon rind, peanut butter, and the turmeric. Add stock from dumpling pot. Simmer 15 to 20 minutes. Remove the lemon rind and pour the coconut milk. Stir well and cook for 1 to 2 minutes, do not boil. Add the noodles, simmer for one minute and add the prawns. Add dumplings and stir in some fresh chopped coriander.

Fish Head Curry

Serves 4

Fish heads reputedly have some of the nicest and tastiest bits such as the cheeks, and heads are part of many special dishes. This recipe works really well and is tasty.

1 large fish head (2 to 3
   pounds snapper)
2 tablespoons salt
3 tablespoons tamarind seeds
3 tablespoons warm water
2 brown onions
4 tablespoons oil
4 cloves garlic
1 teaspoon ginger
3 tablespoons curry powder
3 cups coconut milk
1 cup water
Tamarind extract
3 curry leaves
½ teaspoon sugar
3 quartered tomatoes
6 small okra

Scale the fish head and rub in salt both inside and out. Soak tamarind seeds in warm water, squeeze and then discard the seeds. Rinse and dry the fish head. Finely slice the onions, then gently sauté in oil along with garlic and ginger. Add the curry powder and fry for 2 to 3 minutes. Add the coconut milk, water, tamarind extract, sugar and curry leaves, then stir well. Bring to a boil and then return to a slow simmer for 5 minutes. Add the fish head, tomatoes and okra, then simmer for 20 minutes until head is tender. Serve on boiled rice.

Oriental Fish Bake

Serves 4

2 pounds (1kg) whole fish
½ cup cooked rice
½ cup bean sprouts
¼ cup thinly sliced green
   pepper
¼ cup finely chopped celery
¼ cup chopped shallots
2 teaspoons soy sauce
1 teaspoon finely chopped
   fresh ginger
1 tablespoon extra soy sauce

Scale the fish on both sides, and trim fins and tails. Combine the rice, sprouts, green pepper, celery, shallots, soy sauce and ginger. Spoon the mixture into the stomach cavity, and then put the fish in a baking dish. Brush with the extra soy sauce and cover lightly with greased aluminum foil. Bake at 350°F (180°C) for 15 to 20 minutes or until fish flakes.

Seafood Mousse

Serves 8

1 pound (500g) mixed cooked
   seafood
1 tablespoon gelatine
¼ cup water
½ cup mayonnaise
½ cup evaporated milk or
   cream
¼ cup finely chopped
   cucumbers
Salt and pepper
Parsley
Lettuce leaves
Hard boiled egg

Mince seafood in processor or blend coarsely. Dissolve gelatine in water. Add this to the mayonnaise and evaporated milk. Add the seafood, cucumber and seasonings. Pour into a mold and chill until set. Serve on lettuce leaves and garnish with a wedge of egg. Use your favorite sauce if preferred.

Mineral Water Fish Batter

Serves 4

1 cup plain flour
1 egg
1 cup mineral or soda water

Sift the flour into a bowl, make a well and add the egg and mineral water. Mix to a smooth batter.

Beer Batter

Serves 4

¾ **cup flour**
¼ **teaspoon salt**
1 **egg**
2 **teaspoons melted butter**
¾ **cup flat beer**

Combine and sift salt and flour. Beat the egg and melted butter together. Mix in flour, salt and beer, and stir until smooth.

Sashimi

This is the Japanese term for raw fish. Once you've tasted sashimi you're hooked. When you use the right fish and dipping sauce it is a delightful treat. Most fish can be used for sashimi, but to taste the subtle flavors, the fish has to be really fresh. The Japanese prefer the Southern bluefin tuna. If you cruise in Micronesia, you'll find the tuna is superb and cheap. The alternatives are bream, whiting and yellowfin, although most fish are suitable. Clean and fillet the fish and remove all bones. Wash well. Slice into thin pieces 1¼-inch long by ½-inch wide (3cm x 1cm).

Sashimi Dipping Sauce

1 **teaspoon powdered wasabi (Japanese horseradish)**
1 **tablespoon shoyu (Japanese soy sauce)**
1 **tablespoon mirin (Japanese cooking wine)**

Mix the wasabi powder with just enough cold water to form a thick paste. Mix in a small amount of soy and mirin. Dry sherry can be substituted for mirin.

Tempura

This delightful Japanese food style was introduced by Portuguese traders and sailors who came ashore in the early 1540's during a typhoon. Though some sources say that it was brought by Portuguese Jesuit priests, we'll give the credit to the hapless sailors. The Japanese refined the style to make it distinctly their own. Originally it was purely used with seafood, but it is used also very deliciously on vegetables.

- 6 large or 10 medium sized prawns
- 1 medium squid
- 1 pound (500g) fish fillets
- 1 sliced sweet potato

Tempura Batter

- 1 egg
- 1 cup ice cold water
- Pinch bicarbonate of soda
- ¾ cup unsifted plain flour (the Japanese use tempura flour)

Break the egg into a bowl containing the iced water. Beat until frothy. Add soda and flour and beat just enough for flour to be mixed in. Batter should be very thin.

Tempura Sauce

- 3 tablespoons mirin
- 3 tablespoons Japanese soy sauce
- 1 cup dashi (fish stock)
- Pinch salt
- Grated ginger

Heat the mirin in a small pan. Remove from flame and ignite. Add the soy sauce, dashi and salt, bring to a boil and set aside. Cool to room temperature. Add fresh grated ginger to taste. Put about 2 inches of oil in a wok or skillet. Heat to about 375°F (190°C). Coat the individual pieces of food in the batter and dip in oil. Prawns take around 1 minute per side, vegetables 2 to 3 minutes. Drain on paper towels and serve with the tempura sauce.

Fish Cakes

The humble fish cake is the savior of the many who do not regularly catch larger fish. There are some really good variations that enable a little to go a long way, and are easy to prepare. A breakfast version is given in breakfast ideas.

Thai Fish Cakes

Serves 6

These flavorsome fish cakes will entice you to cruise beautiful Thailand, or voyage back to Phuket. Believe me, the trip is worthwhile.

4 tablespoons coconut cream
2 eggs
1 chopped red pepper
1 chopped fresh chili
1 tablespoon Thai fish sauce
1 pound (500g) fish fillets
2 tablespoons corn flour
1 tablespoon freshly chopped ginger
2 tablespoons chopped shallots
2 tablespoons freshly chopped coriander
1 tablespoon chopped lemongrass, or 1 tablespoon grated lemon rind
2 tablespoons peanut oil

Purée coconut cream, eggs, red pepper, chili and fish sauce in a blender. Add fish fillets, and mince coarsely only. Combine the purée in a bowl with the corn flour, ginger, shallots, coriander, and lemongrass. Mix well into small patties and sauté both sides in peanut oil. Serve with boiled rice and Thai sweet chili sauce, or eat as a snack.

Fish Fritters

Makes 12 to 16

1 pound (500g) fish fillets
½ cup finely chopped parsley
1 clove garlic
Salt and pepper
¼ cup Parmesan cheese
¾ cup chopped celery
3 lightly beaten eggs
Plain flour
Oil

Mince the fillets with a processor or blender. Combine all ingredients except flour and oil. Stir well. Mold balls from mixture and coat with flour. Sauté until golden on both sides.

Fish Sausages

Makes 12

1 pound (500g) white fish
   fillets
2 eggs
¼ cup breadcrumbs
2 shallots
2 tablespoons chopped parsley
1 grated carrot
1 tablespoon lemon juice
Plain flour
2 tablespoons oil
3 tablespoons butter

Mince the fish using a blender or mincer. Lightly beat the eggs, and then combine breadcrumbs, shallots, parsley, carrot, and lemon juice. Stir in the minced fish. Divide the mixture into 12 portions. Roll and shape into sausages. Roll lightly in flour. Sauté in the butter and oil over medium heat for around 10 minutes until golden brown.

SHELLFISH

Mollusks

The mollusk family is extremely diverse to say the least. There are a few groupings as follows:

- **Mussels and clams** (bivalves) While they are available in many locations, make sure you do not miss out in New Zealand.
- **Oysters** (bivalves) The varieties worldwide are amazing; the best oysters are to be found in France as well as Australia.
- **Conches and whelks** (gastropods) The conch is widely located throughout the Caribbean and the Pacific.
- **Octopus and squid** (cephalopods) Most markets will have them around the world.

Mussels

Preparation: Remove the beard, and scrub the shell of debris and mud. Scrub under cold water.

Skillet Mussels

Serves 4

3 cups cooked and shucked mussels
½ cup milk
½ cup flour
½ cup butter
Salt to taste
2 lemons
2 tablespoons chopped parsley

Dip the mussels in milk and then into the flour. Heat half the butter in a skillet, and sauté the mussels until brown. Arrange on a serving plate and sprinkle with salt, juice of 1 lemon and parsley. Heat the remaining butter in the skillet until it begins to foam, then pour over the mussels. Garnish with lemon wedges and parsley.

Moules Marinière

Serves 4

(One of my favorite recipes). The best and most memorable meal of mussels I ever devoured was in St Peter Port, Jersey, Channel Islands.

2 pounds (1kg) mussels,
  scrubbed and beard removed
3 shallots
1 clove garlic
½ teaspoon dried thyme
1 cup dry white wine
6 tablespoons butter or
  margarine
1½ tablespoons flour
1 tablespoon chopped parsley
¼ cup cream
Black pepper

Wash the mussels under cold running water. Put the mussels in a large skillet along with the finely chopped shallots, crushed garlic, and thyme. Add the wine and cover. Bring to a boil and simmer for around 5 minutes, until all the mussels are open. Discard unopened mussels. Put the reserved liquid into saucepan, and boil uncovered until it reduces by half in volume. Cream together the butter and flour with a spatula until a smooth paste is formed. Whisk the butter and flour paste into the liquid gradually, until sauce boils and thickens. Stir in the chopped parsley and the cream. Season with freshly ground pepper. Put mussels into serving bowls and spoon the sauce over them.

Baked Mussels

Serves 4

2 pounds (1kg) scrubbed
  mussels
2 cloves crushed garlic
2 tablespoons butter or
  margarine
2 tablespoons olive oil
¼ cup Worcestershire sauce
2 teaspoons lemon juice
¼ cup grated Cheddar cheese
¼ cup grated Parmesan cheese
¼ cup chopped parsley
½ cup fresh breadcrumbs

Steam the mussels in water until they just open. Remove and discard the half shell. Loosen the mussels. Sauté the garlic in butter and oil, then add the Worcestershire Sauce, lemon juice, cheese, parsley and the breadcrumbs. Stir the mixture well. Spoon 2 teaspoons of the mixture onto each mussel and place on a baking tray. Bake at 350°F (180°C) for 10 minutes or until golden.

Mussels in Tomato Sauce

Serves 4

2 pounds (1kg) mussels
2 tablespoons olive oil
2 cloves crushed garlic
1 quartered and steamed onion
Chili powder
Chopped parsley
2 cups tomato sauce

Put some water in a shallow pan, and steam the mussels for 7 to 8 minutes, covered. Discard un-opened mussels. Heat oil in a skillet and add garlic, onion, chili powder and chopped parsley. Cook very slowly for 5 minutes. Mix in tomato sauce and cook for 3 minutes. Add the mussels, and stir well to warm. Sprinkle with fresh parsley.

Oysters

Oysters are the king of shellfish, with that delicious subtle flavor. You either love them or hate them. Casanova was reputed to consume 40 oysters every morning; you may deduce what you like from that.

Preparation: Insert a strong, short blade knife adjacent to the hinge between the two shell halves. Twist the knife to open the shells. Remove the top shell and carefully loosen oyster meat with the knife. Rinse the oyster in fresh water with a dash of lemon juice before placing back on a washed and dried shell. This removes some of the grit.

Oyster Fritters

Serves 2

24 oysters
2 tablespoons lemon juice
2 tablespoons plain flour
2 tablespoons self-raising flour
¼ teaspoon bicarbonate of
   soda
½ cup water
1 egg white
Cooking oil

Mix oysters with lemon juice and marinate for 15 minutes then drain. Sift the bicarbonate of soda and flours together. Gradually add the water until a smooth batter is formed. Beat the egg white in a bowl until peaks form and blend into the batter. Dip the oysters in the batter and deep fry until golden. Drain on paper towels.

Oysters Bloody Mary

Serves 2

24 oysters
½ can tomato juice
1 tablespoon lemon or lime juice
1 teaspoon Worcestershire sauce
1 teaspoon Tabasco sauce
1 teaspoon vodka
1 tablespoon fresh coriander
1 red finely chopped chili
1 finely chopped tomato

Combine all the salsa ingredients and then let stand for an hour. Place a spoonful on each opened oyster and refrigerate for 30 minutes before serving. Enjoy!

Oysters à la Brasil

Serves 2

¼ cup margarine or butter
1 tablespoon lemon juice
1 tablespoon Worcestershire sauce
¼ teaspoon cayenne pepper
Salt
24 oysters
1 cup coconut cream

Heat the margarine in a skillet and add the lemon juice, Worcestershire sauce, cayenne pepper, and salt. Add the oysters and their juice and bring to a boil. Simmer on very low for 2 minutes. Add the coconut cream and heat. Serve over mold of fresh rice or egg pasta.

Oysters Kilpatrick

Serves 2

24 oysters
4 rashers bacon
Worcestershire sauce
Black pepper

Rinse oysters in lemon and water. Chop bacon into small strips and put over the oysters. Sprinkle a dash of Worcestershire sauce over each and some black pepper. Broil for a few minutes.

Conch

The conch is found all around the world, from Australia to the Caribbean. Buy live conch in Nassau from Bahamian fishermen or dive for them yourself.

Preparation: The conch tends to be on the tough side, so you have to soften it up to eat. Cut the conch flesh into thin strips. Beat the strips with a mallet to tenderize.

Cooking: Personally I like to cook them as you would abalone, sautéed in butter, but the following recipes are equally enjoyable.

Conch Stew

Serves 4

2 pounds (1kg) conch
2 limes
2 tablespoons margarine
1 sliced onion
1 teaspoon minced garlic
½ cup water
1 tablespoon ketchup
1 finely chopped chili
2 ripe and sliced tomatoes
1 clove
Salt and pepper to taste

Rub washed conch with lime halves. Tenderize with a mallet and cut into cubes. Put in a saucepan covered with water, bring to a boil and then simmer for 2 hours. Drain, and then heat margarine in a saucepan. Add the onions, garlic, and gently sauté until onion is soft and golden. Add the conch, ½ cup of water, and the remaining ingredients. Simmer for 20 minutes.

Conch and Soy

Serves 4

2 pounds (1kg) conch
2 limes
1 finely chopped onion
1 teaspoon minced garlic
1 tablespoon minced ginger
¼ cup soy sauce
¼ cup water

Rub washed conch with lime halves. Tenderize with a mallet and cut into cubes. Cook uncovered in a saucepan with water. Bring to a boil and simmer for 15 minutes. Sauté onion, garlic and ginger, then add the diced conch flesh. Add the soy sauce and the water, stir and cover, then simmer for about 25 minutes, stirring occasionally. Serve over boiled rice.

Squid

One of my favorites, go for the baby squid wherever possible.

Preparation: Remove the head and tentacles from the hood. Slide the clear membrane out from the hood. Remove the skin from the flaps by pulling firmly. Cut off flaps if required. Use the various cuts as required. With small tentacles I prefer to leave them as whole little "flowerets" which are delicious in tempura or in stir fry or pasta marinara.

Cooking: Squid has a rather delicate flavor and must never be overcooked as it becomes as tough as old boots. Marinate it in milk or lemon juice for an hour or two before cooking.

Stuffed Squid

Serves 6

Olive oil
1½ pounds (750g) raw prawns
¼ pound (125g) cooked rice
½ pound (250g) drained
    crabmeat
1 cup finely chopped spring
    onions
2 cloves crushed garlic
4 tablespoons finely chopped
    parsley
Basil and celery leaves
1 tablespoon grated lemon zest
Fresh oregano leaves
Salt and black pepper
24 squid, cleaned and skinned
Vermouth

Heat a little olive oil in a pan and cook prawns until pink. Drain and cool, then shell, devein, and chop flesh into small pieces. Combine with the rice and other ingredients. Add salt, and pepper to taste and moisten. Mix well and stuff each squid using a table-spoon to push in so that squid is plump. Put in an oiled baking dish, sprinkle with a little vermouth and brush over with olive oil. Cook uncovered at 350°F (180°C) for 10 to 15 minutes. Cover with foil, and cook until squid is tender, about 20 minutes.

Squid in Olive Oil

Serves 4

1½ pounds (750g) baby squid
Olive oil
Salt and black pepper
1 tablespoon Thai sweet chili
    sauce
½ cup cilantro or coriander

Skin the squid, remove head and insides, remove any black lining with salt and rinse. Slice into several pieces, place in a bowl with oil, salt and pepper and let it stand for around an hour. Turn occasionally. Cook in a frying pan in olive oil for 3 to 4 minutes, do not overcook. To really give it some zip, add a tablespoon of Thai sweet chili sauce, and a handful of fresh chopped cilantro or coriander and serve on boiled rice.

Squid in Tempura Batter

Serves 4

1½ pounds (750g) squid,
   tentacles cleaned
½ cup plain flour
½ cup corn flour
1 teaspoon baking powder
1 cup cold water
Olive oil
Soy sauce
Fresh ginger

Cut squid tentacles into ¼-inch (½cm) rings, and lay onto absorbent paper. Dry well. Combine the plain flour, corn flour and baking powder into a bowl and sift. Gradually add the water and beat lightly. It does not matter if not all the flour is dissolved. Heat oil in a wok or deep skillet until smoking. Dip the squid rings in batter, allow to drain slightly and place in oil for about 3 minutes or until golden brown. Make a dipping sauce of soy and fresh chopped ginger.

Curried Squid on Skewers

Serves 4

1½ pounds (750g) squid
1 tablespoon olive oil
1 thinly sliced onion
½ cup honey
1 tablespoon curry powder
Black pepper

Skin the squid, remove head and insides, remove any black lining with salt and rinse. Slice into quarters lengthwise, then thread onto skewers. Gently sauté the onion in oil, add the honey, curry powder and pepper. Place skewers in a skillet or under a broiler, and spoon over the sauce, cook for around 5 minutes. Turn and baste during cooking. Serve on boiled rice along with remaining sauce.

Mediterranean Squid

Serves 4

Greek islands are made of this.

2 pounds (1kg) squid
3 tablespoons olive oil
2 chopped onions
1 tablespoon chopped garlic
1 can chopped tomatoes
½ cup white wine
1 teaspoon oregano
Black pepper
½ cup fresh parsley (optional)

Skin the squid, remove head and insides, remove any black lining with salt and rinse. Cut into 1-inch (2.5cm) squares. Sauté the onion and garlic gently in oil, then add the tomatoes, white wine, oregano, pepper and squid. Also fresh parsley if available. Cover and simmer until squid is soft and tender. Serve over boiled rice.

Octopus

While sailors of long ago feared giant octopus would rise from the depths and pull their ships down, these are however totally unsuitable for cooking as they are difficult to subdue, tend to be on the tough side, and your skillet will be too small. Go for the smaller denizens, they really are delightful. I will always remember the sight of octopus hanging up to dry on Mykonos in the Greek islands, and savouring the same.

Preparation: Cut off the head from the tentacles just below the eyes. Cut away the eyes from the head and discard. Remove the body beak from the leg center and discard. Gently pull away the skin from the head. Wash prior to use.

Octopus Galicia (Spain) Style
Serves 6

3 pounds (1.5kg) octopus
Olive oil
1 tablespoon paprika
Salt and pepper

Clean the octopus, remove the ink sack and beak and clean out the head. Put on a wooden board and pound using a wooden mallet. Bring a large pot of water to a boil. Dunk the octopus 2 or 3 times, then put it in the pot. Lower the heat and cook for 20 minutes or longer depending on quality and size of octopus. Remove and drain over a large upturned cup. Slice into 1 inch strips. Make a dressing of olive oil, paprika, salt and pepper, and pour over prior to serving.

Charcoal Grilled Baby Octopus

Serves 6

I know harvesting the young is wrong, but this dish is something else.

2 pounds (1kg) baby octopus
½ cup olive oil
¼ cup lime juice
3 cloves crushed garlic
½ bunch chopped coriander

Clean the octopus, remove the ink sack and beak, and clean out the head. Cut into pieces depending on the size of the octopus. Mix the marinade and cover the octopus for about 3 to 4 hours. Cook over charcoal barbecue or in a wok or skillet for 4 to 5 minutes.

Octopus in Curried Coconut Sauce

Serves 4 to 6

A recipe from the Cook Islands.

3 pounds (1.5kg) octopus
Coconut milk
Curry powder
Salt and pepper
Small chopped onion

Clean the octopus, remove the ink sack and beak and clean out the head. Bring a large pot of water to a boil, and dunk the octopus 2 or 3 times prior to putting it in the pot. Simmer until tender. Cut octopus into bite sized pieces. Heat coconut milk and then add other ingredients into a saucepan. Add octopus and heat through. Serve with boiled rice.

Crustaceans

Crustaceans fall into a few distinct groups.

- **Prawns** There are a large variety of prawns, shrimps, langoustines and similar crustaceans. Equally there are as many methods of enjoying them.
- **Crabs** There are a great many varieties of crabs available around the world, and most are delicious, ask locals which are the best. Personally I prefer sand crabs which are sweet, but a good mud crab is hard to beat.
- **Lobsters and crayfish** The pièce de resistance of the ocean pantry. There are many varieties and all are delightful.

Garlic Prawns

Serves 4

1½ pounds (750g) raw king
   prawns
½ cup olive oil
3 teaspoons chopped garlic
½ teaspoon hot chili sauce
¼ teaspoon saffron strands
Salt to taste

Shell and devein the prawns. Leave the tails on. Heat the oil and cook the garlic, chili, and saffron in a heavy skillet until garlic is soft. (If using saffron strands, pound in a mortar and pestle and dissolve in a tablespoon of hot water first). Add the prawns and cook, turning until cooked through. This only takes 3 to 4 minutes. Do not overcook. Place prawns into ramekins and pour over the juice. Serve with freshly baked crusty bread.

Garlic Prawns and Tomatoes

Serves 4

1½ pounds (750g) raw king
   prawns
¼ to ½ cup olive oil
¼ pound (125g) butter or
   margarine
2 teaspoons chopped garlic
1 finely chopped onion
1 pound (500g) canned
   tomatoes
Salt and pepper
Parsley

Shell and devein the prawns. Heat the oil and butter and gently sauté the garlic and onions. Add the drained and finely chopped tomatoes. Simmer uncovered for 2 minutes. Season with salt and pepper. Add the prawns, and cook over high heat for 3 minutes until prawns are tender. Garnish with parsley.

Prawns and Rice

Serves 6

1½ pounds (750g) cooked
    prawns
¼ pound (125g) butter or
    margarine
1 finely chopped onion
2 cups long grain rice
4 cups hot water
½ teaspoon saffron
½ teaspoon paprika
2 chicken stock cubes
Salt and pepper
½ pound (250g) crabmeat or
    mussels
½ cup fresh parsley
1 teaspoon dried fennel

Shell and devein the prawns. Heat the butter and gently sauté the onions. When they are golden, add the rice, water, saffron, paprika, stock cubes, salt and pepper. Simmer uncovered for 20 minutes until rice is nearly done. Add the prawns and seafood, stir and cook for 5 minutes. Add fennel and fresh parsley if available. Cook until all the water has been absorbed. Remove from stove, cover with lid and let stand for 10 minutes.

Spanish Garlic Prawns

Serves 4

1½ pounds (750g) raw king
    prawns
2 cups olive oil
3 teaspoons chopped garlic
2 small red chilies
Salt and pepper
Freshly chopped parsley

Shell and devein the prawns. Leave tails on. Pour ½ cup oil into each of four heatproof ramekins. Add crushed or minced garlic into each (1 clove per bowl). Wash, deseed, chop chilies and distribute between bowls. Season each with salt and pepper. Place ramekins into a moderate oven. Leave oil to bubble for 10 to 15 minutes. Remove and divide prawns evenly between each ramekin. Cook in oven for around 8 to 10 minutes. Sprinkle with chopped parsley and serve.

Prawns in Coconut Milk

Serves 4

1 tablespoon ghee (or oil)
1 large onion, cut into wedges
1 cup coconut milk
Salt
1 teaspoon turmeric
1 teaspoon garam masala
1 teaspoon minced ginger
1 teaspoon ground coriander
1 teaspoon minced garlic
1½ pounds (750g) medium
  prawns
1 teaspoon lime juice
½ teaspoon grated lime rind

Heat ghee in a saucepan, and sauté onion for 3 to 4 minutes. Add the spices and coconut milk, and simmer for 10 minutes, stirring regularly. Stir in the prawns and cook for 5 minutes. Add the lime juice and grated rind just before serving.

Piquant Prawns

Serves 4

2 pounds (1kg) raw prawns
2 apples
3 tablespoons olive oil
1 tablespoon tomato paste
2 teaspoons brown sugar
2 cloves crushed garlic
1 tablespoon chili sauce
1 tablespoon chopped
  coriander
¾ cup sun dried tomato,
  drained
1 tablespoon lime or lemon
  juice

Peel and devein prawns, but keep tails on. Peel, core and thinly slice apples. Heat oil and sauté apples and prawns, 1 minute per each side. Remove and set aside. Add tomato paste, sugar, garlic, chili sauce and coriander to the pan. Cook for 1 minute. Add the prawns and apple, followed by the sun-dried tomatoes. Toss through the chili sauce, sprinkle with lemon juice and heat through. Serve with boiled rice.

Crabs

Crabs are one of nature's great treats, and I personally think every bit as good as lobster and crayfish. Crabs are absolutely delicious boiled and chilled, with rolls of crusty bread, but there are also some great ways to enhance the flavor and enjoyment. For my favorite curried crab recipe, see section on curries. There are a great many crab varieties to try, many prefer the mud crabs, I personally prefer the sand based ones. I shall never forget a restaurant blackboard special on spider crab in the Cornish port of Fowey. The crab had a body larger than a dinner plate. It was pure bliss and it took two tastebud heaven hours to devour the beast.

The most popular way to catch sand crabs is to have a conical trap with a bait in the middle, in which the crabs will entrap or entangle themselves. The mud crabs are more commonly caught by cruisers who seek out an estuarine creek or tidal backwater. Use fresh fish, fish frames from the last catch or a hunk of red meat in the pot. Set the traps in shallow intertidal waters in creeks, rivers and estuaries. Ideally set them near the edges of mangroves. Make sure you can reach them at low tide. Prior to cooking, either kill the crabs by inserting a knife between the base of the claws into the head region or put them in the freezer until they stop moving. Boil in salted water for approximately 10 minutes. Do nature a favor, capture and eat only male crabs, leave the females to breed. Leave the small, undersized ones alone. Check on local bag limits if you are doing well.

Indian Chili Crab   *Serves 4*

8 medium sand crabs
10 tablespoons vegetable oil
3 cloves chopped garlic
2 tablespoons chopped ginger
2 tablespoons chopped fresh
  chilies
2 ripe chopped tomatoes
2 tablespoons chopped
  lemongrass
2 tablespoons lemon juice
1 tablespoon sugar
2 tablespoons tomato paste
4 tablespoons coconut cream
½ cup dry white wine
4 tablespoons chopped
  coriander

Clean and cut the crab into chunky pieces. Stir fry the crab in a wok or large skillet using 4 tablespoons oil. Do not overcook. Set aside crab and in the same pan sauté garlic, ginger and chilies in remaining oil. Add tomatoes, lemon grass, lemon juice, sugar, tomato paste, coconut cream, white wine and fresh coriander. Cook gently and allow a nice sauce to form. Add the crab pieces, coat well with sauce. Cook for 2 to 3 minutes. Serve on boiled rice.

Singapore Chili Crab

Serves 4

2 large crabs
6 tablespoons tomato paste or purée
1 tablespoon sugar
½ tablespoon white vinegar
1 tablespoon salt
Peanut oil
1 sliced onion
1 strip lemon peel
2 cloves chopped garlic
2 teaspoons chopped chili
3 chopped shallots
1 tablespoon chopped ginger
1 tablespoon dry sherry or rice wine
½ pint fish stock
1 tablespoon corn flour (dissolved in 2 tablespoons water)
1 egg
2 tablespoons chopped coriander

Clean and cut the crabs into chunks. Make a sauce mixture by combining tomato paste, sugar, vinegar and salt. Stir fry the crab in a wok or large skillet in 4 tablespoons oil. Do not overcook. Set aside the crab and in the same pan heat 2 tablespoons oil, and sauté the onion slices, lemon peel, garlic, chilies, shallots and ginger until slightly brown. Add the crabs and sauce mixture, sherry and fish stock and cook for 5 minutes. Add dissolved corn flour and egg and stir. Garnish with fresh coriander leaves and serve with boiled rice.

Crab and Corn Pancakes

Serves 4

½ pound (250g) crab meat
2 small grated potatoes
1 medium grated carrot
1 egg
¼ pound (125g) can creamed
　corn
¼ pound (125g) can corn
　kernels
3 chopped scallions
2 tablespoons sour cream
2 tablespoons cooking oil
1 tablespoon chopped parsley

Remove excess liquid out of the crab, potato and carrot. Lightly beat the egg. Mix crab, carrot and potatoes together with corn, scallions, egg, parsley and cream. Heat oil and pour in ¼ cup of the mixture. Flatten out the mixture to form a patty. Cook on medium heat 5 minutes per side, and turn once during the process. Add parsley. Drain on paper towel.

Oriental Crab

Serves 2

2 cooked crabs
1 tablespoon grated ginger
2 cloves crushed garlic
1 finely chopped chili
6 tablespoons coconut oil
1 cup hot water
1 tablespoon brown sugar
2 cups tomato sauce
1 egg

Break crab down into pieces, the claws, legs and halved body. Sauté ginger, garlic and chili in a wok or skillet in the oil for 3 to 4 minutes. Add water, sugar and tomato sauce and heat until boiling. Add the crab pieces and simmer for 3 to 4 minutes. Stir in the egg for 10 to 20 seconds and serve with rice.

Lobster

The king of seafoods. Nothing beats a fresh cooked lobster for lunch or dinner. Try these recipes.

Brazilian Baked Lobster and Pineapple

Serves 4

1 large ripe pineapple
1 tablespoon butter
2 cloves crushed garlic
2 large grated onions
1½ cups chopped canned tomato
1 teaspoon mustard
¼ cup marsala wine
2 sliced spring onions
2 tablespoons chopped parsley
2 pounds (1kg) cooked lobster meat
1 cup white sauce
Salt and black pepper

Cut the pineapple lengthwise. Remove the pineapple flesh, but leave 1¼-inch (4 cm) of shell. Cut the flesh into cubes and put in a colander to drain. Melt the butter and add garlic, onion, tomato, and mustard. Cook and stir for a few minutes. Add the wine, spring onions and parsley and cook for 5 minutes. Stir in the lobster, white sauce and pineapple cubes. Mix well and allow to cool. Dry the pineapple shells, and fill with the mixture. Put in a hot oven for 10 minutes.

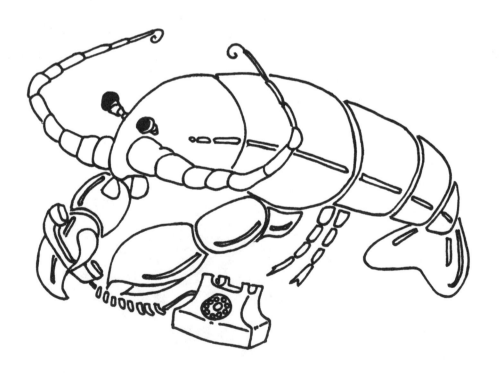

Grilled Lobster

Serves 2

2 medium lobsters
Salt and black pepper
Olive oil
2 tablespoons butter
Lemon juice

Cook the lobsters in boiling salted water for 3 minutes. Split in half lengthwise, and crack the claws. Brush with lemon and melted butter or olive oil, and grill for about 20 minutes.

American Lobster

Serves 4

2 medium cooked lobsters
2 tablespoons olive oil
1 medium finely chopped onion
2 cloves crushed garlic
1 teaspoon dried oregano
2 tablespoons tomato paste
½ cup dry white wine
¼ cup lemon juice
¼ cup water
Fresh breadcrumbs

Split lobsters in half and clean. Remove flesh and cut into cubes. Heat olive oil to smoking point and sauté onion, garlic and oregano. Add the remainder of ingredients, including lobster cubes, and simmer until mixture is heated through. Distribute mixture equally into the lobster shells, and place on a baking tray. Sprinkle with breadcrumbs and bake at 375° (190°C) until breadcrumbs are brown.

FISH SOUPS AND STEWS

Nothing lends itself to stews as well as fish and seafood generally. Obviously the French have made bouillabaisse a classic, and it is memorable when properly done in the true style of its native Provence. There are a number of other great alternatives to cook on board.

Caribbean Bouillabaisse

Serves 4 to 6

Olive oil
1 large chopped onion
2 medium quartered tomatoes
1 clove crushed garlic
1 crushed small chili pepper
Thyme
Grated nutmeg
Salt and pepper
Fish (bonito, etc.), prepared
Small lobster or tail
3 small crabs
1 teaspoon curry powder
Powdered saffron

In a large pan, gently sauté onion, tomatoes, garlic and chili in olive oil. Add some thyme, a dash of grated nutmeg, salt and pepper. Add the seafood. Cover and bring to a boil, and simmer for around 20 minutes. Five minutes before finishing the cooking, add the curry powder, and 2 pinches of powdered saffron.

Fish Soup

Serves 6 to 8

1½ pounds (750g) whole fish
1 sliced brown onion
1 sliced carrot
2 tablespoons butter
1 bay leaf
½ pound (250g) potatoes
½ pound (250g) tomatoes
½ pound (250g) broad beans
1½ tablespoons sweet paprika
2 teaspoons oil
2 cloves chopped garlic
Pinch cayenne pepper
Salt and fresh ground pepper

Prepare and wash the fish, and cut off the head and fins. Sauté the onion and carrot in 1 tablespoon of butter for around 3 minutes in a large saucepan. Add the fish and cover with water. Put in the bay leaf and then simmer slowly for around 10 minutes. Strain the cooked fish, and discard the vegetables. Keep the fish stock. Remove the fish flesh from bones, put the flesh into a large dish, and gently mix in 1 tablespoon paprika. Dice the potatoes into small squares. Heat the oil and 1 tablespoon of butter in a skillet, and sauté potatoes until nearly cooked. Transfer to the dish with the fish and sprinkle a tablespoon paprika over potatoes. Sprinkle beans with remaining paprika. Cut tomato into pieces. Put the tomatoes, fish, potatoes, beans, garlic and fish stock into a large saucepan. Bring to a boil, then slowly simmer for 10 minutes. Add chopped garlic and season with cayenne, salt and pepper to taste.

Seafood Stew

Serves most of the marina.

½ pound (250g) baby cuttlefish
½ pound (250g) mussels
1 pound (500g) small clams
½ pound (250g) small prawns or shrimp
½ pound (250g) crabmeat
½ pound (250g) flounder or sole
½ pound (250g) fish (white flake flesh)
½ pound (250g) spinach or beet leaves
½ cup olive oil
1 diced green pepper
1 can tomatoes
1 small bunch parsley
2 cloves garlic
Pinch dried basil
Salt and pepper

Prepare all seafood and fish. Boil spinach or beet leaves for up to 10 minutes or until tender, but do not overcook. Squeeze out excess moisture. Heat olive oil in large, deep casserole dish. Put in the diced pepper, drained and seeded tomatoes, chopped parsley and garlic, spinach, basil, salt and freshly ground pepper. Sauté the mixture and stir continuously for 5 or 6 minutes. Add the peeled prawns, cuttlefish, crabmeat, then cover and simmer for 15 minutes. If fresh clams and mussels are used, open by heating over high heat, and detach from shells. Cut the fish fillets into chunks and add, then put in clams. Add 1¾ cup water and salt and freshly ground pepper. Bring to a boil and simmer for 15 minutes.

Zarzuela

Serves 4 to 6

The great Spanish seafood stew, do not pass it up if in Spain. Mop up the delicious sauce with crusty bread, and wash down with local wines, it's magic!

2 large finely chopped onions
1 large chopped green pepper
2 teaspoons minced garlic
Olive oil
1 can chopped tomatoes
4 bay leaves
2 pounds (1kg) fish and
   shellfish (mussels, squid)
Saffron
½ cup white wine
½ cup lemon juice
Pepper

Sauté onions, green pepper and garlic in olive oil in a large heavy skillet. Add the tomatoes, bay leaves and seafood, then simmer slowly until seafood is tender. Add the saffron, white wine, lemon juice and pepper, and finish cooking.

Seafood Bake

Serves 4 to 6

4 baby octopus
4 small cuttlefish
4 small squid
2 pounds (1kg) fish
½ pound (250g) prawns
½ cup olive oil
4 medium (parboiled) potatoes
¼ cup Parmesan cheese
3 tablespoons breadcrumbs
1 small bunch parsley
2 cloves fresh garlic
Salt and ground pepper to
   taste

Prepare the octopus, cuttlefish and squid and cut into small pieces. Slice the fish into thin small pieces. Blanch the prawns in salted boiling water for 4 minutes. Drain and then peel. Grease a large casserole dish with 6 tablespoons oil and put in the seafood mixture. Cover with the peeled and sliced potatoes, seasoning to taste with salt and fresh ground pepper. Finally sprinkle the top with Parmesan or any grated hard cheese, breadcrumbs, finely chopped parsley, and the garlic. Sprinkle the remaining oil, cover tightly with a sheet of aluminum foil and bake in a preheated oven set at 425°F (215°C) for 30 minutes. Remove foil and cook for 15 minutes to brown.

Fish Chowder

Serves 4 to 6

1 pound (500g) fish fillets
2 medium potatoes
2 medium carrots
4 cups water
1 teaspoon salt
6 tablespoons butter or
    margarine
1 teaspoon curry powder
3 tablespoons flour
1 tablespoon tomato paste
¼ to ½ cup cream
2 finely chopped shallots
1 tablespoon chopped parsley

Remove skin and bones from the fish and cut into 2-inch pieces. Peel the potatoes and carrots and also cut into 2-inch pieces. Put the water, fish and salt in a pot and bring to a boil. Cover and reduce heat to a simmer. Simmer for 30 minutes. Drain and reserve fish pieces and stock. Melt the butter in a pan, remove from heat and stir in the flour and curry powder, return to heat, and cook and stir for 2 minutes. Gradually add the fish stock, and stir until it boils and thickens. Add the tomato paste, potatoes and carrots. Reduce the heat and simmer uncovered for approximately 20 minutes. Add the fish pieces and cream. Sprinkle with shallots and parsley.

CANNED FISH

Canned fish is still a great meal source. It keeps well and is nutritious and tasty.

Sardines

Fresh sardines are superb as anyone who has bought them fresh off the wharf will agree, particularly in some South American countries, in Portugal, not to mention their namesake, Sardinia. Grilled on the barbecue they are great but there is a certain pleasure in peeling back the lid of a sardine can (assuming the key doesn't snap off on you) and seeing those neat and ordered little rows of silvery fish. Choice is a problem these days: there are sardines in soya oil, vegetable oil, sild oil or mineral water. Then there is a variety of plain, tomato or spicy sauce. My favorite are Norwegian Sild Sardines in sild oil, the smaller double-layered ones. Sardines also are reputed to improve with age like fine wines, and year old or better are tastiest. Many countries incorporate the little tinned fishes into various dishes, so experiment. Personally, I just love them spread onto hot buttered toast.

Sardines and Spaghetti   *Serves 4*

1 pound spaghetti
1 tablespoon olive oil
1 clove crushed garlic
2 sliced spring onions
2 tablespoons raisins
2 cans sardines in tomato sauce
Lemon juice (optional)

Cook spaghetti in boiling water until tender and drain. Heat the olive oil, and add the garlic, onions and raisins. Cook over moderate heat for 2 minutes. Chop sardines into large pieces and stir in the spaghetti, toss and serve. Squeeze in some lemon juice if you wish.

Tuna

Canned tuna has a place in the cruiser's pantry. It is easy to prepare and easy to store.

Tuna and Potato Loaf

Serves 4

2 cups cooked and mashed
  potatoes
1 large can tuna
2 eggs
1 tablespoon finely diced
  onion
Salt and pepper
1 tablespoon chopped parsley

Mix all ingredients well. Put the mixture in a greased loaf pan. Bake in moderate oven for 40 minutes. Garnish with parsley.

Tuna and Pasta

Serves 2

½ pound (250g) pasta
  (spaghetti, macaroni)
2 teaspoons olive oil
1 chopped onion
1 clove chopped garlic
1 stick chopped celery
  (optional)
1 pound (500g) can tomatoes
3 tablespoons tomato paste
1 pound (500g) can tuna
1 teaspoon oregano
¼ cup grated cheese, if
  available
Chopped parsley

Cook the pasta and drain. Gently sauté the onions, garlic and celery in olive oil. Add the tomatoes, and chop roughly. Add the tomato paste and cook for 10 minutes. Flake the tuna, add it with the oregano, and stir through the mixture well. Serve the pasta with the sauce and sprinkle with cheese and parsley.

Curried Tuna Puffs

Serves 4

2½ cups cooked medium grain
    rice
2 eggs
3 teaspoons curry powder
¼ cup skim milk
2 tablespoons chopped parsley
1 pound (500g) can tuna,
    drained and flaked
Juice of 1 lemon
1½ cups dry breadcrumbs
¼ cup oil

Combine all the ingredients, except oil and bread-crumbs. Shape mixture into balls or patties, and roll in breadcrumbs. Cook in oil until golden.

Quick Canned Tuna Casserole

Serves 2

½ pound (250g) can tuna
1 small chopped onion
Oil
½ can tomato soup
2 teaspoons lemon juice
1 cup canned mixed vegetables
1 cup cooked macaroni or
    spiral pasta
½ cup fresh breadcrumbs
1 tablespoon melted margarine
Salt and black pepper to taste

Drain tuna and flake. Sauté the onion in oil in a skillet. Put into casserole dish with tuna. Add undiluted soup, lemon juice, vegetables, pasta and bread-crumbs. Combine mixture well. Toss the breadcrumbs in the margarine and sprinkle over the top of casserole. Bake uncovered at 325°F (160°C) for 30 minutes.

Salmon

The best canned salmon is the red and pink salmon, the tastiest coming from the West Coast and Canada. Sockeye salmon is also good. All are a delight on fresh bread and butter, or with a salad. Of course smoked salmon is a superb gourmet delight, but it is rarely on the cruiser's menu due to price and preservation problems.

Fish Cakes

Serves 2

1 small drained can salmon
1 cooked and mashed medium
   potato
1 tablespoon chopped onion
   (optional)
1 tablespoon lemon juice
1 tablespoon skim milk
   powder
1 tablespoon chopped parsley
   (if available)
Salt and black pepper to taste
Flour
Breadcrumbs

Combine all the ingredients and shape into four patties. Roll the patties in flour and breadcrumbs. Lightly oil a skillet and gently brown the patties on both sides.

Salmon Loaf

Serves 2

1 can salmon in brine
Skim milk
2 tablespoons finely chopped
   onion
4 tablespoons lemon juice
Pinch cayenne pepper
4 tablespoons chopped green
   pepper
4 tablespoons chopped celery
½ cup dried breadcrumbs
1 egg white

Drain the canned salmon, and retain the liquid. Add enough skim milk to make up to half a cup. Mix all ingredients and spoon into a well greased loaf pan. Bake at 350°F (180°C) for 1 hour. Allow to cool for 5 minutes before removing from the pan.

Salmon Quiche

Serves 4

4 well beaten eggs
1 cup milk
½ cup sour cream
¾ cup self-raising flour
2 cans pink salmon
1 small grated onion
1 small grated carrot
2 tablespoons cooked green
   peas (or spinach for color
   and flavor)
1 cup grated cheese (Cheddar)
Salt and freshly ground black
   pepper
½ cup melted butter or
   margarine

Add milk, sour cream and the flour to the eggs and beat to mix thoroughly. Add the salmon, and then the onion, carrot, peas, seasonings, and the cheese. Mix well. Finally add the melted butter. Place mixture into a suitable lightly greased baking pan or quiche mold and cook in a slow oven. Test with skewer after 40 minutes. The quiche should be lightly brown on top.

Chapter 6

Meats

Chicken

Pork

Goat

Lamb and Beef

Sausages

Rissoles

Casseroles

The Barbecue

A chicken in every pot...

and in every galley, too.

Meats in the cruising menu will depend on good and large freezer capacities. Also budget and availability will both be major factors. You can always buy a frozen chicken anywhere, and chicken recipes are the most practical. Besides that, I just love chicken, especially these tried and savored recipes.

CHICKEN

Colombian Style Chicken

Serves 4

Despite the bad press, Colombia is a favorite destination of mine. Whether you go to the Caribbean or Pacific ports, the food is delicious. Try this interesting recipe.

4 chicken thighs
1⅓ teaspoons salt
1 teaspoon sugar
½ teaspoon curry powder
2 bay leaves
2 tablespoons soy sauce
2 tablespoons olive oil
1 tablespoon white vinegar
3 tablespoons olive oil
½ cup flour
1½ cups chicken stock
3 cups hot cooked rice
Chopped parsley

Skin the chicken pieces. Put salt, sugar, curry powder, bay leaves, soy sauce, oil and vinegar into a saucepan and bring to a boil. Pour over the chicken pieces. Cool, cover and refrigerate overnight. Next day remove chicken pieces from marinade and pat dry with paper towels. Dust chicken all over with the flour. Brown in the heated oil in large saucepan or skillet with a lid. When chicken is brown, pour in the marinade and chicken stock, cover and simmer for half an hour or until chicken is tender. Serve on a bed of rice. Reduce pan liquids by rapidly boiling until it has thickened like gravy. Pour over chicken and rice and garnish with parsley.

Mint Chicken

Serves 2

½ pound boneless chicken breasts
2 tablespoons oil
1 teaspoon chopped fresh garlic
1 teaspoon chopped fresh green chili
2 tablespoons fish sauce
½ teaspoon sugar
2 drops sweet black sauce
5 tablespoons chicken broth
15 whole mint leaves

Cut the chicken into 2-inch strips. In a wok or skillet, heat oil and garlic until oil bubbles. Add the chicken and chili. Stir fry until chicken is nearly cooked, about 3 minutes. Add the fish sauce, sugar, black sauce and broth. Stir fry for 4 minutes until chicken is cooked. Add the mint leaves and toss.

Barbecued Chicken Wings

Serves 4

For fellow wing addicts, cheap and yummy!

2 pounds (1kg) chicken wings
1 teaspoon finely grated fresh
  ginger
1 clove minced garlic
¼ cup honey
¼ cup soy sauce
2 tablespoons sherry
1 tablespoon sweet Thai chili
  sauce

Trim and discard wing tips. Rinse the two other joints and dry on paper towels. Mix ginger, garlic, honey, soy, sherry and chili sauce and pour over the wings. Turn continuously. After 1 hour marinating, place in a roasting pan in a medium oven for 20 to 25 minutes. This reduces the times on the barbecue and prevents the sweet glaze from burning. Finish on the barbecue.

Cajun Chicken Wings

Serves 4

2 pounds (1kg) chicken wings
1 cup plain flour
1 teaspoon salt
2 teaspoons white pepper
2 teaspoons black pepper
2 teaspoons cayenne pepper
1¼ cups honey
1½ tablespoons paprika
1 teaspoon dried thyme
1 teaspoon dried oregano

Trim and discard the wing tips. Rinse the two other joints and dry on paper towels. Put all the ingredients in a plastic freezer bag and shake well to mix. Add the wings and shake to coat with mixture. Heat oil in large skillet. Sauté until golden brown and cooked through.

Barbecued Thai Garlic Chicken

Serves 4

3 pounds (1½kg) roasting
  chicken
6 cloves garlic
2 teaspoons salt
2 tablespoons black
  peppercorns
4 fresh coriander plants
3 tablespoons lemon juice

Cut chicken into serving pieces. Crush the garlic and mix with the salt. Crush the peppercorns. Wash the coriander and chop finely. Add the lemon juice and combine all seasonings well. Put in the chicken pieces and toss through so they are well coated. Cover with plastic wrap, and leave to marinate in the refrigerator for at least an hour but preferably overnight. Turn over occasionally. Cook on the barbecue over a low heat, making sure the chicken doesn't burn. Cook until the chicken is tender and the skin is crisp, for about 15 to 20 minutes.

Angelina's Filipina Chicken

Serves 4

2 pounds (1kg) wings and
  drumsticks
3 tablespoons tomato paste
3 teaspoons sugar
Black pepper
4 cloves crushed garlic
1 large chopped onion
3 tablespoons tomato ketchup
1 teaspoon chili sauce, or fresh
  chili
Peanut oil

Mix all the ingredients together and marinate the chicken in the mixture for as long as possible. Pour some peanut oil in a skillet and fry the chicken. After cooking the chicken until tender, put the marinade mixture into the pan and simmer until onions and garlic are cooked. Serve over chicken with boiled rice.

Peanut Chicken

Serves 6

4 double chicken breasts
Salt and fresh ground pepper
Bay leaves
Olive oil
Butter
1 onion
Garlic
1 can tomatoes
2 cups smooth peanut butter
3 cups chicken stock
Parsley or coriander

Season the chicken with salt and pepper. Sauté the chicken in a skillet in a mixture of olive oil, butter and bay leaves. Allow to cool and cut the chicken into small pieces. Preserve the cooking juices. Brown the onion in olive oil with garlic. Add the puréed canned tomatoes and cook on slow heat for 10 minutes. Dissolve the peanut butter in the cold chicken stock, then add the mixture with chicken and chicken juices to the tomato mixture. Cook for 10 minutes until it reaches a creamy consistency. Garnish with chopped parsley or coriander and serve with white rice.

Vietnamese Chicken

Serves 4 to 6

1 3 pound chicken
2 cloves crushed garlic
1 grated onion
2 tablespoons dry sherry
½ teaspoon salt
2 teaspoons 5-spice powder
1 teaspoon sugar
4 tablespoons light soy sauce
1 teaspoon sesame oil

Wash and dry the chicken thoroughly. Mix the garlic and onion and blend with sherry, salt, 5-spice, sugar and soy sauce. Mix until sugar dissolves. Rub marinade well into chicken and leave for around 2 hours. Brush with marinade occasionally. Place chicken on a grid in roasting pan, breast down in preheated oven at 375°F (190°C) for 10 minutes. Turn over and roast for 45 minutes, basting regularly. When cooked, brush with sesame oil and let stand for 10 minutes. Serve with boiled rice and Nuoc Mam salsa (see recipe).

Tandoori Chicken

Serves 6

Not exactly as great as traditional Indian style cooked in a clay tandoor, but an acceptable yacht imitation.

12 chicken pieces
Juice of a lemon
2 tablespoons natural yogurt
1 teaspoon minced garlic
1 teaspoon minced ginger
1 tablespoon ground paprika
1 teaspoon garam masala
2 teaspoons ground turmeric
Olive oil

Trim chicken pieces of fat. Combine all the other ingredients and mix well. Rub the mixture into chicken pieces. Put into a marinade tray, single layer only and cover. Put in refrigerator for 12 to 24 hours. Preheat the oven to 400°F (205°C) and cook for 20 minutes. Brush lightly with oil, reduce heat to 350°F (180°), and bake for a further 40 minutes. Serve with lime wedges and onion slices.

Cooked Chicken

There are many times when it makes good sense and saves on gas to cook two chickens or one large chicken: you will have plenty of leftovers. Enjoy these two great recipes because they are delightful.

Peruvian Chicken

Serves 6

8 slices white bread
1¾ cups milk
⅔ cup olive oil
2 onions
2 cloves garlic
1 tablespoon dried chili
¼ cup honey
½ cup ground walnuts
1 teaspoon salt
Black pepper to taste
3 pounds (1.5kg) cooked
    chicken
Parmesan cheese

Remove the crust and cut the bread into small cubes. Soak in milk for 5 minutes. Mash and mix in a tablespoon of olive oil. Chop onions finely and sauté in remainder of oil with crushed garlic. When soft and golden, add dried chilies, honey, nuts, and salt and pepper. Stir in the bread paste and cook gently until the sauce starts to thicken. Add the cooked chicken pieces and Parmesan cheese. Heat gently for about 3 to 4 minutes. Serve and garnish with olives and 2 quartered hard boiled eggs.

Quick Chicken Casserole
(Heather on *Phantasia*)

Serves 4 to 6

2 large potatoes
2 sliced onions
3 pounds (1.5kg) cooked chicken
1 can leek and potato soup or
1 can cream of mushroom soup
½ cup chicken stock
1 can water
1 cup frozen peas or mixed vegetables
Lemon juice
½ cup breadcrumbs
½ cup grated cheese

Slice the potatoes and layer at the bottom of dish. Add onions. Pour over can of soup. Add chicken stock mixed with a can of water. Microwave on high for 10 minutes. Add cooked chicken and vegetables to dish. Season with black pepper and a squeeze of lemon juice. Mix well. Top with breadcrumbs and grated cheese. Bake at 325°F (160°C) for 15 to 20 minutes.

Chicken Jambalaya

Serves 4 to 6

2 ounces (50g) margarine or butter
½ pound (250g) thinly sliced celery
½ pound (250g) chopped onions
½ pound (250g) chopped green or red peppers
2 cloves crushed garlic
½ pound (250g) cooked chicken
½ pound (250g) long grain rice
1 pound (500g) can tomatoes
Dash Tabasco

Melt margarine into a pan, then add celery, onions, peppers and garlic. Sauté gently until soft and golden. Mix the rest of the ingredients along with ½ pint boiling water. Mash the tomatoes with a spoon. Bring to a boil, cover and simmer for 20 minutes. Cook until rice is dry and fluffy. Serve with a dash of Tabasco.

PORK

Pork is reasonably easy to find. It is the centerpiece of many feasts throughout the Pacific, and a popular meat in Europe and Asia.

Chinese Pork

Serves 4

4 pork spare ribs
1 clove garlic
1½ teaspoons ginger
1 tablespoon soy sauce
1 tablespoon dry sherry
Cooking oil

Remove pork from the bone and cut into small pieces. Mix all ingredients and marinate 1 hour. Heat oil in a wok and add pork mixture. Cook for 10 minutes, stirring continuously. Serve with rice or stir fried vegetables.

Orange Pork

Serves 4

1½ pounds (750g) diced pork
1 cup orange juice
2 cloves chopped garlic
1 teaspoon chopped ginger
1 tablespoon grated orange
   rind
2 tablespoons soy sauce

Mix all ingredients and marinate 1 hour. Place pork pieces on skewers. Barbecue or broil until cooked.

Pork and Seafood Paella

Serves 4 to 6

1 pound (500g) cooked and
    diced pork
1 tablespoon olive oil
1 finely chopped onion
2 chopped tomatoes
1 sliced green pepper
1 teaspoon sugar
2 cups long grain rice
2 cups chicken stock
1½ cups water
Saffron threads
1 bay leaf
½ pound (250g) white fish
12 mussels

Brown pork in a large skillet for 3 to 4 minutes. Set aside. Sauté onion and cook until soft. Add tomatoes, pepper and sugar. Simmer uncovered and reduce liquid 4 to 5 minutes. Stir in rice, stock, water, saffron and bay leaf. Bring to a boil, simmer 10 minutes. Add fish and mussels, cover and simmer for 3 minutes. Add the pork, and cook for another 3 to 4 minutes. Stir rice gently and serve.

Pork Balls

Serves 4 to 6

½ pound (250g) pork mince
½ cup fresh breadcrumbs
    (brown)
1 tablespoon chopped parsley
    and chives
1 egg

Combine mince, breadcrumbs, herbs and egg. Mix well and roll into small balls. Chill balls for 30 minutes. Pan fry until golden, cook for 10 to 15 minutes. Serve with pasta or rice.

GOAT

Goat meat consumption is greater worldwide than the consumption of beef or lamb and mutton. Quality kid meat is beautiful and rivals top quality lamb. Bake or stew like lamb, and the following are a few other recipe ideas. In the Caribbean there are a number of local specialty dishes: try some of them.

Goat Stroganoff

Serves 4 to 6

1½ pounds (750g) goat meat
2 tablespoons plain flour
1 teaspoon mixed herbs
2 tablespoons butter
1 large chopped onion
1 clove crushed garlic
1 can tomatoes
½ cup red wine
1 small can button mushrooms
¼ cup sour cream

Cut the meat into cubes. Combine flour and herbs. Dip the meat in the flour and herb mixture. Sauté onion and garlic in butter for 2 minutes. Add the meat, and sauté until browned for 5 minutes. Add the tomatoes, wine and mushrooms. Cover and simmer for around 3 hours or until meat is tender. Stir in sour cream. Serve with rice or pasta.

Goat Meatballs and Tomato Sauce

Serves 4 to 6

1 pound (500g) lean goat
    mince
1 small chopped onion
1 tablespoon chopped fresh
    mint
1 tablespoon chopped fresh
    parsley
½ cup fresh breadcrumbs
½ teaspoon pepper
1 beaten egg
Corn flour
1 tablespoon olive oil
1 can tomatoes
½ cup red wine

Combine the mince, onion, mint, parsley, breadcrumbs, egg and pepper. Roll into small balls. Chill for 30 minutes. Dust meatballs in corn flour. Sauté in oil for approximately 6 to 8 minutes. To make the sauce, add tomatoes and wine to the pan. Simmer and reduce until thickened. Season to taste. Return the meatballs to the pan and heat through for 5 minutes.

LAMB AND BEEF

There are a few buying tips to remember: The meat should be bright pink to red in color. Do not buy packs where there are meat juices as this is a sign that the meat has lost its juices and may be dry when cooked.

Irish Stew

Serves 4

1 pound (500g) onions
2 pounds (1kg) potatoes
1½ pounds (750g) lamb or
   mutton cubes
2 teaspoons salt
White pepper
2 cups water

Peel onions and potatoes, wash thoroughly and cut both vegetables into thin slices. Put the meat cubes and the onions and potatoes into a saucepan and sprinkle with salt and pepper. Carefully pour water on top. Cover with lid tightly, slowly bring to a boil. Skim off fat, and simmer on low for 1½ hours.

Singapore Satay

Serves 4 to 6

1½ pounds (750g) lamb or
   mutton cubes
1 peeled onion
2 cloves peeled garlic
1 or 2 seeded red chilies
2 tablespoons desiccated
   coconut
3 tablespoons lemon juice
2 tablespoons soy sauce
½ cup peanut butter
½ cup hot water

Process onion, garlic, chilies, coconut, 2 tablespoons lemon juice, and 1 tablespoon soy sauce in food processor. Pour the mixture over meat cubes and marinate 10 minutes. Preheat broiler to high. Put meat cubes onto skewers. Broil 10 to 12 minutes. Combine peanut butter, water and chili over a medium heat, until smooth. Remove from heat and add remaining lemon juice and soy sauce. Serve on boiled rice.

Beef or Lamb Koftas

Serves 6

¼ cup cracked wheat
1 cup water
1½ pounds (750g) minced beef
    or lamb
1 small finely chopped onion
1 clove crushed garlic
1 teaspoon ground cumin
½ teaspoon ground cinnamon
1 lightly beaten egg
¼ cup pine nuts

Soak the cracked wheat in water for 30 minutes. Drain off the water, and squeeze out all excess moisture. Combine with all other ingredients and divide into 12 portions. Roll out each portion into a sausage shape, and push through a metal kebab skewer. Cook under a broiler until brown, or brush with olive oil and cook on the barbecue.

American Spareribs

Serves 4 to 6

1 chopped onion
3 tablespoons olive oil
3 tablespoons tomato purée
4 tablespoons white wine
    vinegar
7 ounces (200ml) chicken
    stock
2 tablespoons honey
1 teaspoon Dijon mustard
1 clove crushed garlic
½ crumbled bay leaf
1 teaspoon dried oregano
Dash of Tabasco
3 pounds (1.5kg) spare ribs
Salt and black pepper

Sauté onion slowly until soft. Mix tomato purée and vinegar to a paste and add to the onion. Heat the stock and then add the honey, mustard and garlic. Add the herbs and simmer for 15 minutes covered. Add a dash of Tabasco and then let cool down. Marinate ribs in marinade for 3 to 4 hours, basting frequently. Broil for 15 minutes per side or you can bake in the oven at 450°F (230°C) for 1 hour.

Canned Corned Beef Packages
(Pauline on *Ruahatu*)

Serves 2

1 small can corned beef
1 cup thick coconut cream
Taro or spinach leaves
1 small finely chopped onion
1 finely chopped tomato
Salt and pepper
½ cup fresh herbs (optional)

Slice corned beef finely and mix with coconut cream. Cut the stalk out of taro leaves and arrange the pieces to overlap in fan pattern, making sure there are no holes. Spoon in a cup full of the mixture into the center of the leaves. Sprinkle with tomato and onion. Season to taste. Add fresh herbs. Wrap to form a small square package. Tie with string. Wrap in foil and bake for 20 to 30 minutes in a moderate oven.

Bubble and Squeak

Serves 2

1 cup canned corn beef
Leftover vegetables, or
Cooked cold cabbage and
    potatoes
Salt and pepper
1 tablespoon butter or
    margarine
Fried egg (optional)

Cube or shred the corned beef. Mix the corned beef and the vegetables. Season with salt and pepper. Sauté the mixture in 1 tablespoon heated butter, and turn until browned on both sides. Serve with a fried egg on top, or with any sauce.

Crumbed Corn Beef

Serves 2

1 small can corned beef
3 tablespoons plain flour
1 beaten egg
1½ cups breadcrumbs
2 tablespoons cooking oil
Fried egg (optional)
Cheese and tomato slices

Slice corned beef into ½-inch pieces. Mix flour and egg and beat into a batter. Roll the corned beef into the batter, then into breadcrumbs. Heat oil in a skillet and fry until golden. As an option, top with a fried egg or put under the broiler. Top with slice of tomato and cheese.

STIR FRY

There are a number of quick and simple stir fry recipes, although, as any good Chinese restaurant will show, there are literally hundreds of possibilities.

Stir Fry Beef and Broccoli

Serves 4

1½ pounds (750g) lean beef
   steak
2 tablespoons corn flour
½ teaspoon 5-spice powder
¼ cup soy sauce
1 tablespoon tomato sauce
¼ cup sherry
1 tablespoon oil
1 onion
2 carrots
1 pound (500g) broccoli
   flowerettes
½ cup beef stock

Slice beef into thin strips. Marinate in mixture of corn flour, 5-spice, soy sauce, tomato sauce and sherry for 15 minutes. Cut onion into eighths, thinly slice carrots and stir fry in hot oil along with broccoli for 2 minutes. Remove from heat. Stir fry the beef in 3 to 4 batches for 2 to 3 minutes. Add the vegetables along with stock and cook for 1 minute. Serve over boiled rice or instant noodles.

Stir Fry Oriental Beef

Serves 4

1 pound (500g) beef strips
2 teaspoons sesame oil
1 teaspoon chopped ginger
1 teaspoon crushed garlic
12 spring onions (white only)
½ pound (250g) broccoli
   florets
¼ pound (125g) snow peas
1 sliced red pepper
2 tablespoons soy sauce
2 tablespoons oyster sauce
1 tablespoon sherry
½ cup unsalted cashews

Brown small quantities of beef in hot oil in a wok or skillet for 2 to 3 minutes. Add the ginger, garlic, onions, broccoli, snow peas and red pepper. Stir fry all for 2 minutes. Stir in soy and oyster sauce, sherry and cashews. Serve on boiled rice.

SAUSAGES

The humble sausage or banger is a great meal in itself, either with traditional mashed potatoes, fried onions, or just wrapped with a slice of bread and butter. If you are cruising Europe, indulge yourself, as sausages are simply superb. Buy a selection of German ones such as knackwurst, bratwurst, bierwurst, weisswurst, then grill or sauté them, serve with mustard, crusty bread and cold beer. If in Spain try chorizo sausages, they are really delicious.

Sausage Hot Pot

Serves 4

8 thick beef sausages
3 rashers lean bacon
2 diced medium potatoes
1 small chopped onion
1 clove crushed garlic
1 can chopped peeled tomatoes
¼ teaspoon Tabasco sauce
¼ teaspoon basil and thyme
1 cup beef stock
2 tablespoons lemon juice
2 tablespoons chopped parsley
1 can of 4 bean mix, drained
Salt and freshly ground black
    pepper

Prick the sausages with a fork, and put into a large pan. Cook them on a medium to high heat for 6 to 8 minutes. Brown evenly by rotating them constantly. Remove from pan and put aside. Add the bacon, potatoes, onion and garlic to the pan and cook for 2 minutes. Mix together the tomatoes, Tabasco, stock, herbs, lemon juice and parsley. Pour in the mix and stir to combine. Return the sausages to the pan and simmer uncovered for 10 minutes. Add the four bean mix, and cook for a further 5 minutes uncovered. Season to taste with salt and freshly ground black pepper.

Curried Sausages

Serves 4

1 ounce (30g) butter or
   margarine
1½ pounds (750g) thick
   sausages
2 peeled and finely chopped
   onions
1 peeled and chopped apple
1 peeled and chopped banana
1 pound (500g) peeled and
   cubed potatoes
1½ teaspoons curry powder
1 can condensed vegetable
   soup
1½ cups water
1 beef stock cube
Salt and ground black pepper
2 tablespoons chopped parsley

Melt butter in a skillet and gently sauté sausages until golden brown. Remove from the skillet and drain off any excess fat, leaving about 1 tablespoon. Add the onions and sauté until golden brown. Add the apple, banana and potatoes and sauté another 2 minutes. Stir in the curry powder and cook for 1 minute. Add soup, water, crumbled stock cube, and season with salt and black pepper. Bring to a boil and reduce to simmer. Simmer for 15 minutes covered until potatoes are just cooked, add the sausages and simmer uncovered for 10 minutes. Garnish with parsley.

Ma's Sausage Stew

Serves 4

2 pounds (1kg) thick sausages
3 peeled and sliced carrots
3 peeled and sliced onions
2 peeled and sliced parsnips
4 large parboiled potatoes
Fresh chopped parsley

Gently fry sausages in a skillet until cooked. Set aside to cool down. When they are cold, skin the sausages and slice into thick chunks. Simmer the vegetables in a large saucepan, and when half cooked add chunks of potato. The potato will thicken the stew. When nearly cooked, add sausage pieces, season to taste. Sprinkle with fresh chopped parsley.

RISSOLES

Strictly speaking, a rissole is a pastry wrapped item, but somehow the meat has assumed the name. It is easy to prepare and even easier to eat.

Basic Rissole

Serves 4

1 pound (500g) ground beef
1 cup fresh breadcrumbs
1 finely chopped medium
   onion
1 beaten egg
Salt and pepper

Combine the ingredients and shape into 8 thick flat rissoles. Sauté on medium low heat, barbecue or broil for 10 to 15 minutes, turning periodically.

Chili Bean Rissole

Serves 4

1 pound (500g) ground beef
1 cup fresh breadcrumbs
1 finely chopped medium
   onion
1 beaten egg
⅓ cup taco sauce
⅓ cup cooked and drained red
   kidney beans
1 teaspoon chili powder
Salt and pepper

Combine the ingredients and shape into 8 thick flat rissoles. Sauté on medium low heat, barbecue or broil for 10 to 15 minutes, turning periodically.

Oriental Rissole

Serves 4

1 pound (500g) ground beef
1 cup fresh breadcrumbs
1 finely chopped medium
   onion
1 beaten egg
1 tablespoon soy sauce
1 teaspoon minced garlic
½ teaspoon 5-spice powder
Salt and pepper

Combine the ingredients and shape into 8 thick flat rissoles. Sauté on medium low heat, barbecue or broil for 10 to 15 minutes, turning periodically.

CASSEROLES

The casserole has as many variations as there are islands in the Pacific. It is the ideal way to consume a variety of "ripe" vegetables, as well as make a little meat go a long way. Use the following basics to make a variety of delicious meals:

- Brown small amounts of diced lean beef in a deep pan. This seals in the meat juices.
- Add vegetables, and when using squash and zucchini, add in the last 30 minutes of cooking.
- Add the seasonings and liquid, which can be stock if a full flavor is required, or red wine, or a combination of both. For a curry flavor use coconut milk, or a dash of fruit juice for extra sweetness. For the Asian flavors stir in soy or oyster sauce. Add tomato and sour cream for European flavors, or add chili and beans for a Mexican taste.
- Do not boil as meat gets stringy. Cover and gently simmer on low heat for 1½ to 2 hours.
- To thicken blend a little corn flour in cold water and stir in.
- Cook casseroles in an around 300°F (150°C) oven.

Osso Bucco Casserole

Serves 4 to 6

2 pounds (1kg) diced lean beef
1 tablespoon oil
2 chopped onions
1 tablespoon crushed garlic
1 tablespoon grated lemon rind
4 medium sliced carrots
2 cans tomatoes
½ cup white wine
Pepper
¼ cup corn flour

Brown small amounts of diced lean beef in a deep pan. Add the onions, garlic, lemon rind and carrots. Cook until onions are well browned. Stir in the tomatoes, wine and pepper. Cover and simmer on low heat for 1½ to 2 hours. Stir occasionally. Blend some corn flour in cold water and stir in until desired consistency is reached.

South American Lamb Casserole

Serves 4 to 6

2 pounds (1kg) lamb
2 tablespoons olive oil
1 sliced onion
2 cloves chopped garlic
1 diced green pepper
1 teaspoon ground coriander
Black pepper
1 teaspoon chili powder
1 can chopped tomatoes
1 cup white wine

Cut lamb into cubes and gently fry until brown. Remove and put aside. Sauté the onion, garlic, green pepper, coriander, chili and pepper until onion is soft. Return the lamb to the pan, stir well. Add the tomatoes and white wine. Bring to a boil and then return to a low simmer. Cook for about 30 minutes until lamb is tender. Serve on boiled or saffron rice.

THE BARBECUE

The backbone of alfresco dining, ashore or afloat is the barbecue. Gas or charcoal, it gets you out of a hot and steamy galley.

Steak

Seal steak on a hot grill over glowing coals, not flames, or on a lightly oiled griddle until juices appear (2 to 3 minutes). Do not turn too often.

Test steak using tongs, do not pierce with knife:

- Springy is rare (2-3 minutes per side)
- Firm is medium (5-6 minutes per side)
- Very firm is well done (10 minutes per side)

Slicing the steak across the grain keeps the meat tender.

Brazilian Beef Brochette   *Serves 4*

If you truly love your meat, a Brazilian barbecue shouldn't be missed. It is the carnivore's finest hour, I assure you.

1½ pounds (750g) rump steak
1 tablespoon honey
1 tablespoon instant coffee
2 teaspoons lemon juice
2 cloves crushed garlic
8 green baby squash
8 yellow baby squash
8 button mushrooms

Cut the steak into 1-inch (2.5cm) cubes. Mix the honey, coffee powder, lemon juice and garlic and marinate meat for 10 minutes. Thread meat cubes onto skewers and alternate with baby squash and mushrooms. Grill on high for around 5 minutes per side. Serve with boiled rice and a salad.

Barbecued Chicken

Seal chicken on a hot barbecue over glowing coals or on a lightly oiled griddle for 2 to 3 minutes. Turn the chicken just once. This will firm up the chicken surface and retain the natural juices, preventing it from drying out and getting stringy while cooking. Do not pierce the chicken when cooking because the juices will escape. If you are using frozen chicken, make sure that it is thoroughly thawed prior to cooking.

Tropical Chicken Kebabs

Serves 4

1 pound (500g) chicken fillets
1 cubed red pepper
Pineapple pieces
2 tablespoons olive oil
2 tablespoons malt vinegar
1 teaspoon lemon juice
1 clove crushed garlic

Cut chicken into ¾-inch (2 cm) cubes. Put in a bowl and add the red pepper, pineapple, and then stir in the remaining ingredients. Marinate for 30 minutes. Thread on the chicken, red pepper and pineapple pieces to skewers, and brush with marinade. Cook on the barbecue for 5 minutes per side, basting with marinade.

Chicken Satays

Serves 4

If using bamboo skewers always soak them in water for about 20 minutes to prevent them from burning and splintering in the chicken during cooking.

12 ounces (400g) chicken
　fillets
1 tablespoon brown sugar
1 tablespoon honey
2 tablespoons soy sauce
1 clove crushed garlic
1 tablespoon lemon juice

Satay Sauce

1 cup crunchy peanut butter
1 cup water
2 tablespoons brown sugar
1 tablespoon soy sauce
1 tablespoon grated onion
½ teaspoon chili powder

Cut chicken into ½-inch (1.5 cm) cubes. Mix the sugar, honey, soy sauce, garlic, and lemon juice together. Pour over the chicken cubes and marinate for several hours. Thread 6 cubes onto each satay stick. Grill on the barbecue and turn frequently while cooking. Brush with marinade during cooking. Serve with Satay Sauce. Heat the peanut butter and water in a saucepan, simmering gently and stirring well. Add the remaining ingredients and simmer for 1 minute.

Chicken Yakitori

Serves 4

1 pound (500g) chicken fillets
½ cup soy sauce
¼ cup honey
1 clove garlic
½ teaspoon ground ginger

Slice the chicken into thick strips. Put in a bowl and add the soy sauce, honey, garlic and ginger. Marinate in the refrigerator for several hours. Thread and weave strips onto the bamboo skewers. Brush with marinade. Heat barbecue to high heat, grease the plate, and arrange on same. Cook each side for 2½ minutes, basting with marinade.

Chapter 7

Rice, Pasta and Legumes

Rice Cooking Methods

Pasta Cooking Methods

Pasta Sauces

Legumes Varieties

Legumes Cooking Methods

Rice is the staple food in most parts of the world. Pasta is the ideal food for long-distance cruising—and for most athletes. Legumes are healthy, inexpensive and available everywhere.

RICE COOKING METHODS

Rice is the staple food for a good part of the planet. It is an ideal food source when cruising, easy to store, nutritious, and economical.

Rapid Boil Method Put 8 cups of water in a large saucepan and bring to a boil. Add salt if required, and slowly add in 1 cup rice. Stir several times with a fork and boil rapidly uncovered for 12 to 15 minutes. Test grains after 12 minutes. Drain in a colander and serve.

Absorption Bring 1½ cups water (or stock if preferred) to a boil in a heavy saucepan. Slowly add 1 cup of rice and salt if required. (For larger quantities add 1 cup water for each cup of rice.) Return to a boil, stir once and cover with a tight fitting lid. Turn the heat as low as possible. Simmer gently for 20 to 25 minutes until the rice is tender and all the liquid is absorbed. Remove the lid, and fork over lightly to allow steam to escape for about 5 minutes.

Steamed Rice

Rinse 1 cup of rice in a colander under cold water until water runs clear. Let the rice drain and dry. Put the rice into a heavy saucepan with a cover in about 1 inch of water. Bring to a boil, and boil rapidly until steam holes appear on the surface of the rice. Reduce heat to the minimum possible, and cover with a tight lid. Simmer for 10 minutes, remove from heat and allow to stand for 10 minutes covered. Uncover and fork over lightly. Allow to stand a further 5 minutes prior to serving.

Fried Rice

Cook the rice using the rapid boil method. Do not overcook. Run under cold water to make sure grains separate and drain well in a colander. Spread the rice on a tray in the refrigerator for at least 2 hours, or ideally in a shallow plastic container overnight.

½ **cup chopped bacon pieces**
½ **cup diced celery**
1 **egg**
3 **cups cooked rice**
½ **cup chopped shallots**
1 **to 2 teaspoons soy sauce**

Cook the bacon and celery until bacon is crisp. Add egg and cook until set. Stir with a fork to break into pieces. Add rice and shallots and cook until rice is very hot. Add soy sauce and mix lightly with a fork.

Saffron Rice

Serves 4 to 6

1 tablespoon butter
1 finely chopped onion
2 cups rice
½ teaspoon turmeric, or ¼
    teaspoon saffron
3½ cups chicken stock
4 cloves
Chopped mint

Sauté the onion and after adding the rice toss for a few minutes. Heat the saffron in another pan then pour the chicken stock over it. Let it boil, and add rice and cloves. Bring to a boil then simmer. Cover and cook until rice is tender. Garnish with chopped mint.

Vegetable Rice Patties

Serves 4

3 cups cooked long grain rice
2 cups grated carrots
2 cups grated zucchini
1 cup cooked and mashed
    pumpkin
¾ cup wholemeal flour
Black pepper
2 egg whites
½ cup mayonnaise
Rice bran
2 tablespoons olive oil

Mix the rice, carrot, zucchini, pumpkin and the flour together and season with pepper. Combine the egg whites and the mayonnaise, and add to the vegetable and rice mixture. Form the mix into patties and coat with rice bran. Sauté in olive oil until golden brown.

Rice Kedgeree

Serves 4

1 small chopped onion
1 tablespoon olive oil
½ cup cooked tuna or flaky
    fish
1 tablespoon sultanas raisins
Salt and pepper
2 finely chopped hardboiled
    egg whites
1½ cups cooked long grain rice
1 tablespoon chopped parsley

Gently sauté the onion in olive oil until tender. Flake the tuna or fresh fish, and add to the onion along with the sultanas and the egg whites. Season to taste and then add rice and turn over with a fork until heated. Garnish with parsley.

Rice and Seafood Fritters

Serves 4

¾ cup self-raising flour
1 cup cooked rice
1 egg
1 cup milk
2 spring onions
1 pound (500g) crab or prawn
  meat
2 tablespoons cooking oil

Sift the flour into a bowl and add rice. Form a well in the mixture and stir in the egg and milk, spring onions and meat. Drop about a tablespoon of the mixture in a preheated skillet. Cook each side until golden brown. Drain on paper towels.

Rice in Coconut Milk

Serves 4 to 6

This is a Malaysian dish.

2 cups long grain rice
1 cup coconut cream
Shreds of ginger
Salt to taste

Wash rice under running water until water runs clear. Put the rice in a saucepan with the coconut cream, ginger and salt and sufficient water to about 1 inch (2.5 cm) above the rice. Bring to a boil, and reduce heat and partly cover with lid. When all the visible liquid has been absorbed, turn off heat, and cover pan tightly. This allows rice to cook in its own steam until soft. Serve in mounds shaped from overturned rice bowl or similar container.

Seafood Paella

Serves 6

I became addicted to paella while living and working in Spain. There are a variety of recipes, and this one works well on board.

½ pound (250g) raw prawns
2 pounds (1kg) mussels
4 tablespoons olive oil
2 large finely chopped onions
6 cloves finely chopped garlic
½ teaspoon saffron strands
1 cup chopped canned
  tomatoes
2 teaspoons paprika
2 teaspoons salt
½ pound long grain rice
4½ cups fish or chicken stock
2 cooked crabs

Wash the prawns and devein, but leave the shell on. Scrub and debeard the mussels. Discard any that are not firmly closed. Steam them in water for 10 minutes and discard any that are unopened. Heat oil in a large saucepan, and sauté onions and garlic until soft and golden brown. Toast the saffron strands in a small dry pan for about a minute until crisp. Crush and dissolve in a tablespoon hot water. Add to the onions and garlic, followed by the tomatoes, salt and paprika. Add the prawns, stir and cook for 5 minutes, lift out prawns and set aside. Add the rice and cook for a few minutes, add the stock and bring mixture to a boil. Turn down to a simmer, cover and cook for 20 minutes. Add the mussels and prawns, cover again and cook for another 5 to 10 minutes. Garnish and serve with crab pieces.

Seafood Risotto

Serves 4

2 tablespoons oil
1 chopped onion
1 clove garlic
1 cup rice
½ pound (250g) diced fresh
   fish
2 peeled and chopped tomatoes
1 tablespoon tomato paste
2 cups chicken stock
1 bay leaf
¼ teaspoon oregano
Salt and pepper
½ pound (250g) fresh prawns
1 cup sliced mushrooms,
   precooked in butter

Heat oil and sauté onion, garlic and rice. Add fish, tomatoes, tomato paste, chicken stock, bay leaf, oregano, salt and pepper. Stir just once to mix the rice evenly . Cover and cook on low heat for 20 minutes. Add the prawns and mushrooms and cook until the rice is tender. Add extra stock if required. Garnish with prawns when serving.

Coconut Rice

Serves 8

This is done in the microwave.

2½ cups coconut milk
½ cup chicken stock
1 teaspoon turmeric
1 bay leaf
1½ cups long grain rice
½ cup toasted and slivered
   almonds
½ cup sultanas raisins

Mix the coconut milk, stock, turmeric, and bay leaf together in microwave casserole dish. Cook on 100% (high) for 6 to 8 minutes, until liquid starts to boil. Stir in the drained rice, sultanas and almonds. Cook uncovered on 100% (high) for 13 minutes. Stir occasionally.

Rice and Bean Soup

Serves 4

This is done in the microwave.

1 finely chopped onion
2 cloves finely chopped garlic
1 finely chopped carrot
2 finely chopped celery sticks
1 tablespoon oil
1 pound (500g) can tomatoes
1 pint (600ml) hot vegetable stock
1 pound (500g) can red kidney beans
3 ounces (75g) long grain rice
1 tablespoon dried basil
2 tablespoons chopped parsley
Pinch sugar
Salt and pepper

Put the onion, garlic, carrot, celery and oil into a dish and microwave on 100% (high) for 4 minutes. Add the tomatoes with their juice and the hot stock. Stir well and cover, cook on 100% (high) for 7 minutes. Allow to partially cool, and purée. Rinse the dish. Add the rice, basil, parsley and sugar. Season to taste. Cover and cook at 100% (high) for 10 minutes. Stir well after 7 minutes. Add the drained beans and finish off on 100% for another 2 minutes.

Rice Pudding

Serves 4

3 cups cooked rice
2 cups skim milk
¼ cup sugar
1 teaspoon vanilla
1 tablespoon butter
Nutmeg and cinnamon
Sultanas raisins

Put the rice, milk, sugar, butter and vanilla into a lightly buttered saucepan. Cook on moderate flame for approximately 30 minutes. Serve and sprinkle with nutmeg or cinnamon. You may also add sultanas.

PASTA COOKING METHODS

The origins of pasta are hazy. Some say Marco Polo brought it to Italy from the Orient, and others say it comes from ancient Greece. Christopher Columbus may have stored pasta before heading off on his voyages. Regardless of origin, pasta is a great food. Pastas are made from durum wheat, semolina and water. There are more than 50 different pastas. Typical pastas for boiling include tagliatelle, spaghetti, and hollow types such as macaroni, rigatoni, penne, as well as shaped pasta shells and spirals. The key to any pasta dish is a great sauce, and that is another subject all together. Sauces range from simple butter with mashed anchovies and garlic to that famous Genovese green sauce called pesto, not to forget the classic sauce bolognaise.

- Always use a large pot so that the pasta can cook without sticking to the sides. The general rule is 4 quarts (4 liters) for every ½ pound (250g) of pasta.

- Add 1 teaspoon of salt for every quart of water.

- Boil water vigorously before adding pasta. Put the pasta slowly in the water so that water keeps boiling.

- Allow 1 pound (500g) pasta for 4 people.

- Add a teaspoon of olive oil to water to prevent the pasta from sticking, especially with lasagne.

- Cook pasta until it is "al dente." This means that it is just firm to the bite.

- To combine pasta and sauce, add part of sauce along with some Parmesan cheese, then toss gently until pasta is coated with sauce.

- When pressure cooking, always reduce pressure slowly. If you use a non automatic manual release cooker, you can release pressure quickly but add 2 minutes to cooking times.

Pasta Cooking Methods and Times

	Pressure Cooker 15 lbs	Stove Top
Spaghetti	3 minutes	12 minutes
Tagliatelle (long ribbon strips)	2 minutes	8-10 minutes
Vermicelli (thin strips)	2 minutes	8-10 minutes
Cannelloni (large pipes)	3 minutes	12 minutes
Macaroni	3 minutes	12 minutes
Noodles	2 minutes	8-10 minutes
Pasta Shells/spirals	2 minutes	8-10 minutes

Minestrone Soup

Serves 6

3 pints beef stock
2 tablespoons tomato paste
½ cup elbow macaroni
1 teaspoon ground paprika
2 teaspoons oregano
2 teaspoons sweet basil
2 teaspoons garlic powder
1 large chopped onion
2 medium chopped carrots
1 small chopped parsnip
2 sticks sliced celery
½ cup chopped French beans
2 cups shredded cabbage
½ pound (250g) red kidney beans
Parmesan cheese

Add tomato paste to stock and bring to a boil. Add macaroni, paprika, oregano, basil, and garlic and simmer for 20 minutes. Add onion, carrots, parsnip, celery and the beans and cook for another 10 minutes. Add the cabbage and drained red kidney beans. Bring back to a boil, and cook until vegetables are tender. Garnish with Parmesan cheese.

Bean and Spinach Lasagne

Serves 4 to 6

1 tablespoon olive oil
2 chopped onions
2 cloves crushed garlic
1 can tomatoes
1 pound (500g) puréed lima beans
1 pound (500g) red kidney beans
1 teaspoon hot chili sauce
1 teaspoon dried oregano
1 bunch spinach, chopped
2 lightly beaten eggs
½ pound (250g) dry lasagne sheets
2 tablespoons Parmesan cheese

Sauté onions and garlic in olive oil in a skillet until tender. Add the tomatoes, lima beans, red kidney beans, chili sauce and oregano. Stir well and bring to a boil, reduce heat, and simmer uncovered for 10 minutes until sauce reduces and thickens. Set aside. Cook the spinach until it wilts, stir in the eggs, and also set aside. Cook lasagne sheets in boiling water until tender and drain. Lay one third of lasagne sheets over the base of a baking dish, cover with a third of the bean sauce and half the spinach. Repeat layers, and top with lasagne sheets and bean sauce. Sprinkle with cheese, and bake at 350°F (180°C) for 30 minutes until golden brown on top.

Pasta and Vegetable Soup

Serves 4

2 cups beef stock
1 sliced carrot
1 medium diced onion
2 sticks diced celery
1 pound (500 g) can tomatoes
1 clove crushed garlic
1 teaspoon sugar
Salt and pepper
½ cup pasta spirals, shell or macaroni

Put all the ingredients except the pasta into a large saucepan, and bring to a boil. Reduce heat to a slow simmer, cover and cook until vegetables are almost done, about 15 minutes. Add the pasta, and cook until pasta is firm but cooked.

Kingfish, Crab and Pasta Soup

Serves 6

1 pound (500g) Kingfish fillets
1 tablespoon oil
1 large finely chopped onion
1 large diced potato
6 cups fish stock
3 medium chopped tomatoes
½ cup pasta shells
4 diced bacon slices
½ pound (250g) cooked crab
   meat
½ cup chopped parsley
Salt and pepper

Remove skin and bone from fish fillets, and cut into bite size chunks. Gently sauté the onion, then add potatoes, stock, tomatoes, pasta and bacon. Simmer 10 minutes until pasta is just tender. Add the fish, crab, parsley, salt and pepper. Cook until fish just starts to flake off, 3 to 4 minutes.

Avocado Fettuccine

Serves 4

1 pound (500g) fettuccine
2 cloves garlic
2 ripe peeled and stoned
   avocados
1 tablespoon fresh squeezed
   lemon juice
½ cup coarsely chopped fresh
   basil
½ cup water
2 tablespoons butter
1 cup cream
Salt and fresh ground black
   pepper

Cook fettuccine in boiling water until al dente. Using a blender or food processor mince fresh garlic, add the avocado, lemon juice, basil and water. Purée and season to taste. Melt butter in a skillet and add the avocado mixture. Heat through, and stir well. Add the cream and cook until sauce just starts to thicken, about three minutes. Serve immediately over pasta.

Fettuccine Marinara

Serves 4

1½ pounds (750g) fettuccine
1 clove garlic
2 teaspoons chopped fresh basil
3 tablespoons virgin olive oil
2 cups tomato sauce
12 scrubbed mussels
½ pound (250g) chopped octopus meat
½ pound (250g) calamari hoods
½ pound (250g) chopped fish fillets
½ pound (250g) raw prawn meat

Cook fettuccine in boiling water until al dente. Using a blender or food processor mince fresh garlic. Mix 1 tablespoon olive oil and basil and set aside. Heat 2 tablespoons oil, add the tomato sauce and cook for about 2 minutes. Add the mussels and cook for 5 minutes. Add the octopus, calamari, fish fillets and prawns, cook for a further 5 minutes. Add the cooked fettuccine and warm through for 5 minutes, stir well. Add the rest of the basil and olive oil.

PASTA SAUCES

The heart of every good pasta dish is the sauce. Everyone has a favorite recipe for a good beef bolognaise sauce. The following are fairly traditional recipes and will make the meal all the more enjoyable. For tomato sauce, add onion and bacon, or perhaps sliced mushrooms and green pepper, or even small shellfish such as clams.

Tomato Sauce

For pizza and pasta dishes.

2 tablespoons olive oil
1 medium onion
1 clove garlic
1 pound (500g) ripe chopped
tomatoes
4 tablespoons tomato purée
1 teaspoon sugar
Small bay leaf
Salt and black pepper
2 teaspoons chopped basil

Heat oil and sauté chopped onion slowly until soft. Peel and crush garlic and add towards the end of cooking. Add the tomatoes and tomato purée. Add sugar, bay leaf, salt and pepper. Simmer slowly for around an hour with the lid off, and allow it to reduce to thick consistency. Stir occasionally, and add the fresh herbs at the end. Freeze if you have any left over.

Tomato Sauce 2

2 tablespoons olive oil
1 finely chopped medium
onion
1 clove crushed garlic
2 teaspoons sugar
Freshly ground black pepper
2 cans tomatoes
2 teaspoons chopped basil
½ teaspoon dry oregano
½ cup red wine

Sauté the onion in olive oil for 2 to 3 minutes. Add garlic, sugar and pepper. Cook gently for around a minute. Add the other ingredients. Reduce over gentle heat to a thick sauce.

Oil and Garlic Sauce

6 cloves chopped garlic
½ cup olive oil
Black pepper
Salt

Sauté the garlic gently in oil. Drain the pasta and pour garlic and oil over it. Stir well and season with salt and fresh ground black pepper.

Pesto

6 tablespoons basil leaves
2 cloves chopped garlic
1 tablespoon pine nuts
5 tablespoons extra virgin olive
   oil
Ground black pepper
2 tablespoons grated Parmesan
   cheese

Put basil, garlic and pine nuts in processor or blender and gradually purée. Pour the oil slowly into the mixture until it has a creamy consistency, adding oil as necessary. Add pepper and Parmesan to taste.

Macaroni in Tomato and Onion Sauce

Serves 4

1 tablespoon oil
1 finely chopped onion
2 cloves crushed or minced
   garlic
1 can peeled tomatoes
1 tablespoon fresh chopped
   basil
1 tablespoon sugar
1 pound (500g) macaroni

Put oil in a skillet and heat slowly. Add the garlic and onion, and sauté gently until transparent. Add the tomatoes, basil and sugar, then cook for 5 minutes, stirring periodically. Cook macaroni in boiling water until tender. Drain, add the sauce and toss to mix.

Chili and Tomato Pasta

Serves 4 to 6

2 tablespoons olive oil
1 sliced onion
1 clove crushed garlic
4 peeled and chopped tomatoes
1 cup dry white wine
1 tablespoon chopped fresh
   basil
Salt and fresh ground black
   pepper
½ teaspoon chopped chili
1 pound (500g) dry pasta of
   choice, cooked
½ cup Parmesan cheese

Sauté onion and garlic in olive oil. Combine the tomatoes, wine, basil, and seasonings until tender, then stir in the chili. Gently reduce liquid. Toss sauce through prepared pasta, and sprinkle well with Parmesan cheese.

LEGUME (DRIED BEANS AND PULSES) VARIETIES

Legumes or beans are available nearly everywhere in the world. They are the staple in many countries. There is a diverse range of beans available, so variety of diet is assured. What is more important is that they are inexpensive, easy to store, and easy to prepare. They will last indefinitely if stored in airtight containers. Beans top the list in nutrition, being rich in complex carbohydrates, vitamins, minerals, fiber and protein. They are low in cholesterol and fat, and recommended by nutritionists.

Black Beans These kidney shaped beans have a shiny black skin and are an essential part of South American and Caribbean cooking.

Black-Eyed Beans Black-eyed beans are small white kidney shaped with a characteristic black spot at the sprouting point. Great in casseroles and salads.

Borlotti or Roman Beans Borlotti beans have a speckled pink, brown or beige color.

Cannellini Beans Cannellini beans are a white, oval and nutty tasting bean. Used in savoury dishes.

Chickpeas Also known as garbanzos, and the essential part of hummus, falafels and of course over couscous.

Dried Peas These are commonly split green or yellow peas, and are the essential part of pea soup. Also good in kedgerees and patties.

Haricot Beans (Navy Beans) Commonly used in baked beans, also great in salads or casseroles.

Kidney Beans Kidney beans come in red, brown, black and white and are the main ingredient of chilli con carne.

Lentils Lentils are small flat seeds that come in red, green or brown. An Indian staple, they are great in traditional dhal.

Lima Beans Lima beans are either pale green or white with a sweet and floury taste. Butterbeans are a type of lima bean. They are good in soups.

Mung Beans These are small green beans and are ideal for growing sprouts. Also good in Indian and Chinese dishes.

Soya Beans Soya beans are pea sized, and have colors ranging from light brown, yellow, green, black or bicolored. The soy bean products are well known, soy sauce to name one. Use them in patties or in casseroles.

LEGUME COOKING METHODS

Legume Preparation Remove foreign material and broken beans. Wash in cold water until water runs clean. Never soak longer than 12 hours as the legumes will ferment. Always discard soaking water and cook in clean water. Use three parts water to one part legume. Use one of the following cooking methods:

- Cook immediately (some require soaking).
- Cover with cold water and soak overnight.
- Cover with cold water, bring to boil, cover tightly, remove from heat and let stand for 1½ hours before cooking.

Legume Cooking Methods and Times

	Pressure Cooker Method	Simmer Method
Black-eye Beans	10 minutes	20 to 45 minutes
Borlotti Beans	15 minutes	20 to 45 minutes
Broad Beans	20 minutes	30 to 60 minutes
Butter Beans	20 minutes	20 to 45 minutes
Cannellini Beans	15 minutes	20 to 45 minutes
Chickpeas	20 minutes	20 to 45 minutes
Haricot (Navy) Beans	15 minutes	20 to 45 minutes
Lima Beans	10 to 15 minutes	20 to 45 minutes
Lentils - Red Split	Not recommended	20 to 30 minutes
Lentils - Green	Not recommended	20 to 45 minutes
Red Kidney Beans	15 minutes	20 to 45 minutes
Split Peas	Not recommended	45 to 75 minutes

Pressure Cooker Tip: Bring the beans to pressure and cook for 5 minutes. Wrap the cooker in a blanket or something to delay cooling down. Allow to stand for 2 hours. Beans are cooked and you save on gas.

Dhal

Serves 4

A red split lentil curry.

½ pound (250g) red lentils
1½ tablespoons ghee
1 large finely sliced onion
2 cloves finely chopped garlic
1 teaspoon minced ginger
1 teaspoon ground turmeric
3 cups hot water
1 teaspoon salt
½ teaspoon garam masala

Wash the lentils well and drain. Heat ghee and sauté onion, garlic and ginger until the onion is soft and golden. Add the turmeric and stir well. Put in the drained lentils and sauté for a couple of minutes. Add the hot water, bring to a boil, and reduce to a simmer. Cover and cook for 15 to 20 minutes or until lentils are half cooked. Add the salt and garam masala, and mix well. Cook until lentils are soft, and the dhal has a porridge like consistency. Serve on boiled rice.

Lentil Patties

Serves 4

½ pound (250g) red lentils
2 cups water
1 egg
1 finely chopped onion
Breadcrumbs
Wheat germ
Sesame seeds

Cook lentils until they are soft. Beat the egg and add half to lentils along with onions. Stir and add enough breadcrumbs to get a solid consistency. Form the mixture into patties. Dip the patties into the remaining egg mixture and roll in a mixture of wheat germ and sesame seeds. Sauté in olive oil until golden, and turn once only. Serve with a peanut sauce.

Lentil Patties 2

Serves 4

1 cup red lentils
1 egg
½ teaspoon salt
½ teaspoon thyme
½ teaspoon turmeric
1 small finely chopped onion
Breadcrumbs
Oil

Cook lentils until they are soft. Beat the egg and add salt, thyme, turmeric and onion. Add cooked lentils, stir well and add enough breadcrumbs to make a thick to solid consistency. Heat oil in a skillet. Place a tablespoon of the mixture into the skillet and flatten it. Sauté until golden brown both sides.

Lentil and Potato Pie

Serves 4

1½ cups lentils
2 cups mashed potatoes
1 tablespoon chopped celery
1 tablespoon chopped parsley
1 tablespoon chopped onion
Grated cheese
Tomato slices

Wash lentils in cold water, drain and cover with cold water. Bring to a boil and reduce heat to a gentle boil until lentils are soft. Mash or purée the lentils and combine with the mashed potatoes and vegetables, and mix well. Put the mixture in a greased pie plate, top with grated cheese and tomato slices, and bake at 350°F (180°C) until brown.

Honeyed Lentil Soup

Serves 6 to 8

3 medium onions
½ pound (250g) orange lentils
1 can tomatoes
1 teaspoon Worcestershire
  sauce
2 teaspoons salt
2 teaspoons honey
¼ teaspoon nutmeg
¼ teaspoon finely grated
  orange peel

Peel and grate the onions. Put all the ingredients in a pan with 2 pints of boiling water, return to a boil, cover and then reduce to a simmer for 45 minutes to an hour.

Chili Beans

Serves 4

2 finely chopped onions
1 teaspoon minced garlic
1 teaspoon thyme
1 teaspoon basil
1 teaspoon oregano
1 teaspoon paprika
1 teaspoon chili powder
Olive oil
2 cups dried red kidney beans
1 can tomatoes
1 can corn kernels
1 finely chopped green pepper
Tomato paste

Sauté the onions, the garlic and the spices in oil. Soak, cook and drain the beans. Add the tomatoes, corn and green pepper. Simmer gently until hot, and then thicken with tomato paste. Stir and simmer until it forms a thick, dry consistency. Serve with tacos, on white rice, as a dip or on its own with grated cheese on top.

Rice and Peas

Serves 4

Almost a West Indian national dish, and eaten throughout the Caribbean. This recipe is a mix of a few recipes that work well on board.

½ pound (250g) red kidney beans
1 finely chopped onion
2 cloves finely chopped garlic
1 chopped chili
4 rashers bacon, chopped
4 tablespoons peanut oil
4 cups water
10 ounces (300g) long grain rice
½ cup coconut cream

Soak beans overnight, rinse and drain. Sauté onion, garlic, chili and bacon until bacon is cooked. Add the kidney beans and water. Bring to a boil and simmer for 1 hour. Add the rice and coconut cream. Season to taste, stir well and cover. Simmer until beans and rice are soft, 25 to 30 minutes. Add water as needed for the rice to cook.

Louisiana Red Beans and Rice

Serves 4

¼ pound (125g) chopped bacon
2 medium chopped onions
1 chopped celery stick
1 red or green pepper
2 tablespoons chopped parsley
1 clove crushed garlic
1 bay leaf
½ teaspoon Worcestershire sauce
2 drops Tabasco sauce
2 tablespoons tomato ketchup
1 pound (500g) red kidney beans

Sauté the bacon over medium heat until fat runs. Add onions, celery and chopped peppers. Sauté gently until soft for about 10 minutes. Stir in the remaining ingredients and mix well. Cover and simmer for 40 minutes, stirring occasionally. Spoon over boiled rice.

Lima Bean and Tomato Casserole

Serves 4

2 cups lima beans
6 cups water
½ cup olive oil
4 chopped spring onions
½ cup chopped green pepper
Sugar to taste
¼ teaspoon cayenne pepper
2 cups canned tomatoes
Parmesan cheese

Rinse and soak lima beans. Drain and then pressure cook with the water and 1 tablespoon of oil for 5 minutes at 15 lbs pressure, or 10 minutes at 10 lbs. Reduce pressure gradually. Sauté onions in oil until golden. Add the peppers and beans, and mix thoroughly. Add the sugar and cayenne, and season to taste. Put in a greased casserole dish and then cover with tomatoes. Sprinkle with cheese, and bake uncovered at 350°F (180°C) for 30 minutes.

Pressure Cooker Ham and Three Bean Soup

Serves 6

Ideal for visitors on cold, wet days when you are stuck in port or anchorages. Serve with thick chunks of bread and talk about tropical places.

½ cup dried chickpeas
½ cup dried lima beans
½ cup dried haricot beans
1 smoked ham hock
½ cup red lentils
1 teaspoon whole black
   peppercorns
3 dried chilies
5 whole cloves
2 tablespoons oil
2 sliced onions
2 teaspoons chopped garlic
1 teaspoon ground turmeric

Put the chickpeas, lima beans and haricot beans in a saucepan, well covered with water. Bring to a boil, cook for 2 minutes, then turn off and let soak covered for 2 hours. Put the ham hock, red lentils, peppercorns, chilies and cloves in another pan with enough water to come half way up the ham hock. Bring to a boil. Heat oil in a skillet and sauté onion and garlic over medium heat until soft and golden. Add the turmeric and fry a few seconds. Add the mixture to the ham hock, and let cook for 1½ hours, and turn the hock half way through, adding more hot water if needed. When the dried beans have soaked, discard the water and put beans in a pressure cooker. Add the ham hock, and everything else from the pan plus water until the pressure cooker is three quarters full. Bring to pressure and cook at low pressure for 35 minutes. After removing pressure, cut ham off bone, and dice it into the thick bean purée. Discard cloves, chilies and peppercorns.

Navy Bean Soup

Serves 6 to 8

No prizes for guessing the source of the name. Haricot beans became a staple of the navy as they stored well and were easy to prepare as well as nutritious.

½ pound (250g) haricot beans
2 carrots
2 leeks
2 celery sticks
4 tablespoons olive oil
1 onion
1 can tomatoes
6 cups chicken stock
Sea salt and black pepper
6 tablespoons chopped parsley

Soak beans in water for 4 hours. Cook until tender in unsalted water for about 45 minutes. Drain beans, and save the water. Prepare vegetables and chop into small pieces. Heat the olive oil in a saucepan and cook onions until softened, don't overcook. Add the vegetables and cook for 5 minutes. Skin and chop tomatoes and add them. Cook for another 4 to 5 minutes and add the stock. If there is not enough, use some of the bean liquid. Bring to a boil, then reduce to a simmer for 30 minutes. The vegetables should be soft when ready. Add salt and pepper to taste, and garnish with parsley. Serve with chunks of fresh bread.

Chickpeas

1. Quick method Put desired amount of chickpeas into a saucepan, and cover with hot water. Bring to a boil and maintain for 2 minutes. Skim as required. Remove from heat, and let stand for 1 hour. Drain and cook in clean water, add salt when peas are nearly tender.

2. Traditional Method Soak peas for approximately 4 to 6 hours. Drain and put in clean water. Simmer 20 to 30 minutes until tender. Add salt when nearly done. Use cooking water as soup base.

Chickpea Pilaf

Serves 4

½ pound (250g) chickpeas
½ pound (250g) rice
Salt to taste
3 tablespoons margarine
¼ cup pine nuts
3 small onions
1 teaspoon turmeric
4 cups chicken stock
2 tablespoons currants

Prepare chickpeas. Add salt and drain when cooked. Rinse rice and drain well. Heat margarine in deep pan with good lid. Add pine nuts and sauté until golden. Remove to a plate. Add sliced onions to remaining margarine and sauté gently until transparent. Add turmeric, sauté 1 minute and add rice, stir on medium heat until grains are coated. Pour in stock and add salt as required. Bring to a boil quickly, stir well and reduce heat to low. Cover with lid and cook on low for 15 minutes. Pour the currants and put drained chickpeas on top. Cover and leave on low heat 10 minutes. Remove from heat and let stand for 10 minutes. Fold currants and chickpeas through rice. Serve hot or cold.

Chickpeas Curry and Rice

Serves 4

3 cups cooked brown rice
1 cup roasted shredded
   coconut
1 large finely diced carrot
½ cup shallots
2 cups cooked chickpeas
1 cup coconut milk
3 teaspoons curry powder

To make the rice, mix the rice, coconut, carrot, shallots and heat through. To make the chickpeas sauce, simply mix together the chickpeas, coconut milk and curry powder and heat through. Pour the sauce over the rice.

Chickpeas and Rice

Serves 4 to 6

2 ounces (50g) dried chickpeas
½ pound (250g) long grain
   rice
½ cup chopped onion
Salt and black pepper
3 tablespoons olive oil
3 tablespoons lemon juice
1 can tuna (optional)
Chervil

Soak chickpeas in water for 4 hours. Drain, put in cold water and bring to a boil slowly. Simmer until peas are soft, about 1 to 2 hours. Drain and allow to cool. Wash and drain rice, and cook in salted water, then drain well. While hot, combine rice and chickpeas and stir in onion, salt and pepper. Stir in olive oil and lemon juice. Drain canned tuna, and break up the fish into flakes, then fork into the rice. Stir in chervil and allow to cool before serving.

Canned Baked Beans

The humble baked bean is much maligned, but in fact it is extremely versatile, and the following recipes will offer a great variety of another essential, canned product.

Baked Bean Dhal

Serves 4

1 can baked beans
1 teaspoon oil
1 clove crushed garlic
¼ teaspoon turmeric
½ teaspoon grated ginger
1 large finely chopped onion
½ cup diced carrot
½ cup chopped green pepper
Chili powder

Purée the baked beans to a paste. Sauté the garlic, turmeric, ginger and onion in oil. Add the remaining ingredients. Serve as a dip.

Baked Bean Rissoles

Serves 4

1 can baked beans
1½ cups cooked brown rice
1 small finely chopped onion
1 clove crushed garlic
½ teaspoon grated ginger
1 tablespoon lemon juice
1 tablespoon soy sauce
¼ cup flour
1 beaten egg

Combine beans, rice, onion, garlic, ginger, lemon juice and soy sauce and chill. Roll the mixture into small balls, roll in flour, egg, then flour again. Sauté until a golden brown then heat in oven at 350°F (180°C) for 10 minutes. Serve with rice and a sauce.

Baked Bean and Sausage Hot Pot

Serves 4

1 can baked beans
4 large sausages, sliced in
    quarters
2 large cubed potatoes
2 large cubed carrots
½ small sliced celery
1 can tomatoes
Fresh oregano

Put all the ingredients in a large casserole dish. Bake at 415°F (210°C) for 30 minutes. Serve with chunks of fresh bread.

Baked Bean and Corn Chowder

Serves 4

1 teaspoon oil
1 small diced onion
1 clove crushed garlic
2 sticks chopped celery
1 can baked beans
1 can creamed corn
2 cups chicken stock
¼ cup chopped parsley
Black pepper
1 cup milk

Sauté onion, garlic and celery, and cook for 5 minutes. Purée the beans and corn. Combine the purée, stock and mixture. Bring to a boil and then simmer for 25 minutes. Stir in the parsley and pepper. Add the milk and heat through just before serving.

Corn and Baked Bean Casserole

Serves 4

1 can tomatoes
1 can baked beans
1 can corn kernels
½ cup cream cheese

Chop the tomatoes, and then put alternate layer of beans, corn and tomatoes into a buttered casserole dish. Cover with lashings of cream cheese. Bake at 350°F (180°C) for 25 to 30 minutes.

Baked Bean Con Carne

Serves 4

1 teaspoon oil
2 finely chopped onions
2 cloves crushed garlic
1½ pounds (750g) ground beef
¼ pound (125g) bacon pieces
3 tablespoons tomato paste
3 cups beef stock
1 tablespoon chili powder
1 can baked beans

Sauté onion, garlic, beef and bacon for 5 minutes. Add the rest of ingredients and simmer for 20 minutes. Serve with rice.

Chapter 8

Vegetables

On board Gardening

Produce Names

Some Vegetables

Leaf Vegetables

Chinese Vegetables

Mixed Vegetables

Eggplants

Okra

Potatoes

Pumpkins

Tomatoes

Zucchini

Be adventurous. Try local vegetables. Most have a real old-fashioned flavor.

A lot of people are turned off local vegetables simply because they do not know them. In most cases, if they look similar to those at home, they generally are similar. Be adventurous and sample a few varieties. One of the best things about market vegetables in many small countries is that they are mostly organically grown, as few can afford the fertilizers and pesticides. Also just as importantly the vegetables have a real old-fashioned flavor.

ON BOARD GARDENING

A little fresh food is readily available by sprouting bean shoots on board. What is more they are very nutritious, and take only 3 to 6 days to grow. To sprout you only need a few basic items:

- a marmalade or instant coffee jar,
- an elastic band,
- a piece of muslin or nylon stocking,
- bean sprouts, which can include Chinese bean sprouts, Mung beans, alfalfa, salad sprouts, lentils, and garbanzos. They all work well. There are some excellent sprouting bean mixes available from health food stores.

To sprout do the following:

- Take a level dessert spoon of seed and rinse thoroughly. Do not use more as seed volume will increase tenfold by the time of harvesting.
- Drain seed and rinse 2 to 3 more times.
- Place the muslin and band over jar opening and then lay on side.
- Repeat this process twice a day, ideally every morning and evening. Use cold or tepid water, and allow to drain.
- You do not need to place sprouts in a light or dark place, but depending on location, you will get either green or white sprouts.

PRODUCE NAMES

When you go to local markets for reprovisioning, you often do not know what it is you are looking at. You feel bewildered and afraid you are going to go hungry. Many items on offer are starch rich staples, mainly based on the vegetable family called tubers. Be assured that if it is good enough for the locals it is good enough for you.

Tubers

Tubers is the name given to root vegetables. They generally are very starchy, and are staples in most Caribbean, Pacific Islands and African cuisines. They are seen in every market, generally at low prices and are a great way to keep fresh food costs down, once you recognize them and cook them correctly.

Cassava

In the Caribbean it is known as gari or yucca. Also commonly called manioc in South American countries. In the Pacific Islands it is also called maniota. Peel the skin off, wash and dice into cubes. Boil in salted water for 15 to 20 minutes. Boil 10 to 15 minutes if frying afterwards. Fry lightly in oil to make cassava chips.

Kohlrabi

In the Cook Islands there is a similar vegetable called kumara. It is also known as cabbage turnip or kiwano. It looks like a turnip but tastes like cabbage. It can be used in stuffings, coleslaw, and in casseroles.

Sweet Potato

In the Caribbean also known as patates douces or patatas dulces. In the United States it is mistakenly called a yam. Sweet potatoes are great as part of a roast dinner. Peel the skin off, wash and dice into cubes. Boil in salted water for 15 to 20 minutes. Mash with butter, pepper and milk.

Taro

Originally a native of India, where it is called katchu. In the Caribbean it is widely known as dasheen or eddo, or cocoyam. It is also called chou chine or chou caraibe in Martinique, madère in Guadeloupe, malanga in Cuba and Haiti, and in Réunion it is songe. Taro can be baked in the skin, or added to casseroles and stews, or frittered. Alternatively you can treat as follows: Peel the skin off, wash and dice into cubes. Boil in salted water for 15 to 20 minutes. For variation, add stock or coconut milk and spices or herbs to the water to give a delicious flavor to the taro. Mash with butter, pepper and milk.

Yam

In the Caribbean it is known as igname. Peel the skin off, wash and dice into cubes. Boil in salted water for 15 to 20 minutes. Mash with butter, pepper and milk, or add to mashed pumpkin.

SOME VEGETABLES

There are a number of vegetables that serve as integral parts of many dishes and these are briefly described.

Garlic

The most widely used of all. Originally from Asia it is an essential part of European and Asian cuisine. Whole garlic cloves last well. Minced garlic in a jar is also very handy. Crush it or chop it any way you like, it adds life to most dishes.

Ginger

This versatile root is used literally in every cuisine in the world. Either fresh, or minced in a jar, it is a galley essential. I freeze roots and grate the ginger when it is frozen. It will keep in the refrigerator for about a week, or it can be peeled and put in a jar with dry sherry, and then it will last 3 weeks. If storing place in a cool, dark and well ventilated area.

Chili

Strange as it may appear, this fiery small vegetable is related to the potato, tomato, sweet pepper and eggplant. There are reputed to be more than 200 varieties of chilies, some mild and piquant, others blast furnace hot. That great seaman and explorer Magellan introduced chili peppers to both Africa and Asia where it has become a mainstay in many cuisines. For pure fire power, choose the small red and green ones, or the Mexican food arsonists favorites, the jalepeño, or the West Indian pepper. Banana chilies are a lot milder, and have a yellow or orange color. The chili is high in vitamin C, although I prefer to get my daily allowance in orange juice. Of course chili is the principal ingredient of the Tabasco sauce, the heart of many great dishes.

Sweet Bell Peppers

Also know as capsicum, or pimiento. Christopher Columbus evidently discovered them in a village market in Hispaniola (now called Haiti and the Dominican Republic). He wrongly assumed he'd found a variety of chilies, which was close in fact. Sweet bell peppers come in many colors ranging from red, green, orange, yellow, purple and black.

Corn (Maize)

Corn is widely available. It has its origins in America, and Christopher Columbus discovered it during his voyages. The Spaniards introduced it to Europe. Corn can be simply enjoyed by boiling and topping with melted butter, or grilled on the barbecue and brushed with butter and sprinkled with salt. Canned corn is used in a number of recipes.

Onions

The essential ingredient in many dishes. The onion has been used for over 5000 years, and everyone is still crying. To stop crying over onions, peel under running water, refrigerate first for an hour, wear goggles or anything else you think might work, especially getting someone else to do it. Brown onions are the best for cooking and white ones are best suited to salads. White onions do not store that well, whereas browns last longer. You can also buy the sweeter Spanish and yellow onions.

LEAF VEGETABLES

Spinach

This name is a generic one that covers a great many similar produce used widely in most cuisines. There is some confusion about names, but in the Caribbean it is generally called dasheen or callaloo. Taro leaves, cassava leaves, and silver beet also fall into the general description, and there is a vegetable in the Cook Islands called rukau. Australia and New Zealand grow a dark spinach that found its way back to Europe with Sir Joseph Banks, botanist with Captain James Cook in 1770.

Caribbean Cabbage and Dasheen Cabbage

Both are used in the Caribbean as a vegetable. Traditionally the cabbage is peeled, washed and sliced before cooking in boiling water. It is mainly used in stews.

Caribbean Callaloo
Serves 4

This is a spinach soup.

Bunch of dasheen
1 cup coconut milk
1 diced onion
2 cloves chopped garlic
6 cups water
2 crabs
½ pound (250g) small okra

Simmer the dasheen, coconut milk, onion and garlic in water for around 15 to 20 minutes (traditional recipes use a piece of salted meat). When tender, add okra and crab meat. Season to taste until soup thickens.

African Spinach and Coconut
Serves 4

Bunch of dasheen
1 cup coconut milk
Ghee (or oil)
1 finely chopped onion
1 chopped tomato
1 teaspoon curry powder

Cook the leaves in coconut milk for 5 minutes. Drain and reserve coconut milk. Sauté the onion, chopped tomato and curry powder for 4 to 5 minutes. Add the cooked leaves and coconut milk. Stir and simmer for 15 minutes. Serve with boiled rice.

Spinach and Lentil Soup
Serves 4 to 6

½ pound (250g) brown lentils
1 pound (500g) bunch of dasheen
1 finely chopped onion
3 tablespoons vegetable oil
2 tablespoons tomato paste
Salt and black pepper

Soak lentils overnight and drain into large saucepan. Cover with water, boil and simmer 45 minutes. Wash and cut dasheen into pieces. Sauté onion in oil and then add dasheen. Sauté over a very low heat. Cover and let stand a few minutes. Pour into pan with lentils then stir in tomato paste, season to taste, and simmer until flavors and colors combine.

CHINESE VEGETABLES

There is an ever increasing range of Asian vegetables with exotic names now available in markets worldwide. Some of the more commonly available are:

Bok Choi or Pak Choi (Chinese chard) Use in stir frying, slice the stems for soups.

Cai Lum (Chinese broccoli) Steam, use in stir frying, slice the stems for soups. Goes well with pork dishes.

Choi Sum (Chinese flowering cabbage) Steam, stir fry. It is great on its own with a coat of oyster sauce after steaming.

En Choi (Chinese spinach) Steam, stir fry or braise. It is also good raw in salads.

Leen Ngau (lotus root) Cook like other starch vegetables, boil, bake, braise, or deep fry.

Loh Baak (white radish) Grate raw into salads, add to braised meat dishes, or pickle in white vinegar.

Sai Yeung Choi (watercress) Use in stocks, steam.

Ts'ung Tau (shallots) Slice into stir frys and soups.

Wong Nga Baak (Chinese cabbage) Steam, braise in oyster sauce or add to stir fry.

Woo tau (taro root) Add to soups to thicken them.

Other Chinese vegetables are Dau Mui (pea sheets), Foo Gwa (bitter melon), Gaai Laan (Chinese kale), Hop Jeung Gwa (choko or chayote), Nga Dhoi (bean sprouts), Ong Choi (water spinach), Saan Choi (slipper vegetable), Taai Gaai Choi (Chinese flat cabbage).

Stir Fry Chinese Leaves

Serves 2 to 4

1½ pounds (750g) Chinese leaves
6 tablespoons oil
1 tablespoon corn flour
6 tablespoons chicken stock
Soy sauce

Cut leaves into wide strips. Add leaves to hot wok and cook for 4 minutes. Mix corn flour to a smooth paste with stock. Blend into leaves, and cook. Stir until mixture thickens. Coat with a little soy or alternatively use oyster sauce.

Curried Lotus Root

Serves 4

½ pound (250g) lotus root
2 ripe tomatoes
1 tablespoon chopped spring
   onions
1 fresh chili, chopped
½ bay leaf
½ teaspoon fenugreek
¼ teaspoon salt
1 cup coconut milk
½ teaspoon turmeric
1 teaspoon curry powder

Peel and slice the lotus root in small pieces. Put in a pan with tomatoes, onions, chili, bay leaf, fenugreek, salt, coconut milk, turmeric, and half the curry powder. Cook gently for 10 minutes. In a wok, stir fry 1 teaspoon onion in oil, then add the mixture and the other half of curry powder. Cook for 3 to 4 minutes.

Stir Fried Water Spinach

Serves 4

You can easily substitute any other leaf vegetable such as beets, spinach or dasheen.

¼ pound (125g) water spinach
½ finely chopped onion
½ teaspoon turmeric
1 fresh chopped chili
½ teaspoon salt
Chopped prawns or crab
   (optional)
2 tablespoons oil

Clean, wash and shred leaves and stems. Mix with other ingredients. Heat 2 tablespoons oil in wok or skillet and when hot add the mixture. Stir fry for 6 to 7 minutes.

MIXED VEGETABLES

Hot Vegetables in Coconut Milk

Serves 4

3 to 4 carrots, or
1 pound (500g) green beans, or
1 small cauliflower head, or
1 pound (500g) broccoli
2 tablespoons oil
1 teaspoon ground cumin
1 teaspoon ground coriander
1 clove crushed garlic
½ medium minced onion
½ teaspoon chili powder
1 cup coconut milk

Steam the vegetables until they are brightly colored. Stir fry oil, spices, garlic with the onions for around 5 minutes. Add the vegetables and coconut milk and reduce to a simmer until vegetables are tender and liquid reduces.

Ratatouille

Serves 4

While serving on a refrigerated cargo vessel, we used to trade back and forth from Morocco (Tangier, Agadir and Casablanca) to European ports carrying courgettes (zucchini) and tomatoes. It was my contention that if we ever collided with a vessel carrying eggplants in the Channel, we would probably have the world's greatest culinary disaster, and what to do with 10,000 tons of ratatouille.Try the following easier recipe and enjoy this classic dish.

1 small eggplant
Salt
2 to 3 tablespoons olive oil
1 pound (500g) sliced zucchini
2 sliced onions
1 sliced red pepper
1 pound (500g) fresh chopped tomatoes
1 clove crushed garlic
2 tablespoons chopped parsley
Salt and pepper to taste

Slice the eggplant, put in a colander and sprinkle with salt. Allow to stand for 1 hour. Rinse, then pat dry. Heat olive oil in a heavy skillet, add eggplant, sliced zucchini, onions and red pepper. Cook for a few minutes. Add tomatoes, garlic, parsley, salt and freshly ground pepper to taste. Cover with a tight fitting lid and cook until vegetables are tender but fairly crisp. Do not overcook.

Canned Corn

Canned corn, either cream or kernels is a versatile and quick meal base. Try these useful meal ideas.

Spicy Corn Fritters

Makes 15

1 small can cream corn
¼ to ½ cup plain flour
1 egg
2 finely chopped shallots
1 stick finely chopped celery
1 small clove crushed garlic
½ teaspoon ground coriander
Salt and pepper
Oil

Mix the corn, sifted flour, egg, shallots, celery, garlic and coriander in a bowl. Mix well and season with salt and pepper. Drop teaspoon of mixture into hot oil and fry until golden brown on one side. Turn over and fry the other side. Remove fritters and drain on absorbent paper.

Sweet Corn and Crab Soup

Serves 4

1 large can creamed corn
1 tablespoon soy sauce
1 teaspoon grated ginger
4 finely chopped shallots
6 cups chicken stock
½ teaspoon sesame oil
2 tablespoons corn flour
¼ cup water
1 cup crab meat
1 beaten egg

In a pan combine the corn, soy, ginger, shallots, stock and sesame oil. Heat until boiling. Mix the corn flour and water to a smooth paste. Blend into the soup mixture, then simmer for 3 to 4 minutes. Finally stir in the crab meat and egg.

Corn and Canned Tuna

Serves 4

1 chopped onion
1 chopped green pepper
1 tablespoon olive oil
1 small can corn kernels
2 cups pineapple pieces
2 tablespoons corn flour
1 cup chicken stock
¼ cup vinegar
1 can tuna
Salt and pepper

Sauté the onion and green pepper in olive oil until onion is soft and golden. Add the corn kernels and pineapple pieces. Blend some corn flour and stock and stir into the mixture along with rest of stock and vinegar. Bring to a boil, stirring constantly. Reduce heat and simmer for 3 to 4 minutes. Add the tuna and season to taste. Serve with steamed rice.

Vegetable Hash Browns

Serves 4

2 peeled and grated potatoes
1 peeled and grated carrot
1 grated zucchini
1 tablespoon coriander
2 lightly beaten eggs
1 tablespoon oil
Fresh ground black pepper

Put the potatoes, carrot, zucchini, coriander and egg into a bowl. Add the black pepper and mix well. Brush a skillet with cooking oil, and bring up to a medium to high heat. Put 2 tablespoons of the mixture into the pan and flatten slightly. Cook 4 to 5 minutes on each side or until golden.

Button Squash Sauté

Serves 4

1 teaspoon butter or margarine
1 clove crushed garlic
2 rashers bacon, cut in strips
2 shallots, cut diagonally
4 sliced golden button squash
4 sliced bright green button squash
4 sliced green button squash

Melt some butter in a pan, then add garlic and bacon. Sauté until brown. Add the shallots and sauté for a further 2 minutes. Add the squash and sauté for 3 minutes.

Vegetable Lasagne

Serves 4 to 6

1 tablespoon oil
1 diced onion
2 cloves crushed garlic
1 large diced carrot
1 cup broccoli flowerets
1 medium diced eggplant
4 chopped golden button squash
1 large diced green pepper
3 medium diced tomatoes
4 tablespoons tomato paste
2 teaspoons oregano
2 teaspoons basil
1 tablespoon butter
2 tablespoons flour
2 cups skim milk
1 cup ricotta cheese
1 packet lasagne sheets
¾ cup grated cheese

Heat the oil in a large skillet, and sauté onion and garlic until transparent. Add the carrot, broccoli, eggplant, squash, green pepper, tomatoes, tomato paste and herbs. Stir and cover, simmer for around 20 minutes, stirring occasionally. Melt the butter in a saucepan and stir in the flour. Gradually add the milk, stirring constantly until the mixture boils and thickens. Finally stir in the ricotta cheese. Butter a baking dish, and lay in alternate layers of vegetables, lasagne sheets and cheese sauce. On the top layer, use lasagne sheets covered with cheese sauce. Sprinkle with grated cheese and bake at 350°F (180°C) for 40 minutes or until lasagne is tender.

EGGPLANTS

They are also known as Brinjals or Aubergines.

The eggplant by strict definition is a fruit rather than a vegetable, and originates from India. You can buy eggplants nearly everywhere, and they can be cooked in a wide variety of styles that includes frying, stuffing, baking, etc. The eggplant is actually closely related to the potato. When choosing eggplants, go for those that are firm and glossy, have a tight skin and no soft patches. Always leave the skin on when cooking as it is rich in vitamins. As the taste can be a little bitter, sprinkle slices with salt and let stand for 30 minutes, and then wipe with paper towel.

Eggplant Caviar

2 medium eggplants
Oil
1 clove crushed garlic
⅛ teaspoon mace
⅛ teaspoon cinnamon
2 tablespoons lemon juice
3 tablespoons chopped parsley

Cut the eggplants in half and score the surfaces. Sprinkle with salt and leave upside down for 30 minutes. Rinse off salt and dry. Put in a baking dish, season and sprinkle with oil. Bake in a moderate oven for about an hour or until soft. Cool and remove the flesh and mash or purée. Add garlic and enough oil to make the thickness of mayonnaise. Add the spices, lemon juice and parsley, and mix well. Chill and serve with corn chips, crackers, toast or as a dip.

Pacific Eggplant

Serves 4

1 medium eggplant
1 beaten egg
Breadcrumbs
6 tablespoons butter

Don't peel the eggplant, cut into thin slices lengthwise. Soak in salted water for half an hour, pat dry and dip in the egg and breadcrumbs. Spread half the butter in a large oven tray and put in a very hot oven. Arrange eggplant flat over the tray and top with a piece of butter. Bake at 375°F (190°C) for 25 to 30 minutes until tops are crisp.

Barbecued Eggplant

Serves 2 to 4

1 large eggplant
Olive oil (extra virgin)

Cut the eggplant into 1-inch (2.5cm) thick slices. Score each slice in a criss-crossed pattern using a sharp knife. Brush with virgin olive oil. Cook for two or three minutes on each side. The flesh should be soft.

Baked Eggplant and Tomatoes

Serves 6

2 small to medium eggplants
1 tablespoon salt
Oil or butter
1 can tomatoes
½ cup chopped parsley
2 cloves finely chopped garlic
½ cup chicken stock or white
　wine
¼ cup grated Parmesan cheese

Put thinly sliced eggplant into a colander and sprinkle with salt. Allow to stand for 30 to 40 minutes. Drain well and pat dry with paper towel. Lightly oil or butter a small baking dish, and put eggplant, tomatoes and parsley in alternate and overlapping rows. Sprinkle garlic between layers and season to taste. Pour stock or wine over all, and sprinkle with Parmesan cheese. Cover and bake at 400°F (205°C) for 30 minutes. Uncover, and continue cooking until browned for approximately 20 minutes. Baste with juices.

Curried Eggplant Purée

Serves 4 to 6

5 to 6 small eggplants
¼ cup oil
1 large chopped onion
½ teaspoon ground coriander
½ teaspoon ground cumin
½ teaspoon turmeric
Chili powder to taste
Fennel seeds
2 large chopped tomatoes
1 tablespoon chopped fresh
　coriander

Bake the eggplant in the oven until soft. When cool, peel, then mash or purée roughly. Heat oil in a pan and sauté gently the onions, ground coriander, cumin, turmeric, chili powder and fennel seeds. Add the chopped tomatoes and the coriander leaves. Cook for a few minutes. Add the eggplant pulp, and cook on low for 5 minutes, stirring constantly. Serve on boiled rice.

Eggplant in Coconut Tempura

Serves 4 to 6

1 medium eggplant, sliced into
　12
Corn flour
½ cup self-raising flour
½ to ¾ cup of water
1 lightly beaten egg
½ cup shredded coconut
½ cup coconut cream
Oil

Toss the eggplant in corn flour and shake off any excess. Put the flour in a bowl, form a well in the center. Combine and gradually stir in the water, egg, coconut and coconut cream. Dip the eggplant slices into the batter. Deep fry a few at a time in hot oil until golden brown. Drain on absorbent paper. Serve with a nice mango or pineapple salsa.

OKRA

Okra is an essential part of Caribbean cookery. It is sometimes called gumbo and it is part of the Louisiana gumbo stew. It has its origins in Africa, and was brought to the Americas by African slaves. Okra is the immature pod of the Ethiopian hibiscus plant and young green pods resemble gherkins in appearance.

Okra with Chickpeas and Tomatoes

Serves 4

1 pound (500g) okra
1 cup chickpeas
3 cups water
1 tablespoon olive oil
8 small onions (pickling size)
2 cloves crushed garlic
1 can tomatoes
1 tablespoon lemon juice
1½ cups tomato juice
2 tablespoons red wine
1 tablespoon fresh chopped oregano
1 teaspoon ground black pepper

Prepare okra, wash and remove the thin skin. In the Middle East, okra is often tossed in vinegar and allowed to stand for 30 minutes prior to rinsing and use. Soak the chickpeas in water for 4 hours. Heat the olive oil in a saucepan and cook onions and garlic for 4 minutes until golden, do not overcook. Add the tomatoes, chickpeas, lemon juice, tomato juice and the red wine and cook for 40 minutes. Add the okra and simmer for another 20 minutes. Stir in the oregano and pepper. Serve with rice or meat, and of course pita bread to mop up the juices.

African Okra Stew

Serves 4

1 pound (500g) okra
3 chopped onions
2 teaspoons turmeric
1 cup oil
2 eggplants
2 tablespoons grated ginger
2 finely chopped chilies
1 can chopped tomatoes
½ pound (250g) crab or fish meat
¼ pound (125g) dried salted fish

Cut okra into ½-inch slices. Sauté the onions in oil and turmeric until soft (if you can use palm oil, delete the turmeric). Add the okra, eggplants, ginger, chilies and tomatoes at intervals of about 2 to 3 minutes. Stir constantly. Simmer slowly for 10 minutes. Add the crab or fish meat and the salted fish. Simmer for a further 10 to 15 minutes. Serve on boiled rice.

Okra Sambol

Serves 2

½ pound (250g) okra
½ pint cooking oil
1 tablespoon lemon juice
¼ teaspoon salt
1 fresh chopped chili
5 finely chopped shallots

Slice okra into small pieces. Sauté okra until golden brown. Combine the other ingredients and then mix in the deep fried okra.

POTATOES

According to some history books, Sir Francis Drake took potatoes back to England from the Americas. He loaded them as part of his provisions in Colombia after spending the cruising season harassing the Spaniards. The potato has its origins in Peru and was discovered there by Pizarro, so Spain may even take the credit. Since I am a proud descendant of Sir Francis Drake, I am totally biased however and will give him the honor. Without this cuisine-wrenching discovery we would never hear those famous fast food words, "Would you like fries with your order?" The potato is one of the most versatile vegetables there is and is entrenched in Western cuisine as a staple. It stores well, has some nutritional value and is easy to prepare.

Jacket Potatoes Roasted with Garlic Olive Oil

Cut some small slices of garlic and drop into olive oil. Let sit overnight. Scrub some potatoes, and dry with paper towels. Prick potatoes with a fork, and paint the potatoes with garlic oil. Roast the potatoes and brush 2 to 3 times again during cooking.

Mashed Potatoes

A great and easy way to enjoy. Cook the potatoes until they are tender but firm. Mash and add some milk and margarine but leave some of the texture. Add a small finely chopped onion, and a raw egg. Mash further and serve. For variation, add some grated cheese on top and brown under the broiler.

Potato Pancakes

Serves 2

½ pound (250g) firm fleshed
  potatoes
Lemon juice
1 small brown onion
3 tablespoons plain flour
Salt
1 egg
¼ cup milk
4 tablespoons ghee

Coarsely grate unpeeled potatoes into a bowl. Add a few drops of lemon juice, and mix well to prevent any browning. Finely chop onions. Add the remaining ingredients except the ghee and mix well. Heat 1 to 2 tablespoons of ghee in a large, heavy non-stick pan. When hot, drop large tablespoons of the mixture into the pan. Allow room for each pancake to spread and cook evenly. When golden brown underneath, turn over carefully with a spatula. The second side takes approximately half the time to cook as the first side.

Potato Cakes

Serves 4

2 cups self-raising flour
2 tablespoons butter
Salt
1½ cups mashed potatoes
¾ cup milk
Caraway seeds

Mix the softened butter with the flour, and add a pinch of salt. Mix the mashed potatoes. Pour in the milk and mix to a soft dough. Roll the dough out on a floured board and cut into small cakes. Sprinkle over the caraway seeds and then bake in a hot oven at 450°F (230°C) for 20 to 30 minutes.

Potato Casserole

Serves 4

1 pound (500g) potatoes
3 thinly sliced onions
6 tablespoons butter or
    margarine
Salt and fresh ground black
    pepper
1 can tomatoes
1 teaspoon basil
Chopped parsley
2 cups fresh breadcrumbs
6 tablespoons extra butter
3 tablespoons grated Parmesan
    cheese

Peel the potatoes and cook in salted boiling water until tender. Drain and cut into thin slices. Sauté onions in butter until soft and translucent. Put half the potato slices in an ovenproof dish, and layer with onions, season with salt and pepper. Put tomatoes and can liquid in a bowl, mash and add basil. Pour over half the tomato mixture onto potato layer. Sprinkle with parsley. Repeat with another layer. Melt the extra butter in the pan, remove from heat and combine breadcrumbs and Parmesan, then sprinkle over the top. Bake uncovered at around 350°F (180°C) for 30 minutes until the top is golden brown.

Chili Bean Filled Potatoes

Serves 4

4 scrubbed potatoes
1 tablespoon tomato paste
½ pound (250g) can red
    kidney beans
1 to 2 tablespoons chili sauce
Paprika

Bake potatoes at 400°F (205°C) until tender and allow to cool slightly. Cut the potatoes in half and scoop out the flesh, leaving a thin shell. Put the potato flesh in a bowl and mash. Add the tomato paste, the beans and chili sauce to taste and mix to combine. Spoon mixture into the potato shells, and dust lightly with paprika. Serve with a salad.

Hashed Brown Potatoes

Serves 4

4 large scrubbed potatoes
2 tablespoons peanut or
    safflower oil
Salt
1 to 2 tablespoons extra oil

Boil the potatoes whole in their skins until tender for around 30 minutes. Drain and cool and put in the refrigerator for an hour to chill. Skin the potatoes and grate coarsely. Heat half the oil in a large skillet over medium to high heat. When hot, add half the potatoes and cover about half the pan base. Sprinkle with salt. Cook until the underside is browned (approximately 5 minutes). Add another tablespoon of oil to the empty side of the pan. Carefully turn the potatoes over to the other side, taking care to avoid breaking them. Cook until golden brown underneath.

Spicy Curried Potatoes

Serves 6

2 pounds (1kg) potatoes
2 tablespoons curry powder
3 to 4 teaspoons sesame oil,
  coconut oil, or light
  vegetable oil
Coarse salt to taste

Boil the potatoes in their jacket until tender but firm. Drain and peel. Cut the potatoes in thick slices and put in a bowl. Sprinkle the potato slices with curry powder while still warm. Sprinkle 3 to 4 tablespoons water over the potato slices and toss water gently to cover them evenly with the curry. Set aside to cool for 15 minutes. Heat the oil in a skillet or wok on high heat for about 2 minutes, add the potatoes and sprinkle with the salt. Reduce the heat and sauté, turning constantly about 10 to 12 minutes, until the potatoes have a crisp crust.

Savoury Fried Potatoes

Serves 4

1 tablespoon ghee
¼ teaspoon black mustard seed
2 finely chopped red onions
½ teaspoon ground turmeric
¼ teaspoon chili powder
1 pound (500g) potatoes
1 teaspoon salt

Heat the ghee in a saucepan, and sauté mustard seed until they start to pop. Add the onions and continue frying on low heat until they are soft and golden. Add the turmeric and chili and stir well. Boil, peel and dice the potatoes. Add the potatoes, sprinkle with salt and then toss gently to mix well. Serve hot or cold.

Stir Fried Spuds

Serves 4

1 pound (500g) grated
  potatoes
3 tablespoons oil
1 tablespoon soy sauce
¼ pound (125g) chopped
  green vegetables
¼ pound (125g) chopped
  carrots
½ pound (250g) cooked and
  chopped chicken
1 teaspoon ginger

Grate potatoes into a sieve and crush to extract as much moisture as possible. Put into a towel and pat dry. Heat oil in a skillet or wok. Sauté potatoes on high heat for 5 minutes. Add the other ingredients, stir fry 5 to 10 minutes.

Sweet Potatoes and Yams

Both can be prepared the same way. They are readily available in many parts of the world and taste delicious.

Sweet Potato Croquettes
Serves 4

2 sweet potatoes
1 large diced onion
1 tablespoon butter
½ cup plain flour
2 eggs
2 cups breadcrumbs
2 tablespoons oil

Peel and quarter the sweet potatoes. Boil the potatoes and the onion in a saucepan until tender. Drain, mash and add the butter. Mold the mixture into sausage shapes about 3 inches (8 cm) long. Roll the shapes in the flour, dip into beaten eggs and then roll into breadcrumbs. Heat the oil in a skillet and cook croquettes until golden brown.

Baked Sweet Potatoes
Serves 4

6 medium sweet potatoes
½ cup water
1 cup apple juice
Maple syrup
1 teaspoon salt
1 tablespoon butter or
   margarine

Boil the sweet potatoes in their jackets until nearly done. Peel, slice and put them in a baking pan. Bring the water to a boil, along with the apple juice, maple syrup, salt and butter. Pour the mixture over the potatoes and bake in a slow oven at 300°F (150°C) for 1 hour or until potatoes are glazed.

Sweet Potato Chips

2 to 3 sweet potatoes (white
   types)
Oil
Cumin
Salt

Peel and thinly slice the sweet potatoes. Sauté in hot oil until golden and crisp. Drain on paper towels and sprinkle with salt and cumin.

Yam Fritters
Serves 4

1 pound (500g) yams
1 tablespoon margarine
1 tablespoon plain flour
½ teaspoon baking powder
2 diced shallots
Salt and black pepper to taste
1 beaten egg
Cooking oil

Peel and grate the yams. Mix with margarine, flour, baking powder, shallots and salt and pepper. Blend the egg in. Heat oil in a skillet. Drop 1 tablespoon of mixture into the oil and fry until golden. Drain on paper towels.

PUMPKINS

The pumpkin is more than a Halloween decoration. It stores extremely well. If possible buy small ones and use them as needed. The pumpkin mixes well with mashed potatoes or sweet potatoes. It also bakes well along with potatoes and sweet potatoes if you doing an old fashioned Sunday roast or a Thanksgiving dinner.

Pumpkin Soup

Serves 4

1 tablespoon butter or margarine
1 medium chopped onion
2 lbs (1kg) pumpkin flesh
1 teaspoon dried rosemary
4 cups chicken stock
3 bay leaves
1 cup skim milk powder
½ cup plain yogurt

Heat the butter and gently cook the onion in large saucepan for 3 to 4 minutes. Cut pumpkin into chunks. Add the pumpkin and rosemary and gently cook, stirring constantly. Add the chicken stock and bay leaves, bring to a boil and then cover and simmer for 12 to 15 minutes, until pumpkin is tender. Purée the soup in batches, adding the skim milk powder. Reheat and serve. If yogurt is available, top the soup with a dollop when serving.

Pumpkin Sauce

½ cup chicken stock
½ cup water
2 cups chopped pumpkin
1 large chopped onion
Fresh ground black pepper

Combine all the ingredients in a saucepan. Simmer over a low flame 15 to 20 minutes. Purée until smooth. Reheat as required.

Baked Pumpkin

Serves 6+

1 butternut pumpkin
2 oranges
Dried rosemary
Salt and ground black pepper

Cut the pumpkin into serving pieces. Scoop out the seeds. Put 3 to 4 slices of the orange on each piece of pumpkin. Sprinkle with salt, black pepper and rosemary. Wrap in aluminum foil and bake at 350°F (180°C) for 1 hour until it is soft.

TOMATOES

The tomato is strictly a fruit. It originated in Peru, and found its way back to Spain in the 16th century. It appears primarily in Mediterranean recipes, and it is very versatile. Canned tomatoes are essential to the cruising pantry and, where fresh tomatoes are available, they become the main ingredient of so many meals and salads. I love ripe tomatoes sliced on crackers with a sprinkle of salt and fresh ground black pepper.

Tomato Preparation

Peeling Tomatoes: Put tomatoes in boiling water for 30 seconds, then allow to cool before peeling off the skin.

Seeding Tomatoes: Halve the tomatoes crosswise, then gently squeeze over a strainer. Seeds and juice squirt out, and the bowl under the strainer catches all the juice.

Sun Dried Tomatoes

These are becoming increasingly popular, and are readily available in the Mediterranean. They are a useful and tasty substitute for tomato purée. They do have a much sharper taste, so use a little less than you would use regular tomatoes or tomato paste.

Sun Dried Tomato Rehydration: Put dried tomato pieces in boiling water for around 30 seconds, drain and use.

Sun Dried Tomato Marination: Marinated sun dried tomatoes are terrific in sandwiches, on pizzas and toasted snacks with cheese, or with cold spicy sausages over boat drinks. They will keep for months, but once they are opened, keep refrigerated and use within 2 to 3 weeks. Once the tomatoes have been used, utilize the oil for salad dressing.

Sun Dried Tomato Dressing

¼ cup balsamic vinegar
¼ cup chopped sun dried
   tomatoes
1 clove chopped garlic
1 tablespoon chopped basil
½ cup virgin olive oil
Salt and pepper to taste

Process or blend vinegar, tomatoes, garlic and basil. Process to a coarse purée. Slowly add the oil, and season with pepper and salt to taste. Serve over pasta, salads, etc.

Marinated Sun Dried Tomatoes

Tomato
1 clove crushed garlic
½ teaspoon dried oregano
½ teaspoon basil
½ teaspoon sugar
Black pepper
Pinch of salt
Olive oil (virgin or extra
   virgin)
1 tablespoon wine vinegar
1 tablespoon lemon juice

Put the tomato in a sterile jar. Add the garlic, oregano, basil, sugar, ground pepper and a pinch of salt. Add enough olive oil to cover the tomatoes. Ideally fill jar to top. Store in a cool dark location. As an alternative, add vinegar and lemon juice for a delicious Italian touch.

Stuffed Tomatoes

4 large tomatoes
1 finely chopped onion
1 clove minced garlic
Olive oil
1 cup long grain rice
1 cup water
Salt and black pepper
2 tablespoons minced
   coriander

Slice off tops of tomatoes. Gently sauté onion and garlic until soft in the oil. Add the rice and sauté for 3 minutes. Add a cup of water. Season with salt and black pepper. Add the coriander, and bring to a boil. Simmer for 12 minutes until rice is al dente. Fill tomatoes with cooled rice mixture. Replace tomato tops and place in a casserole dish. Mix another ½ cup of water with coriander and pour over the tomatoes, then bake in a preheated oven at 350°F (180°C) for 30 minutes.

Fried Green Tomatoes

This old recipe has nothing to do with the Whistlestop Cafe.

Large unripe tomatoes
Plain flour
Salt and black pepper
Oil

Cut unripe or green tomatoes in thick slices. Coat the tomato slices in seasoned flour. Sauté in oil until golden on each side.

Egg Stuffed Tomatoes

Serves 2

2 firm ripe tomatoes
2 eggs
Butter or margarine
Salt
2 tablespoons grated cheese

Preheat oven to 400°F (205°C). Cut off the top of the tomatoes and scoop out pulp. Put on a greased baking pan and add a dab of butter and pinch of salt into each tomato. Cook in hot oven for 3 minutes. Remove and crack an egg into each tomato. Sprinkle with a spoon of grated cheese, return to the oven and cook for 10 minutes or until egg is set.

Tomato Salsa

1 finely chopped onion
4 chopped tomatoes
¼ cup brown vinegar
¼ cup water
1 teaspoon sugar
1 tablespoon olive oil
1 tablespoon chopped fresh
  coriander, or 2 teaspoons dry
  coriander
1 tablespoon chopped fresh
  basil, or 2 teaspoons dry
  basil

Gently sauté onion, tomatoes, vinegar, sugar, and water, stir and cook for around 5 minutes. Add coriander and basil and cook another 2 minutes.

ZUCCHINIS (COURGETTES)

This versatile vegetable is widely available in the United States and Mexico, the Mediterranean and Europe, India and Australia. It is also known as squash or courgette. There are a number of varieties, yellow, green, summer and winter squash. When you buy zucchinis, make sure they are firm to the touch.

Zucchini and Tomato

Serves 4

1 pound (500g) zucchini
4 tablespoons butter or
   margarine
1 can tomatoes
Salt and fresh ground pepper
Pinch of sugar
2 tablespoons fresh chopped
   basil

Cut zucchini into ¼-inch (1 cm) slices. Put into a pan with butter and cook for about 8 minutes. Chop the tomatoes. Add to the pan and simmer for another 8 minutes, stirring constantly. Season with salt, pepper and sugar. Stir in the fresh basil and serve.

Baked Zucchini

Serves 4

4 medium zucchinis
1 tablespoon butter
½ teaspoon crushed garlic
½ cup shredded cheese
2 tablespoons Parmesan cheese
Cracked pepper

Slice the zucchinis lengthwise and score the top diagonally. Put in a baking dish. Baste with melted garlic butter and sprinkle with shredded cheese. Season with cracked pepper. Bake in a moderate oven for 15 to 20 minutes or until crisp and tender.

Zucchini Slice

Serves 6

3 cups grated zucchini
1 large finely chopped onion
3 rashers finely chopped bacon
1 cup self-raising flour
½ teaspoon oregano
½ teaspoon rosemary
½ teaspoon basil
1 stock cube
5 eggs
½ cup milk
1½ tablespoons tomato paste

Combine the zucchini, onion, bacon, flour, seasonings and the crumbled stock cube in a large bowl. Lightly beat the eggs and add the milk and tomato paste. Fold through the zucchini mixture and pour into a lightly greased quiche plate. Bake at 350°F (180°C) for 35 to 40 minutes. Allow to stand for 10 minutes before slicing.

Zucchini and Tomato Curry

Serves 4

1 pound (500g) zucchini
3 tablespoons ghee
1 teaspoon ginger
Chili, or chili sauce
2 cloves minced garlic
1 tablespoon ground coriander
1 teaspoon turmeric
1 teaspoon ground cumin
Pinch ground fennel
1 can chopped tomatoes
Fresh coriander

Wash and slice zucchinis. Chop coriander finely. Heat ghee and add ginger, chili, garlic, ground coriander, turmeric, cumin, and fennel. Sauté gently. Add the tomatoes. Stir well and cook for 5 minutes. Add zucchini and half chopped coriander. Cover and cook for 20 minutes until zucchini is soft. Sprinkle with remainder of coriander, serve with boiled rice.

BREADFRUIT

Breadfruit is common in Polynesia, the West Indies and India. A considerable number of sailors lost their lives and two ships to deliver breadfruit out of the Pacific. As history records, Captain Bligh and the 215-ton *HMS Bounty* were carrying breadfruit seedlings from Tahiti to the West Indies. The now infamous mutiny occurred, as some on board including Fletcher Christian decided that they could not leave such a tropical paradise (and how cruisers can all sympathize with those sentiments!). *HMS Pandora*, which was taking some of the mutineers back to England for trial, also foundered. After making one of history's greatest open boat voyages to safety, Captain Bligh returned on *HMS Providence* and successfully delivered the breadfruit seedlings.

When ripe the skin is a greeny brown or yellow. The flesh is typically white to light yellow; it has a similar texture to bread and is very rich in starch. To eat, peel, remove the seeds, and cook in salted water as you would cook potatoes. Breadfruit can also be roasted, used in stews, or frittered. Breadfruit with seeds can be eaten raw, while those without must be cooked. General preparation is as for sweet potatoes.

Stuffed Breadfruit

Serves 2 to 4

1 hard breadfruit
1 diced onion
3 diced scallions
1 diced green pepper
2 teaspoons oil
1 cup flaked fish
Salt and black pepper

Wash and dry the breadfruit and pierce all over with a fork. Bake in a hot oven at 350°F (180°C) for about 1½ hours. Gently sauté the onions, scallions and pepper in oil until soft and golden. Slice off the top of the breadfruit and scoop out the flesh, leaving ½ inch all around. Mix the flesh and fish together. Put the mixture back into the breadfruit and replace the top. Wrap the breadfruit in aluminum foil. Bake in oven or stove top dutch oven for 35 minutes at 400°F (205°C). To serve, slice into wedges and pour over gravy or a nice fruit sauce. It can be served hot or cold.

Spicy Breadfruit

Serves 2

1 diced breadfruit
2 cups water
½ cup coconut milk
1 teaspoon turmeric
Fresh ground black pepper
1 teaspoon salt
1 tablespoon margarine

Skin, dice and simmer breadfruit in water until tender. Mash the breadfruit, and add the ingredients.

Breadfruit Soup

Serves 4

This soup comes from Trinidad.

½ pound (250g) ham or
   corned beef
4 cups beef stock
1 breadfruit
4 cups coconut milk
1 chopped onion
2 chopped shallots
1 whole chili
Salt and pepper to taste

Dice the meat into small cubes, add to stock and bring to a boil. Strain off the meat from stock. Peel core and slice the breadfruit and add to stock. Boil for 15 minutes. Remove and mash or purée the breadfruit. Put back into pan and add other ingredients. Simmer for 15 minutes.

TARO

The taro root can be found in most markets in the third world cruising countries. It is relatively cheap and can be cooked in several ways. Taro leaves also are a substitute for spinach and silver beet.

Turn Fried Taro

Serves 4

This is an excellent Indian Rajasthani recipe.

1½ pounds (750g) taro root
¾ teaspoon turmeric
¾ teaspoon cayenne pepper
Salt to taste
4 tablespoons peanut oil
½ teaspoon carom seeds (if available)

Boil the taro roots in a covered pot for 12 to 15 minutes or until the taro is tender and can be easily peeled. Drain and cool briefly. Peel the taro and cut into thin slices. Put the slices into a bowl and sprinkle with the turmeric, cayenne and salt, then toss well to cover taro with spices. Heat the oil in a large skillet, and when hot add the carom seeds and allow to sizzle for 10 seconds. Add the spice coated taro, toss and sauté until well browned and fried, about 15 minutes.

Taro Pancakes

Serves 4

¼ cup corned beef
3 cups cooked and grated taro
1 egg
1 finely chopped onion
Salt and black pepper
Flour
Oil

Combine all the ingredients and mix thoroughly. Roll the mixture into small balls and then roll in plain flour. Flatten each ball and fry until golden brown. Eat hot or let cool and eat as a cold snack.

Taro Cakes
(Pauline on *Ruahatu*)

Serves 4

3 cups cooked and grated taro
3 tablespoons grated onions
3 tablespoons chopped parsley
1 beaten egg
1 teaspoon curry powder
Plain flour
Oil
Salt and pepper

Boil the taro roots in a covered pot for 12 to 15 minutes or until the taro is tender and can be easily peeled. Drain and cool briefly. Grate the taro. Combine with onion, parsley, egg and curry powder in a bowl. Blend well and form into small cakes. Roll the cakes in flour and season to taste. Sauté in cooking oil until golden brown each side. Serve as a main meal with rice or as a snack.

Kumara or Taro Puffs

Serves 4

This recipe is from the Cook Islands.

3 cups cooked kumara/taro
2 tablespoons oil
2 tcaspoons salt
1 beaten egg
¼ teaspoon pepper

Boil the taro/kumara in a covered pot for 12 to 15 minutes or until the flesh is tender and can be easily peeled. Drain and cool briefly. Mash the kumara/taro. Combine ingredients together and beat until fluffy. Put large tablespoons of the mixture on a baking tray and bake at 350°F (190°F) until tops are golden brown.

Rarotonga Taro Cakes

Serves 4

This originates also from the Cook Islands.

3 cups cooked and mashed taro
1 finely chopped onion
2 teaspoons salt
4 tablespoons milk
Oil
Plain flour

Boil the taro roots in a covered pot for 12 to 15 minutes or until the taro is tender and can be easily peeled. Drain and cool briefly. Mash the taro. Combine with onion, milk and salt in a bowl. Blend well and form into small cakes. Roll the cakes in flour. Sauté in cooking oil until golden brown on each side.

Fa'ausi

Serves 4

When you next sail into Apia in Western Samoa, try this at Aggie Greys.

Taro root
Coconut cream
Sugar

Shred the uncooked taro root. Mix well with the coconut cream. Wrap in a banana leaf. Wrap in foil and put in a preheated oven at 400°F (205°C). Bake for about 30 minutes. Turn off oven and allow to cook for another 30 to 40 minutes. Cut into 2-inch (5cm) cubes. Make a syrup of sugar and coconut cream, and gently boil until brown. Pour over the cubes and enjoy.

Chapter 9

Fruits and Salads

Tropical Fruit Guide

Apples

Avocados

Bananas

Coconuts

Mangoes

Papayas

Pineapples

Salads

Salad Dressings

Cruising offers the opportunity to try a wide range of rarely available fruits, freshly ripened. The tropical fruit guide will help you identify some of lesser known ones.

Cruising offers the opportunity to try and sample a range of rarely available fruits, or simply to savor fruits that are freshly ripened. Somehow fruits taste a lot better on some tropical island. When you go on one of those enjoyable excursions to a local produce market you ask yourself, as you do when looking at vegetables, "What is that?" The following gives some explanations and descriptions of various tropical fruits, and there are many more.

TROPICAL FRUIT GUIDE

Acerola Found in the Caribbean, it is eaten raw, or use in drinks and jams. It has an astounding 25 to 50 times the vitamin C of an orange.

Ackee Ackee originates from West Africa and was introduced to the Caribbean by slaves. Boiled and combined with saltfish, it forms the national dish of Jamaica.

Ambarella This fruit is found in Polynesia. Eat it fresh or when it is not ripe, use for pickling or in salads.

Araca Araca is found in South America. It is very sour but great and refreshing in a drink.

Avocado The avocado has its origins in South America, and is available all over the world. The Spaniards discovered the plant and transported seedlings to other tropical locations on their galleons and trading vessels. The avocado has a flesh with a butter-like consistency.

Bananas Originally from Asia, and available in most tropical countries. There are many varieties available.

Coconut The coconut is available literally in all cruising areas. It has its origins in Melanesia.

Cristofine In Jamaica cristofine is also called a cho-cho and is eaten raw or cooked.

Durian Originally from Indonesia it has a bad odor, but is eaten fresh and is used to make drinks as well.

Guava Guava originated in Central America. Spain and Portugal spread the fruit around the world. There are several varieties with varying shapes. The strong flavored flesh varies from orange to yellow/white and has a range of flavors from sweet to sour.

Guinep A small green fruit, originally from Surinam.

Jackfruit Originally from India, jackfruit is also found in the Caribbean. It is related to the breadfruit and it is yellow in color. It is often eaten as a vegetable and can be baked or boiled. When ripe it has a strong flavor and is eaten as a dessert.

Mango The mango has its origins in Malaysia and found its way to Africa and South America in the 19th century. Mangoes are used unripe in Asian and West Indian cooking. The mango is typically around 7 to 8 inches in length.

Mangosteen There are two types: The Purple Mangosteen is a delicious fruit eaten fresh, while the Yellow Mangosteen is a very acidic fruit used for drinks.

Ortanique This hybrid citrus was developed in Jamaica from a tangerine and an orange.

Otaheite Apple This apple came from Tahiti with Captain Bligh along with the breadfruit.

Papaya (Paw Paw) The papaya originates from Malaysia. It has a well known smooth yellow skin and orange flesh, with black seeds. These fruits are about 18 to 20 inches long. When ripe the skin turns to a yellow color that is soft to touch. The fruit flesh is an orange color. When green, the papaya should be cooked as a vegetable. Ripe fruits are delicious with rum. The juice also serves as a meat tenderizer.

Passion fruit The passion fruit originates from Central America, and is grown worldwide. Its color is either the familiar purple or yellow. When ripe it has wrinkled skin. The acidic flesh is orange/yellow with small black seeds and smells divine. Eat raw or over fruit salads or desserts.

Pineapple The pineapple comes originally from Brazil and was introduced to France and England in the 16th century.

Sapodilla Sapodilla originates from Central America. In Jamaica it is known as naseberry. It is about the size of a lemon, with a rough grey/brown skin. The flesh is very soft and varies between white to red/yellow and sweet. It is eaten when it is almost overripe, peeled with the seeds removed. Taste is similar to apricot.

Soursop Also known as a guanabana, it originates from the Caribbean and Central America. It is a large heart shaped fruit, with a green prickly skin. The flesh is white with a fragrant and slightly tart flavor.

Sweetsop Also known as a sugar apple, it is similar to the soursop but has a sweet flesh.

Star Apple Also known as caimito, it originates from Central America. The fruit has a thick purple skin. The flesh is sweet and is eaten ripe or in fruit salads.

Tamarind Originally from Africa, it is used in drinks when ripe, and in curries and chutneys when unripe. The ripe flesh is spicy. The tamarind is used as a flavoring in Worcestershire sauce and angostura bitters.

Ugli Jamaican developed hybrid citrus fruit of grapefruit and tangerine.

APPLES

Apples require refrigeration to last well, but if you visit any country with a temperate climate you can buy them fairly cheaply. Use your favorite Mom's apple pie recipe or something different.

Apple Fritters

Serves 4

2 eggs
2 tablespoons sugar
¾ cup milk
½ vanilla essence
1 cup self-raising flour
3 large peeled and grated
  apples
Oil
Sugar
Lemon juice

Whisk the eggs lightly in a bowl. Add the sugar and beat until airy and well combined. Add the milk and vanilla and blend in. Add the flour until the batter is slightly runny. Add the grated apples and any juice to the batter. Stir and put the mixture in the refrigerator for half an hour. Heat a little oil in a skillet. Drop about a tablespoon or two of apple batter into the oil. Cook for two or three minutes until lightly browned on the bottom. Turn over and cook the other side. When cooked, sprinkle each fritter with half a teaspoon of sugar. Sprinkle with lemon juice and sugar when serving.

AVOCADOS

Another great discovery by our travelling gourmet Christopher Columbus. The avocado is a native of the Americas, namely Mexico. It used to be called Midshipman's Butter, usually taken on board as ship stores for consumption by the junior officers. It has also been regarded as an aphrodisiac, which doesn't help the sailors much, I would imagine. Ripeness is tested by pressing a finger against the avocado; if it gives way it is ready to eat. Avocados ripen at room temperature within a few days and can be stored thereafter a few more days in the refrigerator. Prepare avocados only when you are ready to eat them as they very quickly blacken on exposure to air. Once cut or sliced, squeeze some lemon juice over it: this will prevent blackening.

Guacamole   *Serves 8*

2 large ripe avocados
1 peeled and chopped tomato
Tabasco sauce to taste
½ cup finely chopped onion
1½ tablespoon lemon juice
1 teaspoon salt

Peel the avocados and remove the stone. Put in a bowl and mash well with the tomatoes. Add all ingredients. Mix well, cover and refrigerate for at least an hour.

Avocado Snacks

The avocado has great versatility. Try these great tasting ideas.

Avocado Toasties

Mash avocado onto toast and top with cheese (ideally Edam or Gouda, or even Camembert) before broiling.

Sandwich Fillers

- Avocado, chicken and mayonnaise
- Avocado, pink salmon, lettuce and mayonnaise
- Avocado, prawns and bean sprouts
- Avocado, tomato, lettuce, bacon and mayonnaise

BANANAS

I served several times on banana boats around Central and South America. Beside learning the words of the banana boat song, I also developed a taste for these nutritious prepacked meals. They are very nourishing with a high energy value, and rich in potassium, vitamins A, C and K, and starch. The following recipes give just some of the many useful ways to enjoy this relatively cheap fruit. Bananas can be used in different ways according to stage of ripeness. Partially ripe bananas can be baked or cooked as the cooking makes them digestible. The flavor is different from the ripe fruit. Full to over ripe bananas usually have brown spots on the skin. They can be used in baking, desserts, etc.

Banana Fritters   *Serves 8*

¼ pound (125g) plain flour
Pinch of salt
2 eggs
½ cup milk
1 tablespoon oil
¼ cup caster (finely granulated white) sugar
8 firm ripe peeled bananas
Safflower or canola oil
Icing sugar

Sift the flour and salt into a bowl. Form a well in the center. Add 1 egg and the yolk of the second egg. Mix with a whisk and gradually blend in the milk until it becomes a thick and creamy mixture. Stir in the oil and sugar. Cover the mixture and let rest for 30 minutes. Whisk the second egg white until soft peaks are formed and fold through the batter. Peel the bananas and halve lengthwise. Dip one at a time into the batter. Half fill a frying pan with oil and heat so that batter will sizzle, brown, and rise to the surface. Cook the bananas one or two at a time, drain on paper and dust with icing sugar. Serve with boat made vanilla ice cream.

Banana Coconut Cream Pie   *Serves 6*

¼ pound (125g) plain biscuits
6 tablespoons melted butter
½ cup shredded coconut
2 bananas
¾ cup vanilla custard
½ cup shredded coconut
3 tablespoons demerara (light brown raw cane) sugar

Put the biscuits into a blender or processor until crumbed. Pour in the melted butter while still operating. Add the shredded coconut and pulse to blend. Press the mixture firmly on to the base of a 8-inch (20cm) pie plate. Slice the bananas and put over the pie crust. Pour over the custard and sprinkle with more shredded coconut. Sprinkle with sugar, and put under a very hot grill until sugar caramelizes. Allow to cool slightly and serve.

Baked Bananas

Serves 4

½ pint of orange juice
1 tablespoon corn flour
2 tablespoons honey
3 tablespoons dark rum
2 tablespoons demerara sugar
½ teaspoon ground allspice
Pinch ground cinnamon
4 firm bananas
1 orange
Grated orange peel

Blend the orange juice and corn flour together. Put all the ingredients (except the bananas and orange) into a saucepan, mix and bring to a boil, and stir constantly. Peel the bananas, and carefully make a slit along the length of each. Open them slightly, and lay each out on aluminium foil. Cover each with some of the prepared sauce. Reserve some sauce for serving. Seal each banana in the foil and place on a baking sheet. Cook for 10 to 15 minutes at 350°C (180°C). Remove the bananas from the foil and put on a plate along with some orange segments. Pour some re-heated sauce over them and sprinkle with grated orange peel.

Banana Butter

Makes 3 cups

4 ripe bananas
⅔ cup sugar
3 beaten eggs
¼ pound (125g) butter
¼ cup strained lemon juice
1 tablespoon grated lemon rind
½ cup strained orange juice

Peel and chop bananas coarsely. Put in a blender, and blend until smooth. Alternatively simply mash well with a fork. Combine bananas, sugar, eggs, chopped butter, lemon juice, lemon rind, and orange juice in a double saucepan. Stand saucepan over simmering water, and stir until mixture coats the wooden spoon thickly. Pour into hot sterilized jars and seal. Store in the refrigerator.

Banana Fritter Surprise

Serves 4

Batter:

1 egg
6 tablespoons plain flour
Pinch salt
5 tablespoons tepid water
1 tablespoon oil

Separate the egg. Mix sifted flour and salt gradually with water. Beat in the egg yolk and oil to form a smooth batter. Let stand at room temperature for 2 hours. Whisk egg white and fold into batter.

Fritters:

½ pound (250g) rice
1 pint milk
4 to 6 bananas
1 egg
Icing sugar

Cook rice in milk until thick, add milk as needed. Peel the bananas, and cut into small cubes. Mix with the rice, and beat in the egg. Mix with the batter, and fry in oil until golden brown. Dust fritters with sifted icing sugar.

Baked Banana Dessert

Serves 4

4 to 6 bananas
Brown sugar
½ cup orange juice

Peel bananas and put in a casserole dish. Sprinkle with brown sugar. Pour over orange juice. Bake in a moderate oven for 10 minutes. Baste with juice.

Banana Whisk

Serves 2

2 ripe bananas
1½ cups chilled skim milk
1 tablespoon brown sugar
Pinch allspice
½ cup pineapple (optional)
1 tablespoon honey (optional)

Purée the bananas, add the other ingredients and blend until thick. For variety, add ½ cup diced pineapple and 1 tablespoon honey.

Whipped Bananas

Break 4 to 5 frozen bananas into thick chunks. Put in a food processor and blend until thick and creamy. The bananas will form a thick and creamy whip.

Plantain Bananas

Besides the familiar fruit banana, you can find in many Caribbean markets the plantain banana. It has a green skin and a firm pink flesh, and is both longer and flatter than fruit bananas.

The usual method to cook plantains is to drop them in boiling salted water for 15 to 45 minutes depending on maturity, and then fry, mash, or add to stews. This is common in West Indian, South American and African cuisine.

Plantain Chips

A happy hour special, just great with a cold beer.

10 green plantains
Cooking oil
Salt

Peel and slice into small pieces. Fry plantain pieces a dozen at a time turning over once. When golden brown and crisp drain on paper towels, then liberally sprinkle and toss with salt. Store for 2 to 3 days in an airtight container.

Plantain Balls

3 green plantains
1 tablespoon milk
Salt and pepper
2 tablespoons margarine

Boil the unpeeled plantains for about 30 minutes. Cool for several minutes and peel. Chop and then mash, adding milk, salt and pepper. Mix in the margarine. Roll into balls, and serve warm as a side dish.

Fried Plantains

3 ripe plantains
8 tablespoons cooking oil

Slice the plantains into three segments. Slice ¼-inch thick lengthwise. Sauté in hot oil until golden brown.

COCONUTS

The mature coconut has a brown and fibrous outer shell, with the inside consisting of hard white meat. The unripe coconut has a green outer shell; it is filled with that delicious sweet coconut juice that is low in calories and is very different from coconut milk or cream.

Each coconut has three dark colored "eyes." Pierce two of these to extract the juice. After the juice has been extracted, bake the coconut in a preheated oven at about 350°F (180°C) for 15 to 20 minutes. Hit the nut with a hammer and the hard outer shell should break away from the meat.

If you find coconuts on a beach, do not simply appropriate them for yourself. They invariably belong to someone, and are worth money. Always ask someone for permission before taking any; such courtesies will generally ensure hospitality from the local community. Also be very careful when standing under coconut palms, it can be dangerous, even fatal.

Coconut Cream

Put the coconut meat in a food processor or blender, add the coconut juice, and process until the meat is finely pulverized. Place the purée into a tea towel and wring out the liquid into a bowl.

Coconut Milk

Place the remaining coconut from the tea towel into a bowl, and pour a couple of cups of boiling water over it. Allow to stand for an hour, and again pour into a tea towel and wring out as before to extract the liquid.

Palusami

I had my first taste of this at the famous Aggie Greys Hotel in Apia, Western Samoa. It is absolutely delicious. Although it is traditionally cooked in the coals of a fire or umu, you can adapt it to the boat oven.

Taro leaves
Coconut cream
1 chopped onion

Take six baby taro leaves, and make into a cup. Add ½ cup coconut cream, and onion. Fold the leaves, and wrap in a wilted banana leaf. On board you should wrap in foil and bake in a preheated oven of 400°F (205°C) for about 30 minutes, and then turn off and allow to cook for another 30 to 40 minutes.

Cuban Coconut Custard   *Serves 4*

A beautiful and fattening dessert.

1 cup coconut juice
6 ounces (200g) sugar
2 cups coconut cream
6 egg yolks
2 tablespoons white rum
1 teaspoon vanilla essence

Put the coconut juice in a pan and add water as necessary. Add the sugar and stir over high heat until the sugar dissolves. Boil hard for 5 minutes until it reaches a syrupy stage. Remove the pan from the heat and pour in the coconut cream. Beat 6 egg yolks in a bowl, add ½ cup of the cream and syrup mix, and stir well. Pour in the mix back to the saucepan and cook over low heat for about 5 minutes until it forms a custard like consistency. Remove from the heat and stir in the rum and vanilla essence. Serve over sponge cake, or lady finger bananas that have been sprinkled with rum and allowed to soak.

MANGOES

Mangoes are absolutely delicious chilled. If you have ice cream they make great companions. They can be sautéed when they are ripe or baked when unripe. As the mango has a flat, oval shaped clingstone, it requires cutting in a certain way: Cut large slices from both flat sides of the fruit, as close to the stone as possible. Cut the flesh into cubes, but do not cut the skin. Turn the skin inside out. This makes flesh removal easy. To slice either peel or pull off the skin. Slice off segments on the flatter sides of the fruit as close to the stone as possible.

Mango and Ginger

Serves 4

2 large mangoes
1 tablespoon grated ginger
1 lemon or lime
4 teaspoons maple syrup

Peel and cut mangoes into small chunks. Grate the ginger and squeeze the ginger juice over the mango pieces. Peel lemon or lime and slice into thin strips. Squeeze the juice over the mango. Coat the mango with syrup. Sprinkle with lemon or lime rind strips. Marinate for 30 minutes and serve.

PAPAYAS (PAW PAW)

The juice makes a refreshing drink when chilled. For a simple dessert, chill and sprinkle with either lemon or lime juice. When green the papaya can be cooked as a vegetable.

Paw Paw Mousse

Serves 4

1 medium papaya
2 tablespoons honey
1 cup low fat yogurt
1 tablespoon gelatine
¼ cup orange juice
3 medium passion fruit

Peel the papaya and discard seeds. Blend papaya with honey and yogurt. Stir gelatine into orange juice and dissolve over hot water. Add the mixture and passion fruit pulp to the blended papaya. Stir well and place in serving dishes. Refrigerate until set and serve.

Papaya Dip

1 green papaya
1 cup plain yogurt
2 cloves minced garlic
Salt and pepper to taste

Peel the papaya and discard seeds. Grate the papaya. Add the yogurt, garlic, salt and pepper to taste. Cover and chill.

Papaya Frittata

Serves 4

1 green papaya
1 chopped onion
1 clove minced garlic
1 peeled and chopped tomato
½ teaspoon dried basil
½ teaspoon dried oregano
2 tablespoons peanut oil
3 beaten eggs

Peel the papaya and discard seeds. Grate the papaya. Sauté onion, garlic, papaya, tomato and herbs until soft. Pour over the eggs. Stir gently, cover and cook slowly over low heat until eggs set. Invert onto a serving dish and slice into wedges.

Baked Papaya Slices

Serves 2

1 ripe papaya
Honey
Margarine
Brown sugar

Peel the papaya and discard seeds. Cut into thick slices. Lay slices into baking dish. Baste with honey and margarine that have been warmed together. Sprinkle with brown sugar. Bake in a hot oven at 350°F (180°C) until browned.

Green Papaya Curry

Serves 4

2 green papayas
1 finely chopped onion
1 teaspoon crushed garlic
1 teaspoon grated ginger
Ghee
1 tablespoon curry powder
1 teaspoon salt
Pepper
Coconut milk

Peel the papaya and discard seeds. Cut into thick slices. Gently sauté onions, garlic and ginger in ghee. Add curry powder, salt and pepper to taste and simmer for around 5 minutes. Slowly stir in 1 cup coconut milk. Add the papaya and cook gently for 40 minutes. Stir and add coconut milk so that liquid has a nice thick consistency.

Stuffed Papaya

Serves 2

1 small chopped onion
Oil
1 medium half ripe papaya
¾ cup cooked rice
¾ cup cold cooked seafood
(crab meat, lobster or fish
pieces)
1 lightly beaten egg
1 teaspoon salt
Black pepper

Gently sauté onion in oil until soft and golden. Slice top off papaya, and scoop out the seeds. Thoroughly mix all the ingredients together and then put mixture into the papaya. Replace the top and secure with toothpicks or a skewer. Brush the outside with oil, and bake in the oven at 350°F (180°C) for around 45 minutes. Serve with a nice fresh tomato or mango sauce.

Green Papaya Salad

Serves 2 to 4

1 green papaya
3 tablespoons coconut cream
2 tablespoons lemon juice
2 tablespoons oil
1 small finely chopped onion
Salt and black pepper

Peel and grate the papaya. Put in a bowl of salted water for 1 hour. Wash and drain the papaya. Add the coconut cream, lemon juice, oil, onion, and salt and pepper. Let stand for 10 minutes and then serve.

Papaya Cake

Serves 4 to 6

½ cup margarine
1 cup sugar
2 eggs
2 cups ripe papaya
3 cups plain flour
2 teaspoons baking soda
1 teaspoon salt
¼ teaspoon ginger
¼ teaspoon nutmeg
¼ teaspoon cinnamon
2 tablespoons water
1 teaspoon lemon juice
1 cup raisins

Cream the margarine and sugar together. Add the eggs one at a time, and beat the mixture well after each is added. Mash and add the papaya. Sift the flour with baking soda, spices and salt then stir into the papaya mixture. Add the water and juice and gently fold in the raisins. Pour the mixture into a greased baking pan. Bake in a preheated oven at 350°F (180°C) for 45 minutes.

PINEAPPLES

When choosing ripe pineapples, go for the ones that have protruding eyes and, when flicked with a finger, give a solid thud. The aroma should also have that delicious sweet smell. Unlike bananas and apples, they do not get sweeter when left out to ripen. Store ripe fruit whole in the refrigerator with shell and leaves removed. Ideally wrap in plastic wrap or a plastic bag.

Pineapple Salsa

It is ideal with grilled fish.

½ peeled and cored large
   pineapple
½ cup each of red and green
   pepper
½ skinned purple onion
2 tablespoons safflower oil
3 tablespoons coriander leaves
1 tablespoon lime juice
4 tablespoons parsley tops
2 hot chilies
Salt
Freshly ground black pepper

Mince the pineapple or chop in a food processor or blender using pulse mode. Place the pulp into a mixing bowl. Mince or finely chop peppers and onion. Add the oil and chop the coriander leaves. Add lime juice, parsley and chilies. Chop again using pulse until all ingredients are a similar size. Transfer to the pineapple, mix well and season to taste. Cover and let sit for 4 to 6 hours. It lasts for about two days.

Extra Sweet Pineapple

Serves 4 to 6

6 tablespoons caster sugar
6 tablespoons butter
   (preferably unsalted)
2 tablespoons lemon juice
1 cup orange juice
¼ cup rum
8 slices fresh pineapple

Melt the sugar in a pan until caramelization starts. Add the butter, stirring continuously so that both combine. Add the lemon and orange juice, and then the rum. Cook over low heat for 5 minutes, stirring all the time. Add the pineapple slices in and cook another 5 minutes. Serve hot, or with ice cream (preferably coconut).

Creole Pineapple Salad

Serves 4

2 large green peppers
French dressing
1 pound (500g) chopped
   pineapple
4 bananas
4 cups cooked rice

Chop or slice up the peppers. Toss well in the French dressing. Add the pineapple and bananas. Serve the salad mix chilled on top of rice.

SALADS

The salad is the mainstay of on-board cockpit alfresco dining. The following are just a few good variations to add to the repertoire.

Octopus Salad

Serves 4 to 6

2 octopus (1½ pounds each)
1 bay leaf
1 chopped onion
1 carrot
Coarse sea salt
2 waxy potatoes
1 cup green pitted olives
⅓ cup olive oil
Lemon juice (1 lemon)
Sprigs parsley
Salt

Prepare the octopus. Add to a large pan of cold water with the bay leaf, onion, carrot and a tablespoon of coarse sea salt. Bring to a boil and then simmer for approximately 35 minutes. Allow the octopus to cool in the liquid. Boil the potatoes until tender, then peel and dice. Cut the olives in half and mix with the potatoes in a salad bowl. Drain the octopus, remove the suckers, and slice into small pieces. Mix with potatoes and olives. Beat the olive oil, lemon juice and finely chopped parsley together, and add a pinch of salt. Pour over the salad, stir and serve.

Potato and Bean Salad

Serves 4

1 pound (500g) small potatoes
½ pound (250g) green beans
4 tablespoons chopped herbs
   of choice
French vinaigrette

Cook the potatoes in 2 inches (5cm) boiling water until tender but still firm. When they are cooled slice thinly. Trim the green beans, cutting off the tips at both ends. Break them into 2-inch lengths and cook them in a small amount of water until they are tender, but still retain their color. Drain and then toss in the herbs and French vinaigrette while still warm. Add to the sliced potatoes and mix gently. Serve either warm or chilled.

Green Bean and Tomato Salad

Serves 2 to 4

½ pound (250g) green beans
2 ripe tomatoes
1 thinly sliced Spanish onion
Salad vinaigrette
Olives
Feta cheese

Trim the green beans, cutting off the tips at both ends. Break them into 2-inch (5cm) length and cook until they are just crisp. Put in a salad bowl with wedges of tomato and onion. Pour over and mix in about ½ cup mixed salad vinaigrette, sprinkle in some olives and small squares of feta cheese if possible.

Seafood Salad

Serves 4

2 to 3 scallops or cooked white fish
Drained small mussels
¼ pound (125g) crabmeat
¼ pound (125g) peeled prawns
2 tablespoons olive oil
1 tablespoon lemon juice
1 clove crushed garlic
Salt and ground black pepper

Mix seafood (fish or scallops) with mussels, crabmeat and prawns. Mix oil, lemon juice and garlic and toss through the seafood salad. Add seasonings and serve.

Rice Salad

Serves 8

1 cup brown rice
1 cup long grain white rice
8 dried Chinese mushrooms
1 tablespoon soy sauce
1 tablespoon sugar
1 sliced red pepper
½ pound (250g) sliced mushrooms
½ pound (250g) sliced water chestnuts
3 large finely sliced spring onions
3 tablespoons toasted sesame seeds

Cook each rice type separately. Put brown rice in a pan with 2 cups of water, bring to a boil, reduce heat to very low, cover tightly with lid and cook 35 to 40 minutes. Put the rice into a large roasting pan to cool. Cook the white rice the same way, with 2 cups of water, but reduce cooking time to 15 minutes. Spread out to cool. Soak the dried mushrooms in very hot water for 30 minutes, squeeze out the water, cut off stems, and cut into fine strips. Simmer them in a small pan with 1½ of the soaking liquid and a tablespoon each of soy sauce and sugar for around 10 minutes. Combine rice with other ingredients and a basic vinaigrette.

Eggplant and Coriander Salad

Serves 6

2 small eggplants
3 small zucchinis
2 tablespoons olive oil
½ cup fresh chopped coriander
1 tablespoon lemon juice
1 tablespoon orange juice
½ teaspoon ground black
  pepper

Prepare eggplant by cutting into thin slices lengthwise. Put it in a colander and sprinkle with salt. Allow to stand for 20 minutes. Slice zucchini very thinly lengthwise using a vegetable peeler. Wash and pat dry eggplant. Brush both sides with olive oil and put on a baking tray. Cook under a preheated broiler until lightly browned. Allow to cool. Put eggplant, zucchini slices, oil, coriander, juices and pepper into a bowl and toss to combine.

Tahitian Fish Salad

Serves 6 to 8

2 pounds (1kg) fish
Juice 4 to 5 limes or lemons
1 teaspoon salt
1 finely sliced purple onion
1 cup coconut milk
½ teaspoon crushed garlic
½ teaspoon finely grated fresh
  ginger
1 red pepper
6 spring onions

Remove all skin and bones from the fish. Wash and dry and cut the fillets into strips, or dice. Put in a non-metallic bowl and strain lemon or lime juice over. There should be enough juice to cover the fish. Add the salt and sliced onions, and mix well with a wooden spoon. Cover with plastic food wrap and refrigerate for at least 6 hours, stirring a few times. Prior to serving, drain away the lemon juice, and pour over a mixture of the coconut milk with garlic and ginger. Dice the red pepper, chop the spring onions and, after adding to the fish, mix gently.

Canned Tomato Salad

1 can whole tomatoes
Celery salt
Salt
Lemon juice
Brown sugar

Use the firm part of tomatoes. Sprinkle with other ingredients. Serve very chilled.

Lima Bean Salad

Serves 4

1 cup lima beans
Chicken stock
1 chopped onion
2 cloves garlic
2 bay leaves
1 can tomatoes
Thyme
Black pepper
1 cucumber

Soak the lima beans in the chicken stock. Add onion, garlic, bay leaves and cook gently for around 30 minutes. Drain and put in a bowl. Gently simmer tomatoes along with thyme and black pepper for around 10 minutes. Cool and then stir in the cucumber. Add to the beans and toss.

SALAD DRESSINGS

Basic Vinaigrette

½ teaspoon sea salt
1 teaspoon balsamic vinegar
1 teaspoon raspberry vinegar
5 tablespoons virgin olive oil
Freshly ground black pepper

Whisk all the ingredients together in the order given. For variation add the finely chopped flesh of a ripe skinned and peeled tomato, or 1 to 2 teaspoons whole grain mustard.

French Vinaigrette

2 tablespoons oil
2 tablespoons red wine vinegar
¼ teaspoon freshly ground
   black pepper
½ teaspoon mustard (Dijon)
   powder
1 clove crushed garlic

Put all the ingredients into a screw top jar or Tupperware™ Shake-and-Pour. Shake well, and store in the refrigerator.

French Mayonnaise

½ cup vegetable or peanut oil
¼ cup evaporated milk
1 tablespoon prepared Dijon
   mustard
½ teaspoon salt
Dash of black pepper

Put all the ingredients in a shaker or jar, and shake 7 to 8 times. Add 1 tablespoon lemon juice, and shake several times more.

Mixed Salad Vinaigrette

½ cup olive oil
¼ cup white wine vinegar
6 anchovies
1 tablespoon Parmesan cheese

Put all the ingredients in a blender and purée until smooth.

Chapter 10

Baking

Breads

Scones

Muffins

Basic Pancakes, Crêpes and Waffles

Cookies, Cakes and Tarts

Puddings

*Bread making on board is
one of the great challenges
of cruising.*

Bread is the staple of most diets. Most places in the world have good fresh local breads, particularly the former French and Portuguese colonies. On-board bread making is one of cruising's great challenges. There are many methods and recipes, either with an oven or without, in a Dutch oven or pressure cooker, and they all work. Go to any supermarket and the variety of breads is astounding, wholemeal, wholegrain, multigrain, high fiber, white, rye, pita, Lebanese, focaccia, etc. After cooking bread keep in a covered container. Do not store bread in the refrigerator as it actually goes stale faster. Freezing excess is a good option. Don't waste stale bread, cut into small squares and fry in oil until crisp to make croutons, and enjoy with soup.

BREADS

Saltwater Bread
(Neil and Betony on *Island Lady*)

1½ cups warm salt water
1 tablespoon sugar
1 tablespoon dried yeast
4 cups sifted plain flour

Melt the sugar and yeast in warm water. Let stand for at least 5 minutes. Add the sifted flour, stir well. No kneading is really required, but a small amount does help. Grease and flour pressure cooker well. Place dough in and, with lid on, let it rise for 2 hours. Cook over a very low flame for one hour. Tip the bread out, turn over and cook for an additional half hour. Bread should be golden brown and crusty.

Pressure Cooker or Dutch Oven Bread

2 teaspoons sugar
1½ teaspoons salt
1 tablespoon yeast
1½ cups water
2 cups white flour
2 cups whole wheat flour
2 tablespoons oil

Dissolve the sugar, salt and yeast in water. Let it stand for 5 minutes. Blend in the flour and knead the mixture well. Allow to rise until volume doubles. Punch it down and knead again. Grease Dutch oven or pressure cooker and dust with flour. Cover and then cook for 45 minutes, on a very low flame. Do not open and look. If you wish to brown the top, turn the loaf over and cook for another 10 minutes.

Irish Beer Bread

3 cups white flour
1 teaspoon salt
¼ cup brown sugar
3 tablespoons baking powder
1 egg
Small bottle Guinness

Mix all the ingredients together to form a thick, sticky bread dough. Grease Dutch oven or pressure cooker and put the mixture in. Smooth the top over. Cook on moderate heat until brown and turnover and do other side or bake in oven at 350°F (180°C) for 45 minutes.

Traditional White Bread

Makes 2 loaves

1½ teaspoons dried yeast
2 teaspoons sugar
1¾ cups warm water
6 cups plain flour
3 teaspoons salt

Sprinkle the yeast and sugar into warm water and stir until dissolved. Sift the flour and salt in a large bowl and make a hole in the center. Pour in the liquid mixture. Sprinkle a little flour over the liquid and allow to stand for 10 minutes in a warm place. Mix to form a soft dough. Dust a wooden board with flour and knead dough lightly for 10 minutes or until smooth textured. Form dough into a ball and put into greased bowls. Turn dough over so top is also greased. Cover with a cloth and leave in a warm place for 1½ hours. It should double in bulk. Punch down the risen dough and knead lightly to remove bubbles. Divide in two and put in two oiled loaf pans. The dough rolls should be long enough to touch the ends of the pans. Cover the pans and allow to rise until approximately double in size. Place in a preheated hot oven at 400°F (205°C), and bake for 15 minutes, reduce heat to 350°F (180°C) and bake for 20 to 25 minutes until golden brown. Cool on a rack.

Homemade Yeast

This recipe will allow you to make your own yeast. It is an old recipe that goes back to the 1950's or before, but it works well.

1 ounce (30g) hops
2 medium size potatoes
3 pints (1½lts) water
2 tablespoons white sugar
1 cup plain flour

Boil the hops, potatoes and water for 20 minutes. Strain, then add the sugar. Allow to cool. Mix the flour with some of the boiled liquid and add to the boiled yeast liquid. Bottle in a seasoned bottle. To season bottle, make one initial batch, then discard leaving some behind. Always keep some yeast from each batch to start off the next. When bottling, do not cover too tightly. In warm climates allow 8 to 10 hours to ripen, in a cold climate, allow 20 to 24 hours.

Workhouse Bread

6 pounds (3kgs) plain flour
¾ cup yeast
1 cup warm water
1 tablespoon salt

Put flour in a basin and form a well in the center. Pour in the yeast, add the warm water, and mix into a batter. Cover well with flour and let prove overnight. Next morning, sprinkle salt over the flour, add enough warm water to mix into a light dough. Cover bowl with a cloth to prevent crusting and put in a warm location. Allow to rise until it has doubled in size. Knead again to remove gas bubbles. When dough has an elastic feel, shape into loaves. Allow dough to double its size again. Put in a preheated hot oven at 450°F (230°C), then decrease heat. It is ready when the crust is golden brown.

Bread Trouble Shooting

Bread is too small: Oven too hot or dough too cold. Dough should rise at 23 to 30°C.

Dough doesn't rise, or rises very slowly: The yeast is not active, or the dough is cold, or the ingredients used are cold. Water that is too hot kills the yeast, while coldness retards activity. All ingredients should be at room temperature.

Bread does not rise in the oven: The rising period was excessive, or the oven was too hot and the top crusted before it finished rising. Allow the bread to rise only to about double its size. Make sure the oven temperature is correct.

Loaf is large and misshapen: The bread was allowed to rise too long in the pan or too much dough was used for the pan size. The oven temperature was too low.

Indian Chapattis
Makes 12 to 14

2½ cups fine wholemeal flour
1 tablespoon oil
1 cup lukewarm water

Mix the oil with the flour. Add the water and mix to form a dough. Knead for around 10 minutes. Form into a ball, cover with plastic food wrap and allow to rise for an hour. Shape into balls about 2 inches (5 cm) in diameter. Roll out on a floured board into circles. Heat oil in a heavy skillet, until very hot. Place each chapatti in the pan for around 1 minute.

Indian Fried Bread

¾ pound (375g) plain flour
½ teaspoon salt
2 tablespoons ghee or oil
¾ cup hot water
Oil (for frying)

Sift the flour and salt, then rub in the ghee or oil and mix well. Slowly add enough water to form a stiff dough. Knead for 10 minutes and roll out on a floured board. Cut into circles with a scone cutter. Roll each circle out very thinly. Heat oil and fry each side until golden. To get the bread to puff up press with a spatula. Eat hot or cold.

Australian Damper

3 cups self-raising flour
3 teaspoons salt
6 tablespoons butter or
    margarine
½ cup milk
½ cup water

Sift flour and salt into a bowl. Rub in the butter until the mixture looks like fine breadcrumbs. Make a well in the center of the dry ingredients, and then add the combined water and milk all at once. Mix very lightly with a sharp knife, using a cutting motion. Turn the mix out on to a lightly floured board, and knead lightly. Knead the dough into a round shape, and put on a lightly greased baking tray. Pat the dough into a 6-inch circle. Cut two slits across the top in a cross about ½-inch deep. Brush the top with milk, and a little sifted flour. Bake in a hot oven for 10 minutes until golden brown, reduce to 350°F (180°C), and cook a further 15 minutes.

Pita Bread

Makes 12

1 sachet dried yeast
1½ cups lukewarm water
1 teaspoon caster sugar
3½ cups plain flour
2 tablespoons olive oil

Put the yeast, water and sugar into a bowl. Let stand in a warm place for 5 minutes until frothy. Place the flour, yeast mixture and olive oil into a food processor and blend for 30 seconds until the mixture forms a ball. Alternatively mix with a wooden spoon until a smooth dough is formed. Turn out the dough onto a floured board and knead until smooth and elastic. Put into a well oiled bowl, cover with food wrap, and a clean tea towel and allow to rise in warm place for 20 minutes until double in size. Punch air from the dough, and divide into 12 portions. Roll each portion into a round shape. Put on greased baking trays and brush well with water. Let it stand and allow to rise for another 20 minutes. Bake for 4 to 5 minutes in a preheated oven at 450°F (230°C). If the rounds have dried out, brush with water again.

SCONES

Wholemeal Date Scones

Makes 15

1 cup self-raising flour
1 cup wholemeal flour
1 cup unprocessed bran
¼ cup full cream milk powder
2 ounces (60g) butter or
   margarine
¼ pound (125g) finely
   chopped dates
1 cup water

Sift flours into a bowl, and add husks to bowl after sifting. Mix in bran and milk powder. Run in butter, and add the dates. Form a well in center and stir in sufficient water to form a sticky dough. Turn out the dough onto a lightly floured board, and knead gently until smooth. Roll out dough to ½-inch thick, and cut out rounds of about 2-inch (5 cm). Place scones into greased baking tray. Bake in moderate hot oven 15 to 20 minutes. Serve hot with butter.

Foolproof Scones

This is my mother's recipe, designed to make it easy for people like me.

1 egg
1 tablespoon white sugar
1 tablespoon butter
¾ cup milk
2 cups self-raising flour
½ teaspoon salt

Beat the egg and sugar together. Melt butter and add milk to it. Sift self-raising flour and salt together. Make a well in the center and pour in egg mixture. Mix well and then add milk and butter. Mix with a fork. Turn out to a lightly floured surface, and knead lightly. Roll out to ¼-inch (1cm) thick, cut out scones, and put on greased and floured tray. Glaze the tops with milk, and bake in a very hot oven for 10 to 20 minutes.

MUFFINS

Wholemeal Muffins

½ cup butter
1 egg
1 cup milk
2 cups wholemeal self-raising
   flour
¼ cup raw sugar
¾ cup sultanas raisins
¼ pound (125g) grated cheese

Melt the butter. Mix all the ingredients in a bowl (except cheese). Lightly grease muffin tins. Spoon the mixture into the tins, and sprinkle with cheese. Bake for 15 minutes at 400°F (205°C).

Banana Muffins

Makes 18

1¼ cups wholemeal plain flour
1¼ cups wholemeal self-raising
   flour
1 teaspoon bicarbonate of soda
½ cup raw sugar
2 large mashed bananas
1 cup skim milk
1 egg
3 tablespoons melted butter

Combine the flours, soda and sugar. Make a well in the center and add the bananas, milk, egg and butter. Mix until all are combined. Grease muffin tins and bake at 350°F (180°C) for 20 to 25 minutes.

Oat Bran Muffins

3 cups oat bran
2 tablespoons baking powder
1 tablespoon cinnamon
¼ cup brown sugar
1½ cups skim milk
2 egg whites
2 tablespoons olive oil (cold
   pressed if possible)
½ cup chopped dates or
   sultanas, or 2 mashed
   bananas

Mix all the ingredients together as for other muffins. Bake for about 15 to 20 minutes at 350°F (180°C).

BASIC PANCAKES, CRÊPES AND WAFFLES

Basic Pancakes

4 tablespoons plain flour
1 egg
1 egg yolk
1 tablespoon oil
1 cup milk
Salt
Margarine or butter

Sift the flour into a bowl, and add the egg, egg yolk, oil, 2 tablespoons milk and the salt. Beat until smooth with a whisk. Add the remaining milk and allow to chill for half an hour. Grease a heavy skillet, pour thin batter layer and cook until golden brown.

Basic Crêpes

1¼ cups flour
Pinch of salt
3 beaten eggs
1½ cups milk
1 tablespoon brandy
2 teaspoons melted butter
Extra butter for frying

Sift the flour and salt into a bowl. Make a well in the center and add the eggs and milk. Use a wooden spoon and stir from the center to draw the flour in gradually. Add the brandy. Beat well and allow to stand for 1 hour. Heat a little butter in a small skillet and pour off excess. Pour about 1 tablespoon of batter into the pan. Rotate the pan quickly to coat the pan bottom thinly and pour off excess batter. Heat gently and when small bubbles appear after about a minute flip the crêpe over and cook for another 30 seconds.

Basic Waffles

Just heaven if you've stored up with maple syrup, but you can make do with brown sugar syrup.

2 eggs
1 tablespoon sugar
¾ cup milk
½ cup water
1 teaspoon vanilla
Pinch of salt
2 tablespoons corn flour
2 cups self-raising flour
4 ounces butter

Separate the eggs. Beat the yolks and sugar together, and add the milk, water, vanilla and salt. Beat once again. Add sifted corn flour and self-raising flour, then pour in melted butter. Beat mixture well. Lastly fold in stiffly beaten egg whites. Allow the mixture to stand for 10 minutes. The key to good waffles is that the butter must be fairly thin. Spoon into a very hot and greased waffle iron, and cook until crisp and golden brown. Serve with ice cream, maple syrup or boat made brown sugar syrup.

Waffle Brown Sugar Syrup

½ pound (250g) brown sugar
2 tablespoons water
1 tablespoon butter
½ teaspoon vanilla

Boil the brown sugar and water for 5 minutes, then add the butter and vanilla.

Griddle Cakes

1 egg
1½ cups milk
1 tablespoon melted butter
2 cups plain flour
3 teaspoons baking powder
½ teaspoon salt
1 dessert spoon sugar

Combine well beaten egg, milk and butter. Add to the sifted dry ingredients and beat until smooth. Drop spoonfuls onto lightly greased but hot skillet, and cook until bubbles on top burst, turn and cook the other side.

COOKIES, CAKES AND TARTS

Biscuits and boat baked cookies are the snacker's greatest friend. In the days of sail, ships biscuits or hard tack were an essential part of the sailors' diet. There are so many to make or try and the following are just a few tried and proven ones.

Australian Anzac Biscuits

1 cup rolled oats
1 cup plain flour
1 cup sugar
¾ cup coconut
¼ pound (125g) butter
2 tablespoons golden syrup
½ teaspoon bicarbonate of soda
1 tablespoon boiling water

Combine the oats, sifted flour, sugar and coconut. Combine the butter and golden syrup, and stir over low heat until melted. Mix the soda with boiling water. Add to the melted butter mixture. Stir in the dry ingredients. Lightly grease an oven tray and put tablespoons of mixture on the tray. Allow room for spreading. Cook in oven at 300°F (150°C) for 20 minutes. Loosen from the tray while warm, and cool on trays.

Cornflake Cookies

¼ pound (125g) butter
½ cup lightly packed brown sugar
½ cup caster sugar
½ cup coconut
3 cups cornflakes
½ cup mixed nuts
1 egg

Combine the butter, brown and caster sugars in a bowl. Gently heat until butter is melted, then stir in coconut, cornflakes, nuts and the lightly beaten egg. Lightly grease a baking tray, and drop tablespoons of mixture about 2 inches (5 cm) apart. Press the mixture together lightly with fingers. Bake in a moderate oven 350°F (180°C) for about 10 minutes until golden brown. Let it stand for a few minutes until biscuits firm up and cool on wire rack.

Muesli Cookies

1 cup muesli
1 cup coconut
1 cup rolled oats
½ cup self-raising flour
½ cup raw sugar
¼ cup sesame seeds
1 tablespoon honey
1 egg
6 ounces (180g) butter

Combine the muesli, coconut, oats, sifted flour, sugar and sesame seeds in a bowl. Make a well in the center, and add the honey, egg and melted butter. Mix well. Lightly grease a baking tray, and drop tablespoons of the mixture onto the tray. Bake at 350°F (180°C) for 10 to 15 minutes, and cool on trays.

Raisin Cookies

¼ pound butter
¾ cup sugar
1 egg
¾ cup chopped raisins or dates
¼ cup walnuts
1 cup self-raising flour
Crushed cornflakes

Mix the butter and sugar to a creamy consistency. Add the egg, raisins, walnuts and flour. Take large tablespoons of the mixture and roll in lightly crushed cornflakes. Bake in a moderate oven until golden.

Swiss Honey Biscuits

2 tablespoons milk
1 egg
½ cup sugar
Honey
2 cups plain flour
1 cup melted butter
¼ teaspoon ground cinnamon
¼ teaspoon cloves
¼ teaspoon nutmeg

Mix the milk, egg and sugar together. Add the honey and stir. Work the flour and spices in gradually until the mixture forms a dough and allow to stand for 4 hours. Roll out the dough to about ⅓-inch (1cm) thickness, cut into shapes. Put on a baking tray and put in a preheated oven of 350°F (180°C) for about 30 minutes or until brown.

Peanut Cookies

¼ pound (125g) butter
½ cup firmly packed brown
   sugar
1 egg
1 cup self-raising flour
½ teaspoon bicarbonate of
   soda
½ cup rolled oats
½ cup coconut
½ cup salted peanuts
⅓ cup finely crushed cornflakes

Cream the butter and sugar until light and fluffy. Add the egg and beat well. Fold in the sifted flour and soda. Add the rolled oats, coconut, peanuts, cornflakes, and mix well. Lightly grease an oven tray, and put tablespoons of mixture on the tray. Allow room for spreading. Sprinkle extra crushed cornflakes over the top. Bake in oven at 350°F (180°C) for 10 to 12 minutes until golden brown.

Citrus Cookies

2 ounces (60g) margarine or
   butter
1 teaspoon grated lemon rind
½ cup sugar
1 egg
3 teaspoons strained orange
   juice
1¼ cups plain flour
½ teaspoon baking powder
Pinch of salt
Extra sugar and grated lemon
   rind
Icing sugar

Soften the butter, add the lemon rind, then beat in the sugar. Add the egg and beat. Stir in the strained orange juice. Sift the flour, baking powder and salt together, and add to the butter mixture to make a dough. Wrap the dough and chill for 3 hours or until it is firm enough to roll. Roll the dough out, half at one time onto a lightly floured board. Roll to around ⅓-inch thickness. Cut into shapes, and place on an ungreased tray. If frosting is not required, sprinkle tops with sugar and finely grated lemon rind. Bake in a hot oven for 8 to 10 minutes.

Chocolate Banana Cookies

¼ pound (125g) margarine
½ cup caster sugar
⅓ cup brown sugar
1 egg
¼ cup mashed banana
1 cup self-raising flour
½ cup chocolate chips
½ cup rolled oats

Cream the margarine and sugars until they are fluffy. Add the egg, banana, followed by the flour, chocolate chips and oats. Drop a teaspoon of the mixture on a baking tray, then cook in the oven at 350°F (180°C) for about 20 minutes.

Oat Pecan Chocolate Chip Cookies

¼ pound (125g) softened
   butter
⅔ cup soft brown sugar
½ cup sugar
1 egg
1 teaspoon vanilla essence
1½ cups instant oats
½ cup plain flour
1 teaspoon baking powder
⅔ cup dark chocolate chips
¾ cup chopped pecans
¾ cup chopped seeded raisins

Cream the butter and sugar until light and fluffy. Beat the egg and vanilla, then mix in the remaining ingredients. Drop rounded tablespoons of dough onto a greased baking tray. Bake for around 15 minutes at 350°F (180°C) or until golden brown. Allow to cool on wire rack.

Chocolate Banana Cake

¾ pound (375g) margarine
1 cup sugar
2 eggs
Vanilla
2 cups self-raising flour
3 mashed bananas
1 tablespoon cocoa
1 teaspoon bicarbonate of soda
Milk

Cream the margarine and sugar, then add the eggs, vanilla and half the flour. Add the mashed bananas, followed by the remaining flour and the cocoa. Dissolve the bicarbonate in 6 tablespoons milk. Finally add the milk and soda and combine. Place the mixture in a 9-inch square cake tin and bake at 350°F (180°C) for 40 minutes.

Impossible Tart
(Beryl on *Dionysus*)

4 eggs
2 cups milk
½ cup plain flour
Vegetables (onions, peppers, mushrooms)
Bacon, meat or cheese (optional)

For a Savoury Dish: Beat eggs, milk and add flour and seasoning (any mixture of vegetables, along with meat, lightly fried bacon, etc.). Put in a greased dish and cook in a low oven for 40 minutes.

For a Dessert Dish: Use honey, coconut, raisins, dates, cinnamon, apple instead of vegetables and meat.

Chocolate Bread Slice
(Rosemary and John on *Sokari*)

1 pound (500g) bread + 1 slice
2 tablespoons heaped cocoa
1 pound (500g) mixed dried fruit
10 ounces (300g) white sugar
3 eggs
2 ounces (60g) milk powder
¼ pound (125g) butter
½ pound (250g) chopped walnuts
1 cup (big) sweet sherry
½ pound (250g) self-raising flour

Chop bread into small pieces, and cover with water for a short period. Squeeze out excess water gently. Place into a mixing bowl. Add all the ingredients except the flour. Mix well then add the flour. Combine until the mixture is soft but not runny. If it is too hard add some extra milk. Grease a baking tray and place a layer of brown paper on the bottom. Add the mixture and bake for 1 hour at 350°F (180°C). Allow to cool and cut into slices when cold.

Banana Cake
(Maureen on *Bohemian Rhapsody*)

¼ pound (125g) butter
1 cup sugar
2 eggs
3 mashed bananas
Nutmeg
Cinnamon
1 level teaspoon baking soda
2 tablespoons boiling milk
½ pound (250g) flour
2 teaspoons baking powder

Cream butter and sugar together. Add eggs, bananas and spices. Add soda dissolved in milk. Add flour and baking powder. Mix well. Bake 40 to 45 minutes in moderate oven. Eat plain or ice the top.

Coconut Cake

1 cup coconut
2 eggs
⅓ cup oil
½ cup soft brown sugar
2 cups self-raising flour
2 tablespoons powdered milk
2 teaspoons cardamom
1 teaspoon cinnamon

Grate fresh coconut and combine with the eggs, oil, and brown sugar. Sift flour, milk into a bowl and add cinnamon and cardamom. Add the other ingredients and blend well. Bake in a preheated oven 350°F (180°C) for 45 minutes.

PUDDINGS

Some people cannot live without desserts, although most cruising folk opt for single course meals. Nevertheless these recipes are economic essentials.

Nothing Pudding

2 cups soft white breadcrumbs
1 teaspoon bicarbonate of soda
1 cup milk
1 large mashed banana
1 cup mixed dried fruit
Lemon rind

Mix all the ingredients together, and put in a greased pudding pan. Cover with 2 thicknesses of greased greaseproof paper. Steam in a pan of boiling water for 2 hours.

Bread Pudding

3 large eggs
1¼ cups sugar
1½ teaspoons vanilla essence
1¼ teaspoons nutmeg
1¼ teaspoons cinnamon
¼ cup unsalted butter
2 cups milk
½ cup raisins
½ cup pecans
5 cups stale crusty bread

Beat the eggs until they are frothy, and volume increases threefold. Add the sugar, spices and butter and beat well. Blend in the milk. Add the raisins. Dry roast pecans in a skillet, chop coarsely and add. Butter a baking dish. Cut bread into cubes, and put the cubes in the dish. Pour in the egg mixture and toss until bread is soaked. Let stand for 45 minutes, stirring occasionally. Preheat oven to 300°F (150°C). Bake for 40 minutes and increase temperature to 420°F (220°C) for 20 minutes until pudding rises and browns.

Bread and Butter Pudding

4 slices thin buttered bread
1 tablespoon sultanas raisins
2 teaspoon mixed peel
Raw sugar

Custard

2 eggs
2 cups milk
Vanilla flavoring
1 tablespoon raw sugar

Cut up bread into quarters. Place a layer into a greased pie dish. Sprinkle layer with sultanas, some peel and sugar. To prepare custard, lightly beat eggs. Put milk, vanilla and sugar into saucepan and heat to boiling. Pour into eggs and then stir well. Prepare the custard mixture and strain over top layer. Sprinkle with raw sugar, and bake at 350° (180°C) until custard sets and top browns.

Yorkshire Pudding

Simply yummy with a baked dinner, along with roast potatoes, sweet potatoes, pumpkin, peas and other vegetables.

1 cup plain flour
Pinch salt
1 egg
½ pint milk
Oil

Sift flour and salt into a bowl. Make a well in the center, and add the egg. Beat in the flour, and gradually add the milk. Beat constantly and combine the flour from sides of the bowl. After forming a thick batter, beat well for another 5 minutes, stir in the remaining milk, cover and refrigerate for 30 minutes. Put oil in a small baking dish and heat. When very hot, add the batter and bake in a hot oven 20 to 25 minutes until well browned.

Great Grandma's Christmas Plum Pudding

This recipe is from my mother. It is a family heirloom, handed down from my great grandmother and it dates back to last century. Before going away on an extended voyage, I always took one plum pudding with me for that Christmas away at sea. It does require a number of ingredients but if you are near a suitable supply source for these, I can assure you the results are well worth the effort. The plum pudding will last for a year or more so make one or several before the voyage.

½ loaf white bread
2 tablespoons plain flour
1 teaspoon bicarbonate of soda
1 teaspoon mixed spice
½ pound (250g) sultanas
½ pound (250g) raisins
¼ pound (125g) currants
¼ pound (125g) red cherries
¼ pound (125g) figs glacés
¼ pound (125g) apricots glacés
¼ pound (125g) pineapple glacé
¼ pound (125g) dates
½ pound (250g) butter
½ pound (250g) soft brown sugar
6 eggs
2 cups sherry

Grate bread into fine soft breadcrumbs, and put in a large bowl. Sift in plain flour, bicarbonate of soda and the spice into a large bowl, and add the fruits. Make sure that each piece of fruit is coated with flour, as this is the secret of the pudding. Cream the butter and sugar together well, and add eggs to form a light and fluffy mixture. Add half breadcrumbs and half the flour and fruit mixture. Mix and then add the remaining half of breadcrumbs and fruit and flour mixture. Finally add a cup of sherry and mix well to a smooth consistency. Grease a large steaming bowl, and put in the mixture. It should come to around ¾ up the side. Place butter paper on mixture top, a double layer of foil, and then a tea towel. Tie up well, as no water must get in to the mixture. Steam for 6 hours. When cooked pour over another cup of sherry.

Chapter 11

Curries, Salsas, Dips, Marinades, Jams and Pickles

Sample the great flavors of the world. They will enhance any meal, on board as well as ashore.

CURRIES

Indian cuisine is my favorite, and it is easy to prepare on board with tremendous variety. What Indian food is all about is a subtle blend of flavors, and you can make a fine meal out of nearly anything. Curry is the mainstay of Indian cooking, and the following are easy recipes and methods.

Basic Curry Recipe

Serves 4 to 6

This basic recipe can be used for all curries, simply vary the style by adding yogurt for chicken and lamb, coconut cream or coconut milk for prawns and fish. Seafood curries also benefit from the addition of lemon juice.

2 tablespoons ghee
2 large and finely chopped onions
3 garlic cloves
4 curry leaves
6 cardamom pods
1 cinnamon stick
1½ teaspoons fresh ginger
3 tablespoons curry powder
1 teaspoon chili powder
2 teaspoons salt
1 can chopped tomatoes
2 tablespoons chopped fresh coriander
1 chicken cut in pieces, or 2 pounds lamb shoulder cubes, or 2 pounds raw prawns
2 teaspoons garam masala
Yogurt, coconut cream (optional)

Heat the ghee in large saucepan, and gently sauté onion, garlic, curry leaves, cardamom pods, cinnamon stick and ginger until soft and golden. Stir well. The secret of good curry is very slow cooking at this stage. Add the curry powder, chili, and stir for one minute, making sure that ghee and powder all mix in a thick paste. Add the salt, tomatoes, coriander and cook to a pulp. Stir well. Add the chicken (or lamb or prawns) and stir well to coat chicken with mixture. Cover and simmer on low heat for 45 minutes or until meats are tender. Make sure that the mixture does not stick and burn on pan base. Add the garam masala for the last 5 minutes together with yogurt or the coconut cream if used, and simmer uncovered. Sprinkle with fresh coriander or mint.

Curried Crab

Serves 4

The best crab I ever had was in Chittagong, Bangladesh. This recipe will bring back that superb culinary memory.

4 medium sized crabs
3 tablespoons curry paste or powder
1 teaspoon grated lime rind
1 finely chopped medium onion
1 clove finely chopped garlic
1 cup thick coconut milk
6 lime leaves
3 tablespoons grated lemon rind
2 sliced red chilies
3 cups thin coconut milk

Clean, halve and crack crabs. Combine the curry paste, grated rind, onion and garlic in a bowl. Heat the thick coconut milk in a skillet or wok until it goes oily. Stir in the curry mixture and combine the flavors. Add lime leaves, lemon rind, chilies and thin coconut milk. Finally add the crab pieces and simmer for 15 minutes.

Chicken Curry

Serves 4

When I was in the merchant marine, with our Indian or Bangladeshi crew and cooks, chicken curry was the Sunday treat. We had only limited refrigerator and freezer storage space and during the week we ate a variety of other curries.

1 chicken
3 tablespoons ghee
2 large and finely chopped onions
3 garlic cloves
1½ teaspoons ginger
3 tablespoons curry powder
1 teaspoon chili powder
3 teaspoons salt
1 can tomatoes
2 tablespoons chopped fresh coriander
2 teaspoons garam masala
½ cup plain yogurt

Cut chicken into serving sizes. Heat the ghee in a large saucepan, and gently sauté onion, garlic, and ginger until soft and golden. Stir well. Add curry powder, chili, and stir for one minute. Add salt, tomatoes, coriander and cook to a pulp. Stir well. Add the chicken pieces and stir well to coat chicken with mixture. Cover and simmer on slow heat for 45 minutes or until chicken is tender and starting to come off the bone. Make sure that the mixture does not stick and burn on pan base. Add the garam masala in the last 5 minutes with the yogurt, and simmer uncovered. Sprinkle with fresh coriander or mint.

Potato and Eggplant Curry

Serves 4 to 6

1 pound (500g) potatoes
1 large eggplant
Salt
1 finely chopped onion
1 teaspoon minced garlic
1 teaspoon minced ginger
2 tablespoons olive oil
2 teaspoons ground cumin
2 teaspoons chopped fresh chili
1 tablespoon chopped fresh
   coriander
1 cup chicken stock
1 cup coconut milk

Wash the potatoes and chop into cubes, leaving the skins. Simmer in water and boil very lightly for 20 minutes. Cut the eggplant into cubes. Sprinkle cubes with salt, put in a colander and let stand for 20 minutes to allow bitter juices to drain away. Wash thoroughly in clean water, and drain on paper towel. Make a curry sauce by cooking onion, garlic, ginger, and a tablespoon of oil on low heat for 5 minutes. Add cumin, chili, coriander, stock and coconut milk and simmer very slowly. Cook eggplant pieces in remaining oil, brown and soften them but do not cook them completely. Put potatoes and eggplants in casserole dish or heavy saucepan, cover with sauce, and cook slowly on low heat 30 to 40 minutes. Garnish with fresh coriander.

SALSAS AND DIPS

Bring things to life with a salsa, let your favorite meats soak in a marinade, or dunk something into a flavorsome dip. Try these treats.

Salsa

Salsa sounds so much more exciting than sauce, and conjures up vibrant images of South and Central America. Throw away your ketchup, real cruisers only eat salsa! It is easy to make by hand, or really simplify things and get yourself a small Cuisinart, and make any salsa you like. You can make salsa out of plantain bananas, mangoes, pineapples, and anything you like. (See recipe in Fruits section). Salsa often implies hot and spicy. It really depends on your taste and choice of chilies. Go for mild heat with jalapeño or serrano chilies. Go for afterburn with Caribbean Scotch Bonnets or Mexican Habaneros. To turn the heat down, add more olive oil or tomato purée. Remember to wear gloves when handling chilies, and to keep the heat down, remove all seeds and heat causing veins.

Peanut Salsa

Pour this sauce on satays, it is delicious!

2 medium fresh tomatoes
1 onion
2 cups water
2 cloves crushed garlic
1 tablespoon soy sauce
Chili powder to taste
1½ cups crunchy peanut butter

Blend the tomatoes, onion and water in a blender for 3 minutes. Pour the mixture into a saucepan and warm over medium heat. Add the garlic, soy sauce, chili powder and bring to a boil. Simmer for just one minute. Blend in the peanut butter and stir constantly until the mixture boils and thickens. Cool and use with satays.

Vietnamese Nuoc Mam Salsa

This sauce is absolutely divine over chicken.

2 tablespoons sugar
2 tablespoons lime or lemon juice
1 garlic clove
6 tablespoons fish sauce
1 finely chopped fresh chili

Mix sugar and juice together until sugar is completely dissolved. Crush garlic and add to mixture. Add fish sauce and half the chili. Pour over some sauce on chicken, and reserve the rest to dip in.

Cajun Cocktail Salsa

Use as a dip with boiled and chilled shrimps and prawns, or pour over shellfish.

1½ cups ketchup
½ cup chili sauce
½ teaspoon garlic powder
½ teaspoon onion powder
1 tablespoon lemon juice
2 teaspoons Worcestershire sauce
¼ teaspoon Tabasco sauce
¼ teaspoon ground black pepper
2 tablespoons horseradish

Put all the ingredients in a bowl and whisk until well mixed. Cover the mixture and refrigerate until chilled.

Mojo Latino Salsa

¾ cup olive oil
½ cup fresh lime juice
2 tablespoons crushed garlic
1 tablespoon ground cumin
2 tablespoons chopped oregano
1 tablespoon salt

Whisk the oil, lime juice, garlic, cumin, oregano and salt together until well blended. Allow to stand for 4 hours, refrigerate until ready to use.

Chimichurri
(Argentina)

This great salsa is a natural with barbecued meats. The galley made version tastes just great. Or sail on down to Buenos Aires and try it yourself.

6 tablespoons olive oil
4 tablespoons red wine vinegar
3 tablespoons finely chopped onions
3 cloves crushed garlic
3 tablespoons chopped fresh parsley
½ teaspoon oregano
1 finely chopped jalapeño chili
½ teaspoon salt
½ teaspoon black pepper

Whisk the oil and vinegar together. Add the onions, garlic, parsley, oregano, chili, salt and fresh ground pepper. Stir well to combine all the ingredients. Allow salsa to stand for 4 hours before use. Refrigerate until ready to use.

Barbecue Salsa

½ cup chili sauce
2 teaspoons dark brown sugar
1 teaspoon Dijon mustard
1½ tablespoons lemon juice
2 tablespoons molasses
1½ tablespoons light soy sauce
1 clove crushed garlic
2 tablespoons water
Tabasco sauce
½ teaspoon salt
1 teaspoon Worcestershire sauce

Mix all the ingredients in a heavy pan. Bring mixture to a boil and stir to dissolve the sugar. Reduce the heat and simmer 12 to 15 minutes. Reduce further if the mixture is still thin. Alternatively add water if too thick. Sieve the sauce and use to paint barbecue meats and chicken both before cooking and to baste during cooking.

Hummus Dip

1 cup chickpeas
3 cups water
¼ cup lemon juice
¼ cup olive oil
2 cloves chopped garlic
2 tablespoons extra water
½ teaspoon salt
Ground sweet paprika

Soak chickpeas in water for 4 hours or overnight. Drain, put in a pan, add the water and bring to a boil. Simmer uncovered for one hour then drain. Put chickpeas, lemon juice, olive oil, garlic, water and salt in a blender or food processor. Blend using the pulse action for 30 seconds until smooth. Sprinkle with paprika and serve with pita bread.

MARINADES

Marinades make good food even better. You can marinade in anything but personally I think the ideal marinade containers are those from Tupperware. You can easily turn the food without spilling, especially when cooking for a large group, or doing a whole fish.

Spicy Marinade

This marinade works well for lamb, beef and pork.

4 tablespoons sherry, red wine or mirin
1 tablespoon soy sauce
1 tablespoon honey
½ teaspoon chili powder
1 tablespoon fresh chopped coriander
1 teaspoon minced garlic
2 tablespoons olive oil (sesame or peanut for a taste variation)

Combine all ingredients well in a bowl and pour over chicken or fish. Place in a refrigerator for at least 2 to 4 hours or preferably overnight. Turn several times.

Honey Sesame Marinade

This is a marinade for chicken.

½ cup soy sauce
½ cup sherry
3 tablespoons honey
2 tablespoons sesame seeds
2 teaspoons sesame oil
1 teaspoon 5-spice power

Combine all ingredients well in a bowl and pour over chicken. Place in a refrigerator for at least 2-4 hours or preferably overnight. Turn several times.

Lebanese Chicken Marinade

3 tablespoons lime juice
1 teaspoon ground coriander
1 teaspoon ground cumin
½ teaspoon turmeric
1 tablespoon chopped mint

Combine all ingredients well in a bowl. Add chicken fillet strips and leave in a refrigerator for at least 4 hours or preferably overnight. Great for either barbecued chicken, or alternatively for pan frying in olive oil.

Chicken Marinade

½ cup red wine
2 tablespoons oil
2 tablespoons brown sugar
1 tablespoon soy sauce
2 tablespoons tomato paste
1 teaspoon minced garlic
½ teaspoon ground ginger
½ teaspoon paprika

Combine all ingredients well in a bowl. Add chicken fillet strips and leave in a refrigerator for at least 4 hours or preferably overnight. Great for either barbecued chicken, or alternatively for pan frying in olive oil.

Lebanese Fish Marinade

2 tablespoons olive oil
1 clove crushed garlic
1 tablespoon chopped coriander
2 teaspoons ground cumin
1 teaspoon ground black pepper

Combine all ingredients well in a bowl. Brush fish fillets and put in refrigerator for at least 4 hours or preferably overnight. Ideal for use with fish kebabs.

White Wine Marinade

This marinade works well with fish and chicken too.

⅔ cup white wine or ⅓ cup
   lemon juice
⅓ cup wine vinegar
1 tablespoon olive oil
1 small sliced onion
1 bay leaf
1 tablespoon chopped parsley
1 sliced carrot
Fresh ground black pepper

Combine all ingredients well in a bowl and pour over chicken or fish. Refrigerate for at least 2 to 4 hours or preferably overnight.

Lamb Satay Marinade

1 peeled onion
2 cloves peeled garlic
1 to 2 red chilies
2 tablespoons desiccated
   coconut
2 tablespoons lemon juice
1 tablespoon soy sauce

Process all ingredients in a blender. Marinate meat cubes for 30 minutes.

JAMS AND PICKLES

Making jams and pickles out of plentiful and cheap fruits can be worthwhile. The following give a few useful ways.

Banana Chutney

12 medium bananas
2½ cups malt vinegar
1 cup stoned and halved dates
1 cup raisins
1 tablespoon salt
1 cup sugar
1 tablespoon cinnamon
1 teaspoon nutmeg
2 teaspoons turmeric

Peel and slice the bananas. Put in a saucepan with half the vinegar. Bring to a boil and then simmer. Stir and cook for 5 minutes. Add rest of vinegar and stir 3 to 4 minutes. Add remainder of ingredients and simmer for an hour (stirring occasionally). Put into warm, sterilised jars and seal air tight.

Pineapple Chutney

2 medium pineapples
¾ cup cider vinegar
½ cup lemon juice
1 small finely chopped onion
2 small finely chopped red
   chilies
¾ cup raisins or sultanas
¾ cup brown sugar
2 teaspoons salt
2 teaspoons ground ginger
4 cloves
¼ teaspoon cayenne pepper
¼ teaspoon nutmeg

Halve the pineapples, and remove flesh. Put into a saucepan with vinegar, lemon juice, onion, chilies, raisins, and sugar. Stir over low heat 8 to 10 minutes. Add rest of ingredients, and cook gently for 1½ to 2 hours. Stir occasionally. Put into warm, sterilised jars and seal air tight.

Mango Chutney

6 ripe firm mangoes
¼ pound (125g) dates
2 chilies
1 onion
1 teaspoon grated ginger
½ teaspoon salt
1 pint (½ lt) spiced vinegar

Peel and chop the mango flesh. Chop the dates, chilies and onions. Put all the ingredients into a saucepan, bring to a boil, and return to simmer for 1 hour. When mixture has a thick consistency pour into sterilized jars, then seal when cool.

Spiced Vinegar

2 pints (1lt) vinegar
¼ cup white sugar
1 cinnamon stick
8 cloves
½ tablespoon black
    peppercorns

Put all the ingredients into a saucepan and bring to a boil, simmer 10 minutes. Use as needed and bottle the rest.

Green Papaya Chutney

1 coarsely grated green papaya
¼ cup vinegar
1 teaspoon salt
1 teaspoon finely chopped
    ginger
Black pepper

Peel and remove papaya seeds. Grate the papaya, then add the other ingredients. Mix well and serve with curries.

Tomato and Pineapple Relish

2 pounds (1kg) peeled ripe
   tomatoes
2 large cooking apples
2 medium size onions
1 cup finely chopped pineapple
3 cups sugar
¾ cup sultanas and currants
1 tablespoon salt
1 tablespoon whole cloves
¼ teaspoon cayenne pepper
5 cups malt vinegar

Chop the tomatoes coarsely. Peel apples and onions and finely chop. Put all the ingredients except vinegar into pan. Add half the vinegar. Cook gently and stir for 5 minutes. Add rest of vinegar and stir over low heat until sugar has dissolved. Simmer 1½ hours. Put into warm, sterilized jars and seal air tight.

Lime Marmalade

10 small limes
2 pints (1lt) water
2 pounds (1kg) white sugar

Slice limes thinly and put in a plastic bowl. Cover with water and let stand for 12 hours. Put all into a saucepan, boil and then simmer for 45 minutes. Add the sugar, stir until completely dissolved,then boil for around 40 minutes. When it starts to set, pour into warmed jars and seal air tight.

Green Tomato Pickles

2 pounds green tomatoes
½ pound (250g) chopped
   onions
½ cup salt
½ pound (250g) white sugar
1½ cups white vinegar
¼ cup sultanas
2 tablespoons plain flour
1 tablespoon mustard
½ tablespoon curry powder
1 teaspoon turmeric
Black pepper

Cut tomatoes into small pieces, put into a bowl with onions, salt and enough boiling water to cover all. Allow to stand for 12 hours, then strain off the liquid. Put into a saucepan, then add the sugar, vinegar and sultanas. Boil, then remove from stove top and let stand for 5 minutes. Mix the flour, mustard and other spices with a little vinegar to make a paste, add to saucepan and boil for 5 minutes, remove and let stand for 5 minutes then bottle.

Chapter 12

Drinks

Tea

Coffee

Social Icebreakers

Alcoholic Drinks

Home Brewing

Tea has always been associated with the sea, from the clipper ships to the Boston Tea Party, and Sir Thomas Lipton...Social icebreakers are always welcome on board, whether needed or not.

TEA (CH'A, CHAYA, CHAI, THÉ)

Tea has its origins in China, and dates back to something like 3000 BC, before arriving in Japan around 800 AD. Tea conjures up images of graceful clipper ships such as the *Cutty Sark* and *Thermopylae*. The fact is whoever dominated the sea trade dominated the tea trade. The Dutch controlled it first, trading tea out of Amoy in the 16th century. This changed when the Portuguese got access to mainland china through Macau. Finally the English took over. Sir Thomas Lipton became a notable player in the latter tea trading days, and he is responsible for the America's cup, which he never claimed. The Duchess of Bedford made afternoon tea a standard ritual. After tea hit the American market, King George imposed a tax on tea. The American colonists promptly revolted. They put on their Indian fancy dress outfits, boarded the English vessels anchored in Boston, and threw all the tea over the side. This was a non too subtle and politically incorrect way of saying: Keep your tea, we are all drinking coffee from now on.

There are many tea varieties, and we all have a personal preference. You can choose Oolong, Yunnan, Darjeeling, Orange Pekoe, Lapsang Souchong, Assam, Irish Breakfast, a flavored Earl Grey, and many others. The true tea drinker will not use the yachties' best friend, the tea bag. If you are brewing a leaf tea in the pot, remember that black teas should be brewed for 3 to 5 minutes, while green and oolong brew only for 2 minutes. Use fresh boiling water, preheat the pot and the cups, put a teaspoon for each person and one for the pot before adding the water. Stir the pot before pouring. (Do not wash the tea pot with detergent, it will ruin it.)

Indian Iced Tea

2 teaspoons green tea
Boiling water
Fresh mint
Sugar
Rum (optional)

Prepare a pot of tea, ideally green tea. Add a sprig of fresh mint, or leaf from eucalyptus tree. Strain into a jug, and sweeten with some sugar. Allow to cool, then chill in the refrigerator for at least an hour. Serve over crushed ice with a wedge of lemon. For a real bite, add 2 tablespoons of rum just prior to serving.

Moroccan Mint Tea

2 teaspoons China tea
4 tablespoons chopped mint
Boiling water
Slice of lemon
Sugar

Prepare pot with tea and add the mint. Pour over boiling water and allow to stand for 5 minutes. Strain into cups and sugar to taste. Add a slice of lemon. For iced tea add in sugar to the pot, allow to cool and then strain over crushed ice. Serve with ice cubes.

COFFEE

Coffee has its origins in Arabia. History has it that an ancient Abyssinian goat herder was perplexed when his herd became hyperactive (having owned a goat herd, I find this truly an awe inspiring and frightening prospect). The caffeine rich berry was to blame. The Arabians cornered the market until enterprising Dutch traders smuggled plants to Java. The East India Company got very busy bringing Java coffee back to Europe. The French got interested and a French naval captain took a seedling to Martinique. It arrived only after many adventures: a Dutch spy tried to destroy it, pirates attacked the vessel, and a hurricane nearly sunk them. From Martinique, it got to Brazil, and eventually to America where it is the number one beverage. Popularity was boosted by the Boston Tea Party.

Coffee now grows in many locations around the world including New Guinea, Tanzania, Kenya, Mexico, and Ecuador, to name a few. The following are some well-known coffees:

Brazil The premium bean is Bourbon Santos, with a smooth and sweet bodied taste. A medium roasted Arabica bean.

Colombia Medellin Excelso is a dark roasted, coarse ground brew with a rich flavor. One of my personal favorites.

Costa Rica A brew with a full bodied, rich but nutty flavor. It is made with Arabica beans.

Dominican Republic Called Santo Domingos, it has a sweet and full bodied flavor.

Hawaii The best known is Kona, with a strong flavor, full bodied and mellow.

Jamaica The famous Blue Mountain variety, sweet, mellow, with a sense-numbing aroma. Not cheap, but one of the best.

Puerto Rico Available only locally, it is sweet and has a full and rich body.

Venezuela Called Maracaibo, it is rich with a delicate body and full of flavor.

Indonesia Java is still growing a thick, mellow, heavy bodied brew. Other premium varieties include Celebes and Sumatra.

You can rate a good crew on its ability to brew a good cup of coffee. Percolating is a favorite method, but the trick is not to overbrew. It is best to brew 6 to 8 minutes after percolation starts. I personally love thick Turkish style coffee where you can stand a teaspoon in it and it won't fall over. A simple mocca pot is the ideal and easy way. Unlike a percolator, the steam is forced through the grounds. Make sure you put water in before putting the pot on the stove to avoid disaster. Drip filter units are easy and quick, but the glass pots break. The same used to apply to the plunger, but I have now a new German fully insulated plunger unit (Kaffee Therm) which keeps the heat in to ensure a good brew and the extra cups stay hot for up to 2 hours. To improve the palatability of instant, freeze dried coffee, make the coffee in a pot. Heat the pot, add 1 teaspoon per cup, pour boiling water, stir and serve in preheated cups.

SOCIAL ICE BREAKERS

Citrus Granitas

1 cup caster sugar
2 cups water
½ cup freshly squeezed citrus
    juice

Stir the sugar into the water and bring slowly to a boil, stirring to dissolve the sugar. Add the citrus skins for flavor. Boil 2 minutes and leave to cool off. Strain off the skins and discard them. Stir in the juice and pour into a jug through a strainer. Pour into ice cube trays and freeze overnight. Crush 4 to 5 cubes at a time in an ice crusher or blender until evenly crushed. Spoon into long chilled glasses and serve with a straw.

Red Wine Granita

1 cup water
1 cup caster sugar
1 orange and 1 lemon
1 bottle light red wine

Stir water and sugar together in a heavy pan. Carefully pare the zest off the citrus fruits using a vegetable peeler. Add to the sugar mixture and bring slowly to a boil, stirring to dissolve the sugar. Boil for 2 minutes, and remove from heat and cool. Squeeze fruits and strain juice into syrup. Stir and strain through a fine sieve into a glass jug. Pour into ice cube trays and freeze overnight. Crush 4 to 5 cubes at a time in an ice crusher or blender until evenly crushed. Spoon into long chilled glasses and serve with a straw.

Mango Frappés

1 large mango
⅓ basket of strawberries
1 cup crushed ice
Sugar syrup to taste

Put all the ingredients into the blender, purée until smooth. Ha! Bliss! (Sugar syrup is made with equal quantities of caster sugar and boiling water, stirred until dissolved.)

Lemonade

Lemon juice
Sugar
Still or aerated water (soda
    stream or spritzer)

Add 3 tablespoons lemon juice to a chilled glass. Dissolve the sugar into the juice, add some ice, preferably crushed, and then put in chilled water. Put a wedge of lemon in the glass. As a guide, 1½ tablespoons lemon juice to 3 to 4 tablespoons sugar and ⅛ teaspoon salt to 1 cup water.

ALCOHOLIC DRINKS

The "happy hour" or "drinkies" is an important part of the cruising social life. Any time after 1200 hours, when the sun is well and truly over the yardarm, is an acceptable time to host a small and relaxing get-together. There is something magical about the ritualistic preparation of a favorite drink. Some drinks are an essential part of cruising. My personal favorite is the Margarita.

The Perfect Margarita

The following was extracted from the Parrot Head Handbook, which comes with Jimmy Buffet's quintessential cruising music 4 CD set, Boats, Bars, Beaches and Ballads on MCA and Margaritaville Records.

1 lime
Cuervo 1800
Jose Cuervo White
Roses Lime Juice
Bols Triple Sec
Bols Orange Curaçao

Fill shaker with broken ice. Squeeze 2 fresh lime wedges into shaker. Add 2 ounces of Cuervo 1800. Add ½ ounce of Jose Cuervo White. Add 1¼ ounces of Roses Lime Juice. Add ½ ounce of Bols Triple Sec. Add a splash of Bols Orange Curaçao. Cover shaker and vigorously shake mix. Rim the outside of the glass with lime peel and salt. Put in fresh ice. Strain the mixture over the ice. Squeeze in 1 lime wedge. Now sit back and savor the drink and sing along with Jimmy Buffet and Margaritaville, *Adios ground control.*

Standard Peasants Margarita

Lime or lemon wedge
Coarse salt
2 ounces tequila
⅓ cup lime or lemon juice
1 ounce Cointreau or Curaçao
Ice

Rub the rims of 2 glasses with the lime wedge. Dip the wet edges into coarse salt. Combine the tequila, lime juice, cointreau and ice in a shaker. Shake and strain into the glasses.

Kava

If you cruise the Pacific, you will inevitably run into kava. Mostly found in Samoa, Fiji and the central Pacific islands, this mixture is either made fresh or it even comes in an instant pack form. Traditionally, kava is used in greeting ceremonies and it is important to drink it; your hosts will be insulted if you don't. I personally don't find it too intoxicating. In Pohnpei (Ponape), they have a much stronger brew called "sakau." Like kava, it is made from the pulverised roots of the sakau plant. It is more potent because it is prepared and consumed immediately. Both are served in a half coconut shell.

Rum

Well, naturally rum would have its origins with sailors and explorers. The history books tell us that Columbus introduced sugar cane to the West Indies from the Canary Islands (originally it came from the Far East). Rum distillation started from cane sugar and by-products around the turn of the 17th century in Hispaniola. Evidently this was pretty rough stuff but, as it improved, sailors developed a taste for it, and subsequently introduced it to England, Spain and France. The Caribbean has been long recognized as the home of rum. My personal favorite is one that I acquired a taste for in the merchant marine, aptly named "Four Bells," smooth as silk! Australia, being a sugar producer, also has a fine local rum that is affectionately known as "Bundy," an abbreviation of Bundaberg Rum. Puerto Rico is the largest rum producer, followed by Jamaica. Other fine rums are made in Trinidad, Barbados (Mount Gay) and Guyana. Tortola in the British Virgin Islands is the home of British Royal Navy Pusser's Rum. This rum like another from Martinique (Negrita) is distilled from cane juice, rather than molasses.

Royal Navy Rum Terms

The following was extracted off a small flask of Pusser's Rum that I have:

Grog: Traditionally this consisted of 2 parts of water with 1 part of Pusser's Rum.
Tot: ⅛th pint of rum, which was the standard daily ration.
Sippers: A small, and gentlemanly sip from a friend's rum issue.
Gulpers: A single large swallow from another's tot.
Sandy Bottoms: To finish off whatever is left in a mug when offered by a friend.
Splice the Main Brace: This is an invitation aboard for a drink.
Long Swig at the Halliards: Means to "tie one on."

Rum is used a lot in cookery. On board use it to flavor sweet potatoes, pineapples, bananas and fruit salads. Also add it to marinades and sauces for extra flavor and aroma. Of course the other use of rum is to drink it, either a traditional Cuba Libre, or in a punch. White rum is often used in punches but these recipes use dark rum. Of course Kahlúa and Tia Maria are wonderful rum liqueurs.

Trinidad Rum Punch

1 quart water
1 pound (500g) sugar
1 bottle dark Caribbean rum
Juice of 8 limes or lemons
Several dashes Angostura
  bitters
Nutmeg or ginger

Heat water until boiling. Add the sugar. Stir until sugar dissolves, then add the rum, lime juice and Angosturas. Serve cold in a tall glass, and sprinkle with nutmeg or ginger.

Planters Punch

Juice of 1 lime
2 teaspoons caster sugar
2 ounces dark rum
Dash of Angostura bitters
Soda water
Slice of lemon

Fill three quarters of a tall glass with crushed ice. Pour the lime juice, caster sugar, rum, bitters and stir until glass is frosted. Top up with soda water while stirring. Serve with a slice of lemon.

Barbados Coconut Rum Punch

3 teaspoons syrup
1 teaspoon lime juice
4 teaspoons rum (light or dark)
½ cup young coconut juice

To make the syrup, dissolve 4 parts sugar into 2 parts water. Put all the ingredients into a cocktail shaker along with ice cubes. Strain into a long cool glass and enjoy.

Hot Buttered Rum

An essential soul restorer for those cold, wet nights.

¼ cup dark rum
Cinnamon stick
Twist of lemon peel
2 cloves
1 bottle cider
1 tablespoon unsalted butter
Sugar
Nutmeg

Put the rum, cinnamon, peel and cloves into a large mug. Heat the cider until it boils. Pour into mug with other ingredients. Add butter and stir, sugar to taste. Sprinkle with nutmeg. Feel the warmth return.

HOME BREWING

Beer (Birra, Cerveza, Bière, Bier)

Beer is available wherever you cruise. There is nothing so refreshing as an ice cold beer after a hot tropical day in paradise. Most cruisers will delight in sampling the local brews; almost every country, however small, has a local brewery. In the Caribbean, for example, currently available brews are Piton Lager in St Lucia, Red Stripe in Jamaica; Trinidad has Carib, Barbados has Banks and Tiltman, St Vincent has Hairoun and Antigua has Wadadli's. In Martinique you find Bière Lorraine. Give the local breweries a taste. But beer costs can blow out a cruising budget. You can save a lot by brewing your own beer. Most kits and cans of beer mixture are easy to use following instructions. The essential rules are to ensure sterility of all items used in making the brew, maintain correct temperatures when brewing and lastly bottle correctly.

Bottling

Traditionally you can use brown bottles, however the Dutch brewers Grolsch have great little bottles with integral clamp on lids which are perfect for yachts. Another successful method is using Coke or other PET plastic screw top bottles. I have found this works well.

Beer Faults

- **Beer is too gassy** It is either a result of excessive sugar or incomplete fermentation.
- **Beer lacks head** Froth has been lost either through the fermenter air lock or lost during bottling. Never skim off the head.
- **Excess water added** This will produce a thin, bland beer with minimal head retention.
- **Unpleasant odor** Usually because of poor cleaning and sterilization.

Acknowledgments and References

The Book of Coffee, Jacki Baxter. Quintet Publishing, 1995.

Colin Spencer's Vegetable Book, Colin Spencer. Conran Octopus, 1995. A very useful guide.

The Complete Asian Cookbook, Charmaine Soloman. Summit, 1975. This book is my favorite. Indispensable on any yacht, Asian cookery at its very best.

The Complete Caribbean Cookbook, Pamela Lalbachan. Lansdowne, 1994. A culinary voyage, great onboard reference for the region.

Larousse Gastronomique. Hamlyn, 1989. The greatest cookery encyclopedia ever, do not sail away without a copy! Pack it in the panic bag, a desert island best book selection.

Latin American Cookbook, Lynette Tume. Ure Smith, 1979. A good introduction to South American cuisine.

Lonely Planets Guides for South America, Fiji, Vanuatu, Tahiti and French Polynesia, Micronesia, Tonga, Samoa. I strongly suggest you carry a copy of every area you plan to visit. Good general and useful food information.

The Marine Electrical and Electronics Bible, John C. Payne. Sheridan House, 1994.

A Taste of Africa, Dorinda Hafner. Simon and Schuster, 1994. (A culinary adventure, this book is essential.)

Special thanks to the following people:

Joanna Harrop, Charlie and Pauline Taylor, Betony Bickford, Karen Truelove, Frank Thomson, Angelina, Bertolli (olive oils), Nestlé, SPC Foods, Australian Meat and Livestock Corporation, Queensland Fruit and Vegetable Growers Co-operative, Cruising World Magazine, MCA Records, Cruising Equipment Company, Broadwater Stoves, Prestige (pressure cookers), Islands Magazine, and the countless magazines and newpapers from which recipes were found, tried and adapted, and the patient chefs and cooks who showed me so much. Thank you all!

Extra special thanks to Greg Horder for his wonderful cartoons.

A

African Okra Stew 153
African Spinach and
  Coconut 145
American Lobster 83
American Samoa 38
American Spareribs 105
Angelina's Filipina
  Chicken 97
Antigua 37
Apples 173
  Apple Fritters 173
Australia 41
Australian Anzac Biscuits 200
Australian Damper 195
Avocados
  Avocado Fettuccine 125
  Avocado Snacks 174
  Avocado Toasties 174
  Guacamole 174
Azores 42

B

Bacon
  Breakfast Fritters 46
  Egg and Bacon Pie 47
  Impossible Tart 204
Bahamas 37
Baked Banana Dessert 177
Baked Bananas 176
Baked Beans
  Baked Bean and Corn
    Chowder 137
  Baked Bean and Sausage
    Hot Pot 137
  Baked Bean Con
    Carne 138
  Baked Bean Dhal 136
  Baked Bean Rissoles 137
  Corn and Baked Bean
    Casserole 138
Baked Eggplant and
  Tomatoes 152

Baked Mussels 68
Baked Papaya Slices 182
Baked Pumpkin 159
Baked Sweet Potatoes 158
Baked Zucchini 163
Balearics 42
Bananas
  Baked Banana Dessert 177
  Baked Bananas 176
  Banana and Ginger
    Fillets 58
  Banana Butter 176
  Banana Cake 205
  Banana Chutney 220
  Banana Coconut Cream
    Pie 175
  Banana Fritter Surprise 177
  Banana Fritters 175
  Banana Muffins 197
  Banana Whisk 177
  Chocolate Banana
    Cake 204
  Chocolate Banana
    Cookies 203
  Whipped Bananas 177
Barbados Coconut Rum
  Punch 232
Barbecue 112
  Barbecue Salsa 216
  Barbecued Chicken 113
  Barbecued Chicken
    Wings 96
  Barbecued Eggplant 151
  Barbecued Thai Garlic
    Chicken 97
  Brazilian Beef
    Brochette 112
  Chicken Satays 114
  Chicken Yakitori 114
  Steak 112
  Tropical Chicken
    Kebabs 113
Basic Crêpes 198
Basic Curry Recipe 211
Basic Fish Cooking 56
Basic Frittata 47

Basic Pancakes 198
Basic Rissole 110
Basic Vinaigrette 188
Basic Waffles 199
**Beans (*See Baked Beans
  also*)**
  Bean and Spinach
    Lasagne 124
  Chili Bean Filled
    Potatoes 156
  Chili Beans 132
  Lima Bean and Tomato
    Casserole 134
  Louisiana Red Beans and
    Rice 133
  Navy Bean Soup 135
  Potato and Bean Salad 185
  Pressure Cooker Ham and
    Three Bean Soup 134
  Rice and Bean Soup 121
Beef
  American Spareribs 105
  Baked Bean Con
    Carne 138
  Basic Rissole 110
  Beef or Lamb Koftas 105
  Brazilian Beef
    Brochette 112
  Canned Corned Beef
    Packages 106
  Chili Bean Rissole 110
  Oriental Rissole 110
  Osso Bucco Casserole 111
  Stir Fry Beef and
    Broccoli 107
  Stir Fry Oriental Beef 107
**Beer (Birra, Cerveza, Bière,
  Bier) 233**
Beer Batter 63
Bouillabaisse, Caribbean 84
Brazilian Baked Lobster and
  Pineapple 82
Brazilian Beef Brochette 112
Bread
  Australian Damper 195
  Banana Muffins 197

Bread Trouble
    Shooting 194
Foolproof Scones 196
Indian Chapattis 194
Indian Fried Bread 194
Irish Beer Bread 192
Oat Bran Muffins 197
Pita Bread 195
Pressure Cooker or Dutch
    Oven Bread 191
Saltwater Bread 191
Traditional White
    Bread 192
Wholemeal Date Scones
    196
Wholemeal Muffins 197
Workhouse Bread 193
Bread and Butter
    Pudding 207
Bread Pudding 206
Breadfruit 165
Breadfruit Soup 166
Spicy Breadfruit 166
Stuffed Breadfruit 165
Breakfast Ideas
Breakfast Fritters 46
Fish Flapjacks 46
French Toast 45
Norris Family Scottish
    Hotcakes 46
Pacific Toast 45
Porridge Oats 45
Quick Bubble and
    Squeak 45
Broccoli, Stir Fry Beef
    and, 107
Bubble and Squeak 106
Button Squash Sauté 150
Buying Fish 54

C

Cajun Chicken Wings 96
Cajun Cocktail Salsa 215
Cakes
Banana Cake 205

Chocolate Banana
    Cake 204
Coconut Cake 205
Papaya Cake 183
Canned Goods
Canned Baked Beans 136
Canned Corn 149
Canned Corned Beef
    Packages 106
Canned Fish 88
Canned Food
    Preservation 22
Canned Tomato Salad 187
Carbohydrate Loading 4
Carbohydrate Sources 4
Caribbean 37
Caribbean Bouillabaisse 84
Caribbean Cabbage and
    Dasheen Cabbage 145
Caribbean Callaloo 145
Cassava 142
Casseroles
Corn and Baked Bean
    Casserole 138
Lima Bean and Tomato
    Casserole 134
Osso Bucco Casserole 111
South American Lamb
    Casserole 111
Catching Fish 51
Charcoal Grilled Baby
    Octopus 75
Chicken
Angelina's Filipina
    Chicken 97
Barbecued Chicken 113
Barbecued Chicken
    Wings 96
Barbecued Thai Garlic
    Chicken 97
Basic Curry Recipe 211
Cajun Chicken Wings 96
Chicken Curry 212
Chicken Jambalaya 100
Chicken Marinade 218
Chicken Satays 114
Chicken Yakitori 114

Colombian Style
    Chicken 95
Cooked Chicken 99
Lebanese Chicken
    Marinade 218
Mint Chicken 95
Peanut Chicken 98
Peruvian Chicken 99
Quick Chicken
    Casserole 100
Tandoori Chicken 99
Tropical Chicken
    Kebabs 113
Vietnamese Chicken 98
Chickpeas
Chickpea Pilaf 135
Chickpeas and Rice 136
Chickpeas Curry and
    Rice 136
Hummus Dip 216
Okra with Chick Peas and
    Tomatoes 153
Chili
Chili 143
Chili and Tomato
    Pasta 128
Chili Bean Filled
    Potatoes 156
Chili Bean Rissole 110
Chili Beans 132
Chimichurri 216
Chinese Pork 101
Chinese Vegetables 146
Chocolate
Chocolate Banana
    Cake 204
Chocolate Banana
    Cookies 203
Chocolate Bread Slice 204
Oat Pecan Chocolate Chip
    Cookies 203
Chutneys
Banana Chutney 220
Green Papaya Chutney 221
Mango Chutney 221
Pineapple Chutney 220
Ciguatera Poisoning 53

Citrus Cookies 202
Citrus Granitas 228
Coconut
  African Spinach and
    Coconut 145
  Banana Coconut Cream
    Pie 175
  Barbados Coconut Rum
    Punch 232
  Coconut Cake 205
  Coconut Cream 179
  Coconut Fingers 36
  Coconut Milk 180
  Coconut Mousse 36
  Coconut Rice 120
  Cuban Coconut
    Custard 180
  Eggplant in Coconut
    Tempura 152
  Fa'ausi 168
  Hot Vegetables in Coconut
    Milk 148
  Octopus in Curried
    Coconut Sauce 75
  Palusami 180
  Prawns in Coconut
    Milk 78
  Rice in Coconut Milk 119
Coffee 227
Colombian Style
  Chicken 95
Companion Storage 24
Conch
  Conch and Soy 71
  Conch Stew 71
Condensed Milk 35
  Coconut Fingers 36
  Coconut Mousse 36
  Papaya Mold 35
  Quick Mayonnaise 35
Cookies
  Australian Anzac
    Biscuits 200
  Chocolate Banana
    Cookies 203
  Citrus Cookies 202
  Cornflake Cookies 200

Muesli Cookies 201
Oat Pecan Chocolate Chip
  Cookies 203
Peanut Cookies 202
Raisin Cookies 201
Swiss Honey Biscuits 201
Cooking Data 18
Cooking Equipment 13
Cooking Oils 33
Cooking Stove 9
Corn
  Baked Bean and Corn
    Chowder 137
  Corn and Baked Bean
    Casserole 138
  Corn and Canned
    Tuna 149
  Crab and Corn
    Pancakes 81
  Spicy Corn Fritters 149
  Sweet Corn and Crab
    Soup 149
Corned Beef
  Bubble and Squeak 106
  Crumbed Corn Beef 106
Cornflake Cookies 200
Courgettes 163
Crab 79
  Caribbean Callaloo 145
  Crab and Corn
    Pancakes 81
  Curried Crab 212
  Indian Chili Crab 79
  Kingfish, Crab and Pasta
    Soup 125
  Oriental Crab 81
  Singapore Chili Crab 80
  Sweet Corn and Crab
    Soup 149
Creamed Fish with Rice 58
Creole Pineapple Salad 184
Crêpes, Basic 198
Crumbed Corn Beef 106
Crustaceans 76
Cuban Coconut Custard 180
Curried Eggplant Purée 152
Curried Lotus Root 147

Curried Sausages 109
Curried Squid on Skewers 73
Curried Tuna Puffs 90
Curries 211
  Basic Curry Recipe 211
  Chicken Curry 212
  Chickpeas Curry and
    Rice 136
  Curried Crab 212
  Fish Head Curry 61
  Green Papaya Curry 182
  Potato and Eggplant
    Curry 213
  Zucchini and Tomato
    Curry 164

D

Desserts
  Australian Anzac
    Biscuits 200
  Banana Cake 205
  Baked Banana Dessert 177
  Banana Coconut Cream
    Pie 175
  Bread and Butter
    Pudding 207
  Bread Pudding 206
  Chocolate Banana
    Cake 204
  Chocolate Banana
    Cookies 203
  Citrus Cookies 202
  Coconut Cake 205
  Coconut Mousse 36
  Cornflake Cookies 200
  Cuban Coconut
    Custard 180
  Great Grandma's Christmas
    Plum Pudding 208
  Muesli Cookies 201
  Nothing Pudding 206
  Oat Pecan Chocolate Chip
    Cookies 203
  Papaya Cake 183
  Peanut Cookies 202

Raisin Cookies 201
Rice Pudding 121
Swiss Honey Biscuits 201
Dhal 131
Drinks
Barbados Coconut Rum
   Punch 232
Citrus Granitas 228
Energy Drink 6
Hot Buttered Rum 232
Kava 230
Lemonade 228
Mango Frappés 228
Perfect Margarita 229
Planters Punch 232
Red Wine Granita 228
Standard Peasants
   Margarita 229
Trinidad Rum Punch 231
Dry Food Preservation 22

E

Eggplant
African Okra Stew 153
Baked Eggplant and
   Tomatoes 152
Barbecued Eggplant 151
Curried Eggplant
   Purée 152
Eggplant and Coriander
   Salad 187
Eggplant Caviar 151
Eggplant in Coconut
   Tempura 152
Pacific Eggplant 151
Potato and Eggplant
   Curry 213
Ratatouille 148
Eggs
Basic Frittata 47
Egg and Bacon Pie 47
Egg Storage 27
Egg Stuffed Tomatoes 162
Fettuccine Frittata 48

Frittata Pottatta 48
Pasta Frittata 5
Rice and Vegetable
   Frittata 47
Tropical Scrambled
   Eggs 48
Energy Drink 6
Extra Sweet Pineapple 184

F

Fa'ausi 168
Fettuccine Frittata 48
Fettuccine Marinara 126
Fiji 39
Fish
African Okra Stew 153
Banana and Ginger
   Fillets 58
Beer Batter 63
Caribbean Bouillabaisse 84
Creamed Fish with Rice 58
Fish Cakes 65, 91
Fish Chowder 87
Fish Flapjacks 46
Fish Foil Recipes 56
Fish Fritters 66
Fish Head Curry 61
Fish Sausages 66
Fish Soup 84
Fish Storage 55
Ika Mata 58
Indian Fried Fish 59
Kingfish, Crab and Pasta
   Soup 125
Kokoda 59
Lebanese Fish
   Marinade 218
Marinated and Grilled
   Yellowfin Tuna 57
Mineral Water Fish
   Batter 62
Oka 60
Oriental Fish Bake 62
Rice Kedgeree 118

Sashimi 63
Sashimi Dipping Sauce 63
Seafood Laksa 61
Seafood Mousse 62
Steamed Fish in Banana
   Leaves 60
Tahitian Fish Salad 187
Tempura 64
Thai Fish Cakes 65
Thomo's Gameboat Fish
   Recipe 57
Tropical Snapper or
   Bream 57
Food Preservation 22
Foolproof Scones 196
French Mayonnaise 188
French Toast 45
French Vinaigrette 188
Fresh Food Substitutes 34
**Fresh Vegetables and
   Fruit 23**
Fried Green Tomatoes 162
Fried Plantains 178
Fried Rice 117
Frittatas
Basic Frittata 47
Fettuccine Frittata 48
Frittata Pottatta 48
Papaya Frittata 182
Rice and Vegetable
   Frittata 47
Fritters
Apple Fritters 173
Banana Fritter Surprise 177
Banana Fritters 175
Fish Fritters 66
Oyster Fritters 69
Rice and Seafood
   Fritters 119
Spicy Corn Fritters 149
Yam Fritters 158

G

Galley Cleaning 16
Galley Fires 15
Galley Safety 15
Garlic 143
   Garlic Prawns 76
   Garlic Prawns and
      Tomatoes 76
Gas Safety 15
Gibraltar 42
Ginger 143
   Banana and Ginger
      Fillets 58
   Mango and Ginger 181
Goat
   Goat Meatballs and Tomato
      Sauce 103
   Goat Stroganoff 103
   Great Grandma's Christmas
      Plum Pudding 208
Green Bean and Tomato
      Salad 186
Green Papaya Chutney 221
Green Papaya Curry 182
Green Papaya Salad 183
Green Tomato Pickles 222
Grenada 37
Griddle Cakes 199
Grilled Lobster 83
Guacamole 174
Guam 41

H

Ham
   10 Minutes Pressure
      Cooker Hot Pot 6
   Pressure Cooker Ham and
      Three Bean Soup 134
Hashed Brown Potatoes 156
Herbs, Spices and
      Condiments 31
Home Brewing 233

Homemade Yeast 193
Honey Sesame Marinade 217
Honeyed Lentil Soup 132
Honiara 39
Hot Buttered Rum 232
Hot Pots
   Baked Bean and Sausage
      Hot Pot 137
   Sausage Hot Pot 108
Hot Vegetables in Coconut
      Milk 148
Hotcakes, Norris Family
      Scottish 46
Hummus Dip 216

I

Ika Mata 58
Impossible Tart 204
Indian Chapattis 194
Indian Chili Crab 79
Indian Fried Bread 194
Indian Fried Fish 59
Indian Iced Tea 226
Irish Beer Bread 192
Irish Stew 104

J

Jacket Potatoes Roasted with
      Garlic Olive Oil 155

K

Kava 230
Kingfish, Crab and Pasta
      Soup 125
Kohlrabi 142
Kokoda 59
Koror 40
Kosrae 40
Kumara or Taro Puffs 168

L

Lamb
   Basic Curry Recipe 211
   Beef or Lamb Koftas 105
   Irish Stew 104
   Lamb Satay Marinade 219
   Singapore Satay 104
   South American Lamb
      Casserole 111
Lasagne
   Bean and Spinach
      Lasagne 124
   Vegetable Lasagne 150
Leaf Vegetables 145
Lebanese Chicken
      Marinade 218
Lebanese Fish Marinade 218
Legume (Dried Beans and
      Pulses) Varieties 129
Legume Cooking
      Methods 130
Lemonade 228
Lentils
   Dhal 131
   Honeyed Lentil Soup 132
   Lentil and Potato Pie 132
   Lentil Patties 131
   Lentil Patties 2 131
   Spinach and Lentil
      Soup 145
Lima Beans
   Lima Bean and Tomato
      Casserole 134
   Lima Bean Salad 187
Lime Marmalade 222
Lobster
   American Lobster 83
   Brazilian Baked Lobster and
      Pineapple 82
   Grilled Lobster 83
Long Life Milk 36
Long Life Vegetable Bag
      23

Louisiana Red Beans and
  Rice 133
Luganville 39

M

Macaroni in Tomato and
  Onion Sauce 128
Madeira 42
Maize 144
Majuro 40
Mango
  Mango and Ginger 181
  Mango Chutney 221
  Mango Frappés 228
Marinades
  Chicken Marinade 218
  Honey Sesame
    Marinade 217
  Lamb Satay Marinade 219
  Lebanese Chicken
    Marinade 218
  Lebanese Fish
    Marinade 218
  Spicy Marinade 217
  White Wine Marinade 219
Marinated and Grilled
  Yellowfin Tuna 57
Marinated Sun Dried
  Tomatoes 161
Marmalade, Lime 222
Marshall Islands 40
Ma's Sausage Stew 109
Mashed Potatoes 155
Mayonnaise
  French Mayonnaise 188
  Quick Mayonnaise 35
Mediterranean 41
Mediterranean Squid 73
Melanesia 38
Micronesia 40
Microwave 10
Mineral Water Fish Batter 62
Minestrone Soup 123
Mint Chicken 95

Mixed Salad Vinaigrette 188
Mojo Latino Salsa 215
Mollusks 67
Moroccan Mint Tea 226
Moules Marinière 68
Muesli Cookies 201
Muffins
  Banana Muffins 197
  Oat Bran Muffins 197
  Wholemeal Muffins 197
Mussels
  Baked Mussels 68
  Moules Marinière 68
  Mussels in Tomato
    Sauce 69
  Skillet Mussels 67

N

Navy Bean Soup 135
New Caledonia 39
New Zealand 41
Norris Family Scottish
  Hotcakes 46
Northern Marianas 41
Nothing Pudding 206
Noumea 39

O

Oats
  Oat Bran Muffins 197
  Oat Pecan Chocolate Chip
    Cookies 203
Octopus
  Charcoal Grilled Baby
    Octopus 75
  Octopus Galicia (Spain)
    Style 74
  Octopus in Curried
    Coconut Sauce 75
  Octopus Salad 185
Oil and Garlic Sauce 127
Oka 60

Okra
  African Okra Stew 153
  Okra Sambol 154
  Okra with Chick Peas and
    Tomatoes 153
On Board Gardening 141
Onions 144
Orange Pork 101
Oriental Crab 81
Oriental Fish Bake 62
Oriental Rissole 110
Osso Bucco Casserole 111
Oysters
  Oyster Fritters 69
  Oysters à la Brasil 70
  Oysters Bloody Mary 70
  Oysters Kilpatrick 70

P

Pacific Eggplant 151
Pacific Islands 38
Pacific Toast 45
Paella
  Pork and Seafood
    Paella 102
  Seafood Paella 119
Palau 40
Palma 42
Palusami 180
Pancakes
  Basic Pancakes 198
  Crab and Corn
    Pancakes 81
  Potato Pancakes 155
  Taro Pancakes 167
Papaya
  Baked Papaya Slices 182
  Green Papaya Chutney 221
  Green Papaya Curry 182
  Green Papaya Salad 183
  Papaya Cake 183
  Papaya Dip 181
  Papaya Frittata 182
  Papaya Mold 35

Paw Paw Mousse 181
Stuffed Papaya 183
Pasta
Avocado Fettuccine 125
Bean and Spinach
Lasagne 124
Chili and Tomato
Pasta 128
Fettuccine Frittata 48
Fettuccine Marinara 126
Kingfish, Crab and Pasta
Soup 125
Macaroni in Tomato and
Onion Sauce 128
Minestrone Soup 123
Pasta and Vegetable
Soup 124
Pasta Frittata 5
Sardines and
Spaghetti 88
Tuna and Pasta 89
Vacuum Flask Pasta 5
**Pasta Cooking Methods
122**
Pasta Sauces
Oil and Garlic Sauce 127
Pesto 128
Sun Dried Tomato
Dressing 160
Tomato Sauce 127
Tomato Sauce 2 127
Paw Paw 181
Paw Paw Mousse 181
Peanuts
Peanut Chicken 98
Peanut Cookies 202
Peanut Salsa 214
Peas
10 Minutes Pressure
Cooker Hot Pot 6
Rice and Peas 133
Perfect Margarita 229
Peruvian Chicken 99
Pesto 128
Pickles, Green Tomato 222

Pie, Banana Coconut
Cream 175
Pineapple
Brazilian Baked Lobster and
Pineapple 82
Creole Pineapple Salad 184
Extra Sweet Pineapple 184
Pineapple Chutney 220
Pineapple Salsa 184
Tomato and Pineapple
Relish 222
Piquant Prawns 78
Pita Bread 195
Planning 21
Plantains
Fried Plantains 178
Plantain Balls 178
Plantain Chips 178
Planters Punch 232
Pohnpei 40
Polynesia 38
Pork *(See Bacon and Ham
also)*
Chinese Pork 101
Orange Pork 101
Pork and Seafood
Paella 102
Pork Balls 102
Porridge Oats 45
Port Vila 39
Potatoes
Chili Bean Filled
Potatoes 156
Frittata Pottatta 48
Hashed Brown
Potatoes 156
Jacket Potatoes Roasted
with Garlic Olive Oil 155
Lentil and Potato Pie 132
Mashed Potatoes 155
Potato and Bean Salad 185
Potato and Eggplant
Curry 213
Potato Cakes 155
Potato Casserole 156
Potato Pancakes 155

Savoury Fried
Potatoes 157
Spicy Curried Potatoes 157
Stir Fried Spuds 157
Tuna and Potato Loaf 89
Vegetable Hash
Browns 150
Powdered Milk 36
Prawns
Garlic Prawns 76
Garlic Prawns and
Tomatoes 76
Piquant Prawns 78
Prawns and Rice 77
Prawns in Coconut
Milk 78
Spanish Garlic Prawns 77
Pressure Cooker Ham and
Three Bean Soup 134
Pressure Cooker or Dutch
Oven Bread 191
Produce Names 142
Provisioning Checklists 28
Puddings
Bread and Butter
Pudding 207
Bread Pudding 206
Great Grandma's Christmas
Plum Pudding 208
Nothing Pudding 206
Rice Pudding 121
Yorkshire Pudding 207
Pumpkin
Baked Pumpkin 159
Pumpkin Sauce 159
Pumpkin Soup 159

Q

Quiche, Salmon 92
Quick Bubble and Squeak 45
Quick Canned Tuna
Casserole 90
Quick Chicken Casserole 100

Quick Mayonnaise 35

R

Raisin Cookies 201
Rarotonga Taro Cakes 168
Ratatouille 148
Red Wine Granita 228
Refrigeration Systems 10
Relish, Tomato and
    Pineapple 222
Rice
    Chickpea Pilaf 135
    Chickpeas and Rice 136
    Chickpeas Curry and
        Rice 136
    Coconut Rice 120
    Fried Rice 117
    Louisiana Red Beans and
        Rice 133
    Prawns and Rice 77
    Rice and Bean Soup 121
    Rice and Peas 133
    Rice and Seafood
        Fritters 119
    Rice and Vegetable
        Frittata 47
    Rice in Coconut Milk 119
    Rice Kedgeree 118
    Rice Pudding 121
    Rice Salad 186
    Saffron Rice 118
    Seafood Paella 119
    Seafood Risotto 120
    Steamed Rice 117
    Vacuum Flask Rice 5
    Vegetable Rice Patties 118
Rice Cooking Methods 117
Risotto, Seafood 120
Rissole
    Baked Bean Rissoles 137
    Basic Rissole 110
    Chili Bean Rissole 110
    Oriental Rissole 110
Rough Weather Foods 4

10 Minutes Pressure
    Cooker Hot Pot 6
Energy Drink 6
Pasta Frittata 5
Vacuum Flask Pasta 5
Vacuum Flask Rice 5
Rum 230

S

Saffron Rice 118
Saipan 41
Salads
    Canned Tomato Salad 187
    Creole Pineapple Salad 184
    Eggplant and Coriander
        Salad 187
    Green Bean and Tomato
        Salad 186
    Green Papaya Salad 183
    Lima Bean Salad 187
    Octopus Salad 185
    Potato and Bean Salad 185
    Rice Salad 186
    Seafood Salad 186
    Tahitian Fish Salad 187
Salad Dressings
    Basic Vinaigrette 188
    French Mayonnaise 188
    French Vinaigrette 188
    Mixed Salad
        Vinaigrette 188
Salmon, Canned
    Fish Cakes 91
    Salmon Loaf 91
    Salmon Quiche 92
Salsa 214
    Barbecue Salsa 216
    Cajun Cocktail Salsa 215
    Chimichurri 216
    Mojo Latino Salsa 215
    Peanut Salsa 214
    Pineapple Salsa 184
    Tomato Salsa 162
    Vietnamese Nuoc Mam

Salsa 214
Saltwater Bread 191
Sandwich Fillers 174
Sardines and Spaghetti 88
Sashimi 63
Sauces
    Pumpkin Sauce 159
    Sashimi Dipping Sauce 63
Sausage
    Baked Bean and Sausage
        Hot Pot 137
    Curried Sausages 109
    Fish Sausages 66
    Ma's Sausage Stew 109
    Sausage Hot Pot 108
Savoury Fried Potatoes 157
Scones
    Foolproof Scones 196
    Wholemeal Date
        Scones 196
**Seafood *(See individual
    listings also)***
    Caribbean Bouillabaisse 84
    Pork and Seafood
        Paella 102
    Rice and Seafood
        Fritters 119
    Seafood Bake 86
    Seafood Laksa 61
    Seafood Mousse 62
    Seafood Paella 119
    Seafood Risotto 120
    Seafood Salad 186
    Seafood Stew 85
    Zarzuela 86
Singapore Chili Crab 80
Singapore Satay 104
Skillet Mussels 67
Social Ice Breakers 228
Society Islands 38
Solomon Islands 39
Soup
    Baked Bean and Corn
        Chowder 137
    Breadfruit Soup 166
    Caribbean Bouillabaisse 84

Caribbean Callaloo 145
Fish Chowder 87
Fish Soup 84
Honeyed Lentil Soup 132
Kingfish, Crab and Pasta
    Soup 125
Minestrone Soup 123
Navy Bean Soup 135
Pasta and Vegetable
    Soup 124
Pressure Cooker Ham and
    Three Bean Soup 134
Pumpkin Soup 159
Rice and Bean Soup 121
Spinach and Lentil
    Soup 145
Sweet Corn and Crab
    Soup 149
South American Lamb
    Casserole 111
Soy Milk 36
Spanish Garlic Prawns 77
Spiced Vinegar 221
Spicy Breadfruit 166
Spicy Corn Fritters 149
Spicy Curried Potatoes 157
Spicy Marinade 217
Spinach 145
    African Spinach and
        Coconut 145
    Bean and Spinach
        Lasagne 124
    Caribbean Callaloo 145
    Spinach and Lentil
        Soup 145
Squid
    Curried Squid on
        Skewers 73
    Mediterranean Squid 73
    Squid in Olive Oil 72
    Squid in Tempura
        Batter 73
    Stuffed Squid 72
    Tempura 64
St Lucia 37

Standard Peasants
    Margarita 229
Steak 112
Steamed Fish in Banana
    Leaves 60
Steamed Rice 117
Stew
    Irish Stew 104
    Ma's Sausage Stew 109
    Seafood Stew 85
    Zarzuela 86
Stir Fry
    Stir Fried Spuds 157
    Stir Fried Water
        Spinach 147
    Stir Fry Beef and
        Broccoli 107
    Stir Fry Chinese
        Leaves 146
    Stir Fry Oriental Beef 107
Storage
    Cheeses 27
    Egg Storage 27
    Meats 27
    Typical Average Fruit
        Storage Life 26
    Typical Average Vegetable
        Storage Life 25
Stove Gimballing 9
Stuffed Papaya 183
Stuffed Squid 72
Stuffed Tomatoes 161
Sun Dried Tomatoes 160
    Sun Dried Tomato
        Dressing 160
Sweet Bell Peppers 143
Sweet Corn and Crab
    Soup 149
Sweet Potatoes
    Baked Sweet
        Potatoes 158
    Sweet Potato Chips 158
    Sweet Potato
        Croquettes 158
    Yam Fritters 158
Swiss Honey Biscuits 201

Syrup, Waffle Brown Sugar
    199

T

Tahiti 38
Tahitian Fish Salad 187
Tandoori Chicken 99
Taro 167
    Fa'ausi 168
    Kumara or Taro Puffs 168
    Rarotonga Taro Cakes 168
    Taro Cakes 167
    Taro Pancakes 167
    Turn Fried Taro 167
**Tea (Ch'a, Chaya, Chai,
    Thé) 225**
    Indian Iced Tea 226
    Moroccan Mint Tea 226
Tempura 64
10 Minutes Pressure Cooker
    Hot Pot 6
Thai Fish Cakes 65
Thomo's Gameboat Fish
    Recipe 57
Tomatoes
    Baked Eggplant and
        Tomatoes 152
    Canned Tomato Salad 187
    Chili and Tomato Pasta
        128
    Egg Stuffed Tomatoes 162
    Fried Green Tomatoes 162
    Garlic Prawns and
        Tomatoes 76
    Green Bean and Tomato
        Salad 186
    Green Tomato Pickles 222
    Lima Bean and Tomato
        Casserole 134
    Marinated Sun Dried
        Tomatoes 161
    Okra with Chick Peas and
        Tomatoes 153

Stuffed Tomatoes 161
Sun Dried Tomato
    Dressing 160
Tomato and Pineapple
    Relish 222
Tomato Preparation 160
Tomato Salsa 162
Tomato Sauce 127
Tomato Sauce 2 127
Zucchini and Tomato 163
Zucchini and Tomato
    Curry 164
Tonga 38
Traditional White Bread 192
**Trash Control And
    Disposal 17**
Trinidad Rum Punch 231
Trolling 52
Tropical Chicken Kebabs 113
Tropical Fruit Guide 171
Tropical Snapper or
    Bream 57
Truk 40
Tubers 142
Tuna
    Corn and Canned
        Tuna 149
    Curried Tuna Puffs 90
    Quick Canned Tuna
        Casserole 90
    Tuna and Pasta 89
    Tuna and Potato Loaf 89
Tunisia 41
Turn Fried Taro 167

V

Vacuum Flask
    Vacuum Flask Pasta 5
    Vacuum Flask Rice 5
    Vacuum Flask Yogurt 36
Vanuatu 38
Vegetables *(See individual
    listings also)*
    Button Squash Sauté 150
    Curried Lotus Root 147
    Hot Vegetables in Coconut
        Milk 148
    Impossible Tart 204
    Pasta and Vegetable
        Soup 124
    Ratatouille 148
    Rice and Vegetable
        Frittata 47
    Stir Fried Water
        Spinach 147
    Stir Fry Chinese
        Leaves 146
    Vegetable Hash
        Browns 150
    Vegetable Lasagne 150
    Vegetable Rice Patties 118
Vietnamese Chicken 98
Vietnamese Nuoc Mam
    Salsa 214
Vinegar, Spiced 221

W

Waffle Brown Sugar
    Syrup 199
Waffles, Basic 199
Western Samoa 38
Whipped Bananas 177
White Wine Marinade 219
Wholemeal Date Scones 196
Wholemeal Muffins 197
Workhouse Bread 193
**Worldwide Provisioning
    Guide 37**

Y

Yam Fritters 158
Yap 40
Yeast, Homemade 193
Yorkshire Pudding 207

Z

Zarzuela 86
Zucchini
    Baked Zucchini 163
    Zucchini and Tomato 163
    Zucchini and Tomato
        Curry 164
    Zucchini Slice 164